Modeling Legal Argument

Artificial Intelligence and Legal Reasoning
L. Thorne McCarty and Edwina Rissland, editors

An Artificial Intelligence Approach to Legal Reasoning, Anne von der Lieth Gardner, 1987

Modeling Legal Argument: Reasoning with Cases and Hypotheticals, Kevin D. Ashley, 1990

Modeling Legal Argument
Reasoning with Cases and Hypotheticals

Kevin D. Ashley

A Bradford Book
The MIT Press
Cambridge, Massachusetts
London, England

© 1990 Massachusetts Institute of Technology

All rights reserved. No part of this book may be reproduced in any form by any electronic or mechanical means (including photocopying, recording, or information storage and retrieval) without permission in writing from the publisher.

This book was set in Computer Modern by The MIT Press and printed and bound in the United States of America.

Library of Congress Cataloging-in-Publication Data

Ashley, Kevin D.
  Modeling legal argument: reasoning with cases and hypotheticals/ Kevin D. Ashley.
    p. cm.—(Artificial intelligence and legal reasoning)
  Based on author's dissertation.
  "A Bradford book."
  Includes bibliographical references.
  ISBN 0-262-01114-X
  1. Information storage and retrieval systems—Law—United States 2. Law—United States—Methodology. 3. Artificial intelligence.
I. Title. II. Series.
KF242.A1A7 1990
340'.11—dc20   89-29963
                                                                            CIP

To my wife, Alida Merlo Ashley

Contents

	Series Foreword	xi
	Acknowledgments	xiii
1	Introduction	1
2	The Law as a Paradigm of Case-Based Argument	9
2.1	A Scenario	9
2.2	What a Legal Argument Should Be	10
2.3	Hypo: An Alternative	20
3	Introduction to Hypo and Its Adversarial Reasoning Process	25
4	The Hypo Program: An Overview	35
4.1	Hypo's Reasoning Process	36
4.2	Knowledge Sources in Hypo	36
4.3	Hypo's Architecture	38
5	Hypo in Action: An Extended Example	45
5.1	The Case Editor	46
5.2	The Session Manager	51
5.3	The Case Analyzer	52
5.4	The Case Positioner	55
5.5	The Best Case Selector	57
5.6	The 3-Ply Arguer	62
5.7	The Explainer	75
5.8	The Hypo Generator	84
6	The Case Knowledge Base	87
6.1	Legal Case Frames	87

6.2	Factual Predicates	98
6.3	Indexing a Case in the CKB	102
6.4	Aspects of Legal Precedents Represented	105
7	A Dimensional Index	107
7.1	The Primary Function of Dimensions	107
7.2	Hypo's Dimensions	108
7.3	A Dimension's Structure and Function	115
7.4	Advantages of Dimensions	125
8	Basic Mechanisms of Case-Based Reasoning	127
8.1	Ordering Analogous Cases	128
8.2	Selecting Most-Analogous Cases	139
8.3	Identifying Configurations of Counterexamples	144
8.4	Hypothetical Modifications to Explore Contingencies	147
8.5	Comparing Case-Based Analyses of Different Problem Situations	154
9	A Theory of Case-Based Argument in Hypo	157
9.1	Computationally Defining Salience and Significance	157
9.2	Argument Roles for Precedents	161
9.3	Evaluating Precedential Arguments	166
9.4	An Example of Computing Salience	167
9.5	Factor Weights	174
9.6	Computing Citation Labels	178
9.7	Conclusion	180
10	Evaluating Hypo's Performance	183

10.1	Comparing Hypo's Points and Responses to Court Opinions	183
10.2	Comparing Hypo's Citation Displays to Treatise Notes	191
10.3	Discussion	193
11	Adversarial Case-Based Reasoning beyond the Law	195
11.1	Examples	195
11.2	The Adversarial Case-Based Reasoning Process	202
11.3	Characteristics of Good Domains for Adversarial Case-Based Reasoning	203
11.4	Computationally Implementing Adversarial Case-Based Reasoning	205
11.5	Adversarial Case-Based Reasoning in AI	207
12	Extending Hypo's Model of Case-Based Legal Argument	223
12.1	Other AI Models of Legal Reasoning	223
12.2	Jurisprudential Debate about Analogical Reasoning	229
12.3	The Importance of Modeling Hypothetical Reasoning	232
12.4	Extending Hypo	238
13	Conclusion	249
13.1	A Model of Adversarial Case-Based Reasoning	249
13.2	Contribution to AI	250
13.3	Contribution to Legal Philosophy	253
A	The Uniform Trade Secrets Act	255
B	A Restatement of Torts—Section 757	257

C	A Complete List of Legal Case Frames	259
D	Factual Predicates	261
E	Cases in the Case Knowledge Base	265
F	Implemented Dimensions in Hypo	273
G	Argument Evaluation Criteria	279
H	Sample Hypo Outputs	281
I	Excerpts from Opinion and Briefs in the *USM* Case	299
J	Implementation of Hypo	303
	Glossary	307
	Bibliography	315
	Index	323

Series Foreword

The law, with its diverse modes of reasoning, provides a rich area for the study of both human and artificial intelligence. The reasoning can involve cases, rules, or text. Cases can be real or hypothetical; rules, well- or ill-formulated; text, free or highly structured. And the reasoning can be deductive, inductive or analogical. It is a perfect arena in which cognitive scientists and artificial intelligence researchers can merge interests.

Although jurisprudence has traditionally grappled with problems of legal reasoning, it has not been able to describe them at the level of specificity that artificial intelligence and cognitive science strive for. Armed with new techniques of knowledge representation, procedural specification, and the like, artificial intelligence researchers now believe that a more detailed analysis of legal reasoning is possible. But artificial intelligence, which has has some practical successes in areas like medicine and geology, has not yet had much empirical experience in a domain with such hybrid modes of thought as the law. The law challenges AI on all fronts, from natural language processing to computational architectures combining rule- and case-based paradigms.

A joint endeavor in artificial intelligence and law will strengthen and inform both disciplines.

L. Thorne McCarty
Edwina L. Rissland

Acknowledgments

Edwina Rissland was my mentor throughout my graduate school career in computer science. She was the chairperson of my dissertation committee at the University of Massachusetts, where I carried out the research and wrote the doctoral dissertation on which this book is based. She teaches by example to look beyond the bounds of one's own expertise, to be energetic and creative in searching for ideas and ways to test them, and to write well. Her overriding concern on behalf of her students has always been to get them to "think good thoughts." Working with Edwina, it is hard not to.

A number of people have provided invaluable critiques of and suggestions for this book. Wendy Lehnert of the University of Massachusetts and Paul Brest, dean of the Stanford Law School, as members of my doctoral dissertation committee, helped me to see how my dissertation research fit into the larger pictures of research on Artificial Intelligence and jurisprudential theory. Donald Berman of Northeastern University Law School and Anne vdL. Gardner, author of an important previous work in this series, reviewed my doctoral thesis. Their critiques helped me to revise and restructure my dissertation to create this book.

The IBM Thomas J. Watson Research Center supported me through much of this work, both with an IBM Graduate Research Fellowship and more recently as a visiting scientist. I am very greatful to them and, in particular, to Se June Hong, for their continuing good will and support. Additional support for this research came from the National Science Foundation, grant IST-8212238, the Advanced Research Projects Agency, Department of Defense, monitored by the Office of Naval Research, contract no. N00014-84-K-0017, and the University Research Initiative, award no. N00014-86-K-0764.

Most of all, I thank my wife, Alida, who has supported me in my peregrinations through Harvard Law School, a Wall Street legal practice, graduate school in computer science, and most particularly through my dissertation and the writing of this book. Her wise counsel, unflagging optimism, and patient understanding are the mainstays of my life.

Modeling Legal Argument

1 Introduction

Scholars who think abstractly about reasoning have new descriptive tools in artificial intelligence (AI). Practitioners of AI attempt to design computer programs that behave in an intelligent manner. AI research has focused on many kinds of intelligent behavior, including symbolic reasoning. The goal is not necessarily to design a program that reasons in the same way as a human but whose outputs are, within certain constraints, as intelligent as those of a human reasoner. The constraints involve the range of the program's intelligent behavior. Expert systems designers, for example, build programs whose problem-solving behavior, though comparable to that of a human expert, is limited to a narrow domain of expertise, such as diagnosing a particular kind of bacterial infection or analyzing a particular kind of organic molecule or geological data.

AI researchers are in the historically unique position of building working models of some extremely abstract phenomena, like diagnosis, design, and argument. Working models of freight locomotives or steam turbines are familiar enough; they show on a small scale the work that the machine does. In AI the model is a computer program whose organization and control help to concretize in a simplified way something that cannot be directly observed: the way in which an expert reasons.

This book describes an exercise in building a working model of an abstract reasoning phenomenon: the way in which attorneys argue with cases, real and hypothetical. The computer program, called Hypo, analyzes problem situations dealing with trade secrets disputes, retrieves relevant legal cases from its database, and fashions them into reasonable legal arguments about who should win. The arguments demonstrate the program's ability to reason symbolically with past cases, draw factual analogies between cases, cite them in arguments, distinguish them, and pose counterexamples and hypotheticals based on past cases.

The model has practical ramifications. It demonstrates how to build a program for assisting attorneys in an important part of legal practice. Attorneys make arguments for a living. A program that, given a problem situation, determines the relevance of legal cases based on their utility in legal arguments is a significant improvement over the prevailing keyword-driven legal database retrieval systems.

The model also has theoretical ramifications. Part of intelligent behavior is reasoning from past experiences. Legal argument is interesting as an example of a highly developed system for reasoning from past experiences, cases, as a supplement to deductive reasoning. By modeling this kind of reasoning in a domain where it is a refined art, one can learn how to approach modeling more informal kinds of reasoning from past experiences in every day life.

The legal domain is a special challenge for AI because it is intensively linguistic and complex, only partially logical, adversarial, and analogical. Unfortunately for AI, legal reasoning involves interpretation of textual materials. Understanding natural language is a notoriously difficult problem for computer programs, one that will take years, perhaps decades, of research. This is especially true in law, where the problems and situations are as complex and diverse as human experience and the prose is so atrociously poor.

The legal domain is harder to model than mathematical or scientific domains because deductive logic, one of the computer scientist's primary tools, does not work in it. Although deductive reasoning plays an important role in law, legal rules tend to be incomplete, logically and semantically ambiguous, sometimes inconsistent, and frequently hard to find or even to identify. Second, the law is adversarial; legal problems frequently have no one right answer. Usually there are at least two opposing viewpoints, and the arguments on either side may be quite reasonable, although only one side wins. Finally, legal reasoning involves reasoning by analogy. Lawyers argue by drawing analogies to past cases and posing hypotheticals. This kind of reasoning is not yet well understood in AI, especially in a domain where there is no strong theoretical model of a solved problem to guide analogizing as there are in scientific analogies.

These challenges, however, make the legal domain an interesting one from the viewpoint of AI research. The legal domain is midway between logical or mathematical domains that are amenable to computer science techniques and the domains of commonsense reasoning and ordinary discourse that AI so wishes to tackle. Studying how knowledge is structured in this intermediately formalized field may lead to useful insights. One particularly promising avenue is the legal system's institutionalized use of adversarial reasoning by analogy as a way of dealing with the problems of logical reasoning with rules.

To the mathematically minded, legal decision making may seem chaotic, but it is an organized chaos. By building a working model of making reasonable arguments in law, AI succeeds in modeling intelligent behavior in a messy domain, one that lacks a strong theoretical model that would support deductive reasoning techniques.

Since the problems of modeling the legal domain are too big for any one AI research effort, the approach has been to simplify and to focus on one piece of the general problem: adversarial reasoning with cases, or the way in which attorneys argue how to decide a dispute by drawing comparisons to past legal cases or precedents.

Adversarial case-based reasoning involves justifying a conclusion about a problem by drawing an analogy to a similar past case and arguing that the problem should be decided in the same way. This kind of reasoning comprises a variety of tasks, including, drawing factual analogies to past cases, distinguishing past cases, citing past cases as counterexamples, posing made-up cases or hypotheticals, and evaluating the strength of case-citing arguments.

Adversarial case-based reasoning is a kind of reasoning from experience. It is adversarial because there are at least two sides—one that favors and one that opposes a decision. It is case based because the experience is recorded not necessarily in generalized rules but in discrete, specific historical cases.

Adversarial case-based reasoning is a paradigm for legal argument. The legal system institutionalizes argument. In court, a judge decides a case after hearing at least two adversaries argue both sides of an issue. The attorneys justify an analysis or argument by citing and reasoning about past legal cases. To justify an assertion that a client should win in a particular fact situation, attorneys draw analogies to prior cases where similarly situated parties won. They distinguish away troublesome cases that would lead to contrary conclusions by pointing out the legally important dissimilarities and cite other cases as counterexamples.

Attorneys employ this style of arguing before trial when attorneys try arguments out on their associates to assess the pro's and con's of a client's position, at trial when the judge directs each side to brief a legal issue, and after trial in arguments before a judge on appeal of a lower court decision.

Lawyers have no choice but to argue from cases. Arguing from precedents is formally ensconced in Anglo-American law in the rule of stare decisis, the rule followed in common law jurisdictions that "a holding by a court in a previous case is binding on the same court (or an inferior court) in a similar case"[Berman and Greiner 1980]. Moreover, the law's many statutory, constitutional, and administrative rules lack intermediate rules that define the legal predicates. Lacking authoritative definitions, courts and advocates who must decide whether a general rule of law applies to a specific dispute cannot settle the matter by logical deduction. Instead they justify a rule's application by arguing analogically that the dispute is similar to a precedent where the court decided that the rule applied.

The model of adversarial case-based reasoning implemented in the Hypo program and described in this book comprises

- a conceptual structure for case-based legal arguments;

- computational definitions of how cases are relevantly similar and different;

- a computational definition for qualitatively measuring which cases are most analogous (i.e., most on point) with respect to a problem and which cases are the best to cite in favor of a party's position;

- definitions of four roles precedents play in legal arguments, including four types of counterexamples;

- knowledge representation structures and a control structure for implementing the definitions so that the Hypo program can select relevant cases, choose the most-on-point cases, cite them in arguments, distinguish them, pose cases as counterexamples, and pose hypotheticals based on precedents to show how to strengthen an argument.

The model functions in the domain of trade secrets law. Trade secrets disputes usually involve corporate competitors, one of whom complains that the other gained an unfair competitive advantage by illegally obtaining the former's commercial secrets. Case-based argument is very important in trade secrets law because the statutory rules are extremely general and provide little guidance. The work tackles issues that are vital to the design of expert systems in areas outside law as well.

Designers of expert systems in all fields need to focus on building systems that present alternatives. To many, a computer is a machine that accepts a question and returns the answer. The answer is either right or wrong, and if it is wrong, we call the repairman or sue the manufacturer. That model does not work in a domain where there is no right answer and where the most important function of a computer is to assist, not supplant, the decision maker by providing a range of alternative reasonable courses of action. Building expert systems that assist decision making by focusing the user on relevant alternatives will also ameliorate the expert systems providers' potential legal liability for mistaken advice.

Expert systems designers need to focus on improving a system's ability to explain its advice. One effective way of explaining advice, and persuading us of its value, is by demonstrating how well the advice worked in a similar past case. Another is to pose horrible hypothetical cases to demonstrate potential problems in the advice.

Yet another effective way of explaining advice is by arguing in favor of a conclusion. We judge a human advice giver's level of expertise and the quality of that advice, in part, by whether the person can argue like an expert. Any profession has standards of what a reasonable argument in that domain looks like. An important part of professional education is teaching students how to recognize, make, and evaluate reasonable arguments in that domain. If the advice giver does not know how to package the argument in the traditional garb, we conclude that he or she is no expert. The fluency with which he or she argues and anticipates responses and contingencies has a direct bearing on whether we are persuaded. The same considerations apply to expert systems. If the system can argue in favor of its advice, the human user is also in a much better position to understand and assess the value of the advice.

Finally, the field of expert system design is taking note that humans expect experts to be able to reason with cases and hypotheticals. In design, strategic planning, estimating values, tutoring, as well as argument and explanation, we expect experts to compare our problem symbolically with past cases and to pose hypothetical variations. For example, in design, we are not prepared to pay an expert to reinvent the wheel. If a previously designed widget could satisfy our problem with a little tweaking, then we expect the expert to start with the previous design, not with first principles. In strategic planning, we expect experts to have considered the best- and worst-case scenarios, the most likely case scenario, and the most similar past case. A good real estate appraiser knows what comparable houses have sold for recently. A good ethics tutor knows how to pose a series of hypotheticals that make a clear moral judgment seem more and more dubious. Why would we expect less from expert systems?

Beyond expert systems design, the model addresses a central problem of AI: controlling the complexity of inference required for a system to locate relevant information. In the short run, AI's principal contribution to society may be to provide intelligent access to our vast databases of information, in particular, helping us to select and organize information that is relevant.

The Hypo program's conceptual structures for argument and knowledge representation techniques for indexing cases allow it to use the context of an argument to assess the relevance of a case and the features of a case that are salient. In other words, the model takes into account the context in which an object sought from the database will be used in dynamically assessing the relevance of retrieved objects and how to describe them.

The model's emphasis on argument is important philosophically as well. Theories of argumentation have long been juxtaposed to analytical reasoning. Aristotle drew a distinction between rhetoric and dialectics on the one hand and analytical reasoning on the other. (Plato ascribed the origins of the study of rhetoric to an ancient legal dispute. To help exiles returning to Syracuse in a lawsuit to regain their lands, teachers offered them instruction in rhetorical techniques.)

A theory of argumentation deals with justification and persuasion, not logical demonstration; potentially it provides structure for a vast range of discourse for which formal logic does not, value judgments. The Hypo model's computational knowledge structures and definitions are a first step toward more systematically describing value judgments.

The model also represents a start at a more accurate description of analogical reasoning in a domain where it is highly developed but not well understood. The model focuses on what improvements would allow the program to perform more complex kinds of legal analogies. It also focuses AI research on drawing analogies where the analog is not necessarily a highly structured object that can be mapped onto something else.

In short, this research extends AI into the realm of practical reasoning where there are no right answers and no internally consistent and well defined theories for making and explaining decisions but only arguments justifying alternative possible conclusions based on the experience of prior cases. In this realm, where experts do not agree what the rules are or what they mean, where reasoning is not just repeated applications of *modus ponens*, and explanations are not simply daisy chains of rules from axioms to conclusion, arguing with cases and hypotheticals is an effective methodology.

Chapter 2 illustrates the crucial role of adversarial case-based reasoning in legal argument by presenting an actual legal problem. It provides a brief description of a precedent-citing legal argument and some of the problems attorneys encounter in making such arguments.

Chapter 3 introduces the Hypo program and describes what it does, its inputs and outputs, and, in very general terms, how it works. In order to perform its adversarial case-based reasoning process, Hypo needs a computational definition of relevant similarities and differences. The chapter introduces the notions of factors and Dimensions and describes how they are employed in defining relevance.

Chapter 4 presents an overview of Hypo's knowledge sources, reasoning process, architecture, modules, major algorithms, and data structures. Chapter 5 works through an extended example of Hypo's reasoning process from start to finish, illustrating the inputs to and outputs from the process and providing a running commentary of the steps. (Other sample Hypo outputs are shown in appendix H.)

Chapters 6, 7, and 8 focus on selected aspects of Hypo's function and design. Hypo's two languages for representing legal cases and their facts, Legal Case Frames and Factual Predicates, its Case Knowledge Base (CKB) of actual legal cases, and the Dimensional Index to the CKB are discussed in chapters 6 and 7. Details about Hypo's implementation are contained in appendix J. Chapter 8 identifies basic operations of case-based reasoning and how they are performed in Hypo, including comparing cases, selecting the most analogous cases, and posing hypotheticals. Hypo's use of Claim Lattices in selecting most analogous cases and identifying configurations of counterexamples is discussed in detail.

The partial computational theory of adversarial case-based reasoning that Hypo in effect implements is set out in chapter 9. The chapter formally defines relevant similarities and differences in terms of factors and provides expressions for the best cases to cite and the features of a case that are salient in various argument roles. The chapter describes how Hypo uses citation labels from the *Blue Book: A Uniform System of Citation*, familiar to attorneys, to characterize the significance of cases and how Hypo deals symbolically with factor weights.

Chapter 10 presents an evaluation of Hypo's performance in the examples of chapter 5 and appendix H by comparing the outputs to the arguments that lawyers and judges made in the actual legal cases on which the example fact situations were based.

In chapter 11, I present some examples of adversarial case-based reasoning in nonlegal domains and discuss the kinds of domains where this case-based reasoning process works well and the problems of computationally implementing it. The chapter compares, in a general way, the approach taken in designing Hypo with that of various lines of research in artificial intelligence, including argument discourse analysis, analogical, case-based, and example-based reasoning, and explanation.

Chapter 12 compares Hypo's model of legal reasoning with that of other researchers. I examine the jurisprudential debate about analogical legal reasoning and discuss the importance of modeling hypothetical reasoning in law. The roles of hypotheticals in legal argument are illustrated with some exchanges from actual oral arguments before the U.S. Supreme Court. The chapter concludes with some specific suggestions for extending Hypo's reasoning process to account for more sophisticated kinds of precedential reasoning, including arguing about the meanings of abstract legal predicates and posing more sophisticated hypotheticals.

2 The Law as a Paradigm of Case-Based Argument

Case-based argument plays an essential role in legal argument. An attorney's law school training and legal practice inculcate standards of legal argument, and those standards strongly prefer arguments whose conclusions are justified by citing precedents (prior legal cases). In the American legal system, there is also a strong theoretical reason that case-based arguments are preferred. Under the common law doctrine of *stare decisis*, like cases are decided alike. Courts are bound to decide a case in accordance with the most analogous precedent.

2.1 A Scenario

Let us examine the quandary of a fictitious attorney in dire need of an argument.

It was 5:55 P.M. An associate of a major New York law firm sat in the walnut-paneled library at 13 Wall Street. He had opera tickets in his pocket for 8:00 that night, *Pagliacci*, and his socialite fiancée and her parents were to meet him at the Met. At 5:00, just before leaving for the day, Howe, a partner in the firm, buttonholed the associate in the elevator and recounted to him a telephone conversation between Howe and the house counsel of one of the firm's big oil company clients, Amexxco. The house counsel had been very angry. She complained that Amexxco was getting "shafted" by a particular former employee named G. Whiz. Mr. Whiz had developed a computer program, called Dipper, for analyzing drilling logs of oil wells. Last week Whiz quit, started his own consulting company, and was about to enter into a contract with Amexxco's competitor, Exxssinc, for computerized analysis of oil drilling logs. The house counsel wanted to know ASAP whether Amexxco could get an injunction against Whiz and Exxssinc to prevent Whiz from using or disclosing anything about the Dipper program. Howe promised to have an answer by 10:00 A.M. the next day. And that is why the associate sat in the walnut-paneled library as the hands of the brass pendulum clock showed 6:00.

There was more to Howe's story. Apparently Whiz, an expert on drilling log analysis, has a background in some arcane computer science specialty. Howe thought she said "AY." "Just like Howe to get it wrong," thought the associate. The house counsel had told Howe she was particularly worried about the fact that although Whiz was on the

Amexxco payroll, he had developed the Dipper program on his own initiative. For four years, Amexxco had repeatedly directed Whiz to drop the Dipper in favor of another approach. Then, a couple of weeks ago, in an experiment cooked up by Whiz, the Dipper actually discovered a major producing well. Last week Whiz quit over a dispute about salary and the use of the Dipper program. "At least," thought the associate, "Howe had sense enough to ask the house counsel whether Whiz had signed a nondisclosure agreement with Amexxco." Whiz had signed such an agreement when he first began working for Amexxco, long before he started work on the Dipper.

Trade secrets law wasn't exactly the associate's field. On the one hand, the facts that there was a nondisclosure agreement and that Whiz was an Amexxco employee when he developed the Dipper program seemed to him to help Amexxco's position. On the other hand, it sounded as if Whiz had been right about the Dipper program all along and Amexxco had been wrong. If Whiz hadn't been persistent enough to continue working on Dipper over Amexxco's objections, there wouldn't be a Dipper program to scrap over. Whiz ought to have some rights to the program. But what rights? All? None? "If it were up to me," the associate thought, "I'd give the guy a break, but Howe isn't billing me out at $250 per hour to do justice, and now its 6:10 and the taxi ride is going to take at least 45 minutes."

The associate knew that whatever conclusion he might come to, the house counsel was not going to take his word for it, or Howe's for that matter. She would have to be convinced, and it would take a legal argument to convince her. And at 6:15 P.M. a legal argument was precisely what the associate did not have. "Muffy and her parents have probably left Manhasset by now," he thought as he glanced at his watch.

2.2 What a Legal Argument Should Be

The associate needs to make an argument fast. Although he may not be an expert on trade secrets law, he knows what a legal argument looks like and how to tell if it is a good one. He knows what the facts of the dispute are, or at least some of them, and his firm's library contains most of the world's recorded knowledge on the subject of trade secrets misappropriation. The trick is to find the most relevant bits of that mountain of arcana to justify Amexxco's position.

The associate has been asked to provide a specific kind of information: a legally justifiable argument in favor of Amexxco on which to base a decision by Amexxco to commence a lawsuit against Whiz and Exxssinc to enjoin them from using Dipper. The associate knows who the parties to the lawsuit will be—Amexxco will bring suit as the plaintiff against Exxssinc and Whiz as defendants—and that he represents the plaintiff's side.

The associate's answer will take the form of a legal memorandum setting forth

- a summary of the facts of the dispute as he knows or assumes them to be;

- a description of the claims that Amexxco can bring against Whiz and Exxssinc (a claim is a recognized form of complaint for which the courts will grant relief, such as trade secrets misappropriation, breach of contract, copyright or patent infringement, or negligence);

- for each claim, a summary of the legal points that can be made for or against Amexxco's position on the claim.

Although there are no hard and fast rules for what a point in a legal argument should be, attorneys would expect to see three components:

1. A legal conclusion. Of the many kinds of legal conclusions, we will be concerned primarily with assertions that a side in a particular fact situation should win or lose a claim.

2. A justification. In a legal argument, a justification is a citation to an authority in support of the legal conclusion. There are four main kinds of authorities to cite in a legal argument: legal cases; court-made rules or principles; provisions of statutes, constitutions, and administrative regulations; and so-called secondary authorities, including scholarly legal works such as treatises.

3. A rationale why the justification applies. For each kind of authority there is a fairly standard way of substantiating that the authority cited in the justification applies to the particular facts of the current dispute.

The associate's task, then, is to determine what points can be made in a legal argument in favor of Amexxco. He must decide what kinds of legal claims Amexxco can assert against Whiz and Exxssinc, search his legal library for authorities to cite, and explain why the authority justifies the conclusion that Amexxco should win those claims.

2.2.1 Justifying by Citing Precedents

In the context of planning a lawsuit, the most important points the associate can turn up are those that cite precedents as authorities. The partner and house counsel will feel secure about assessing a lawsuit's prospects only if they can see and compare their client's fact situation with the cases they would cite in making an argument before the court and the cases that Whiz and Exxssinc would cite against them.

When the justification cites a legal case, the argument is an argument by analogy. The advocate asserts the legal conclusion that the current dispute should be decided in the same way as the cited case. His rationale is to draw an analogy between the current dispute and the cited case by pointing out the important similarities between them.

For purposes of drawing an analogy to a prior case or precedent, the similarities that matter involve facts that constitute strengths or weaknesses in the plaintiff's position on that claim. The plaintiff can make a strong point for its position on a particular claim if it can cite a case won by a plaintiff, involving the same kind of claim, and having the same plaintiff's strengths and weaknesses in common with the current dispute.

Even when the cited authority is a statute or a court-made rule or policy, the preferable way to make an argument is still to draw an analogy to precedents in addition to citing the statute. An advocate who seeks to show that a statutory provision or court-made principle applies to a client's facts finds other previously decided cases, selects those in which courts have decided in favor of the same side that the provision or principle applied, and argues by analogy that the court should decide in favor of the client because the client's facts are the same as those presented in the precedent.

The question of what strengths and weaknesses matter for a particular claim is important and controversial. One answer is that a strength or weakness matters if there is case (either the cited case or some other precedent) where the court has held that the facts associated with the strength or weakness made a difference in the outcome of the case, in favor of either the plaintiff or the defendant on that claim. A holding is the conclusion of the court as to the legal effect on each claim of the facts of the case, in favor of the plaintiff or the defendant. When asserting that a particular strength or weakness in a side's position makes a difference to the outcome, an attorney is always in a better adversarial position if he or she can cite a case where a court held that a similar strength or weakness mattered for that type of claim.

There are other answers to the question of what strengths and weaknesses matter for a claim. The issue is bound up with the controversial question of what determines the importance of similarities and differences in analogical legal reasoning. Despite the existence of a jurisprudential debate, in practice attorneys make arguments by analogy all the time.

2.2.2 What Precedents to Cite in a Point

The associate must find the right precedents to cite on behalf of Amexxco, but what are the right precedents? There are five basic criteria:

1. Same claim. The precedent should involve the same claim as the conclusion for which the attorney is arguing.

2. Same side. The side who won the precedent should be the same side for whom the attorney is arguing.

3. On point. A precedent is on point to the extent that it shares the same strengths and weaknesses as are present in the current dispute.

4. Most on point. The goal is to find the most-on-point precedents— the cases sharing the most strengths and weaknesses in common with the current dispute. These are the cases most analogous to the current dispute. In particular, the goal is to find cases that are more on point than any cases that held for the opponent's side.

5. Highest pedigree. All courts are not equal, and thus neither are all precedents. They have pedigrees. Precedents are better authorities to the extent that they were

- decided by a court of the same state whose law applies, a court of the relevant jurisdiction (figuring out which state's law applies may be a complicated issue that will also require case-based arguments to resolve),
- decided by the highest court of the relevant jurisdiction,
- decided after a full trial on the merits of the claim,
- never overturned, distinguished, or questioned by a subsequent court of the same or higher rank.

The associate's goal is clear: he must find the most-on-point cases with the highest pedigrees that favor Amexxco as the plaintiff, the side he represents. For example, he needs some precedent cases with claims for trade secrets misappropriation or breach of a nondisclosure agreement where an employee who signed a nondisclosure agreement worked on a product and then left to work on his own or for someone else using the information about the product and where the plaintiff won despite the fact that the employee was the sole developer of the product. He can use these cases to make strong points for Amexxco.

If the associate cannot find cases that are exactly on point, that is, that share all of the strengths and weaknesses in common with the current dispute, then he will settle for cases that are as on point as possible. His points, however, will not be as strong to the extent that his cited cases are not on point or there are even more-on-point cases for the opponents to cite in response.

2.2.3 Responding to Precedents

Since the associate can be sure that his opponents will point out the failings of his cited cases, he must consider their possible responses to his points in order to evaluate the strength of his side's argument. In general, responses to a precedent-citing point in a legal argument consist of combinations of the following: distinguishing the cited case, citing a real (or hypothetical) case as a counterexample, attacking the cited case's pedigree, and citing a contrary statutory provision or policy.

Distinguishing a cited case is a primary means of responding to it. An advocate argues that the case is not analogous to the fact situation by pointing out strengths and weaknesses that they do not share and that justify not treating the former as a precedent for the latter. If the point being responded to was made on behalf of side 1, facts that favor side 1's opponent, side 2, in the current dispute but were not present in the cited case, or that favored side 1 in the cited case but were not present in the current dispute, are distinctions. According to this kind of response, there is no need to follow the cited case as a precedent if the current dispute presents relative strengths for side 2 not considered in the cited case.

Citing another precedent as a counterexample is a second important way of responding to a point. A counterexample is a case that shares some of the same strengths and weaknesses with the case at hand as side 1's cited case but held nevertheless for side 2. By citing a counterexample, side 2 makes a point for its own side (it draws the analogy between the counterexample and the case at hand) and uses the contrasting result to show that the analogy drawn by side 1 is not compelling. Some counterexamples are better than others. A counterexample might be a hypothetical case, a made-up factual dispute that has not been decided by an actual court. In general, however, a counterexample is more persuasive to the extent that it is an actual decided case that is

- more on point than the cited case, that is, to the extent it has more strengths and weaknesses in common with the case at hand than the cited case, or

- an extreme example of some of the same pro-side 1 features as the cited case but still held for side 2.

A response can also attack the cited case's pedigree. Essentially the attorney argues that the court is not bound to follow the cited case because the cited case was

- decided by a court from another jurisdiction,

- not decided by an equivalent or superior court in the judicial hierarchy,

- overturned, distinguished, or questioned by a subsequent higher-ranking court, or

- involved a procedural setting that did not fully present the issues.

Statutory provisions, court-made rules, and policies also can be cited in response to a point. Side 2 may cite a provision or policy that contradicts the point's conclusion. Such a response would be improved by citing a case where the court expressly applied the provision or policy in holding for Side 2.

2.2.4 What about Other Facts?

As the associate builds his points and responses, inevitably he must worry about whether he has all of the facts. The house counsel may not have told Howe all of the facts relevant to the dispute. She may not have conducted a thorough investigation; she even may not know all of the kinds of facts that would be relevant. Even if facts are known, they still must be proved at trial. If the precedents indicate that a particular fact is crucial, the associate must plan for the contingency that his side will fail to prove it. Also he does not know what facts the opposing side may prove.

The associate's memorandum should flag these contingencies. It should pose hypotheticals like the following: What if Amexxco has disclosed information about Dipper to customers or in professional articles or sales literature? What if Amexxco has failed to take adequate measures to protect its trade secret information in Dipper?

2.2.5 Evaluating a Legal Argument

After the associate has assembled all of the on-point cases he can find for both sides, he, Howe, and the house counsel will have to assess how strong an argument each side can make. They must try to decide whether they have adequate grounds to commence a lawsuit and whether they have a winning argument. They will ask questions like the following:

- Do we (representing plaintiff) have cases to cite on a claim?
- Do they (representing defendant) have cases to cite?
- Are our cases distinguishable?
- Are any of their cases more-on-point than any of ours?
- Can either side cite any cases for which there are no more-on-point counterexamples?

- Have any of the cases been overturned?
- Are there significant contingencies for which we do not have information?
- What cases can we cite if the contingencies occur?

It is noteworthy that the attorneys cannot deduce how strong their legal argument is from the language of the statutes or the restatements of the law in the legal treatises. Appendixes A and B show excerpts from some representative statutory provisions and restatements. The definitions are far too general to determine whether the concepts apply to the fact situation. Even if they do apply, no attorney would be satisfied with citing just such a provision in support of his argument but would also seek to cite cases as authorities.

Similarly, the various statements of the elements of a legal claim propounded by courts or scholars are unavailing. The elements of a claim are generalized statements of the facts that must be proved in order to prevail on the claim. There is little agreement about the elements of a trade secrets claim. Compare the statement in [Gilburne and Johnston 1982, p. 215] that there are three elements as a condition of the existence of the trade secret: "novelty, secrecy and value in the trade or business of the putative trade secret owner" with the fact that neither [Milgrim 1985] nor [Nimmer 1985] is willing to list definitively the elements of a trade secrets claim. The primary utility of these statements of a claim's requirements are not as definitions but as annotated guides to cases.

The drafters of the Restatement (appendix B) were remarkably frank about the limitations of their definition of trade secrets:

An exact definition of a trade secret is not possible. Some *factors* to be considered in determining whether given information is one's trade secret are:
(1) the extent to which the information is known outside of his business;
(2) the extent to which it is known by employees and others involved in his business;
(3) the extent of measures taken by him to guard the secrecy of the information;
(4) the value of the information to him and to his competitors;
(5) the amount of effort or money expended by him in developing the information;
(6) the ease or difficulty with which the information could be properly acquired or duplicated by others. Res. (First) of Torts Sec. 757 comment b.

In order to supplement the deficiencies in their definition of trade secrets, the drafters of the Restatement described various factors that attorneys and judges should look for in the cases. "It is most common to discuss trade secrets in terms of the factors... tending to define a trade secret" [Nimmer 1985, pp. 3–4]. In the next chapter, we will see how factors play an important role as a way of indexing and organizing cases in a computerized database.

2.2.6 Finding the Cases

How can the associate come up with the right cases to cite in a legal argument? The firm's legal library offers the associate many routes into cases that he may cite. There are four major ones:

1. Digests. The associate can search manually through one of the many legal digests. The digests have hierarchical indexes to cover major areas of the law such as trade secrets. The attorney needs to examine the many entries to the index looking for promising entries such as "employee" and "nondisclosure agreements," turn to the digests, and manually scan the annotations for cases that appear to have interesting similarities to the current dispute. One especially useful index would include factors like those in the Restatement's commentary. If the associate knows or can find out what trade secret factors apply to his problem and if a digest indexed cases by those factors, he would be able to find useful cases.

2. Annotated statutes and treatises. The associate can examine the case annotations listed in the statutes and legal treatises dealing with trade secrets misappropriation. Reporting services index cases interpreting a particular statutory provision. The attorney must know what statutory provisions might be relevant to his fact situation. In treatises, legal propositions are annotated in footnotes containing cases that are examples of or counterexamples to the proposition. In order to find relevant propositions and cases, the attorney must scan the Contents or use the index of legal concepts to find potentially useful propositions and then scan the footnotes.

3. Full-text retrieval systems. The Lexis and Westlaw systems contain immense databases of the full text of legal cases. See [Sprowl 1976a, Sprowl 1976b]. The attorney fashions queries using logical

strings of keywords like "trade secrets," "employee," "nondisclosure agreement," or "sole developer." The system retrieves all cases evidencing the keywords ranked according to statistical criteria. The attorney must know what keywords to use and be prepared to scan the cases returned by the system.

4. Other computerized legal databases (Shepardizing). If the attorney knows of a relevant legal case, he may easily find all other cases that cite the case approvingly or disapprovingly, some of which are likely also to be relevant. The cross-references among legal cases are extensively documented in physical volumes and computerized databases.

All of these routes of access have disadvantages. Manual searches are time-consuming. Index entries may be too general to focus the attorney quickly on cases that share important analogous features. The indexes tend to have numerous entries, any of which might contain relevant information and all of which have to be examined. The visual scan of the annotations under each entry is thwarted if the descriptions of the cases are too general to disclose the particular features.

The full-text retrieval schemes have all of the problems of keyword searches [Blair and Maron 1985, Hafner 1987]:

- Ambiguity. The same keywords have different meanings in various legal areas, leading to retrieval of irrelevant cases.

- Synonyms. Relevant cases are omitted because they employed synonyms of keywords.

- Query composition. The attorney may not know the best, or even appropriate, keywords to use.

- Screening. The statistical criteria used to rank retrieved cases have little to do with the actual relative utility of the cases for the attorney's purpose. In attempting to pare down the list of retrieved cases to a manageable number, the attorney is forced to add logical qualifications to the query that arbitrarily skew the search, discarding potentially relevant cases.

2.3 Hypo: An Alternative

Alternatively the associate could use the computer program Hypo. With Hypo, the associate describes the facts of the problem. In response to inputting into Hypo the *Amexxco* fact situation, the program outputs (1) a summary of the best cases for the plaintiff or defendant to cite, (2) arguments showing how those cases can be cited and responded to, and (3) suggested hypothetical modifications of the problem that show how either side's argument could be improved. Hypo's Citation Summary of the *Amexxco* fact situation shows the best cases that each side can cite:

> **Citation Summary for *Amexxco* Case**
>
> On a claim for Trade Secrets Misappropriation, both sides can make a strong argument.
>
> Plaintiff can cite the following cases for which there are no more-on-point counterexamples:
>
> Structural Dynamics Research Corp. v. Engineering Mechanics Research Corp., 401 F. Supp. 1102 (E.D. Mich. 1975)
>
> Defendant can cite the following cases for which there are no more-on-point counterexamples:
>
> Amoco Production Co. v. Lindley, 609 P.2d 733 (Okla. 1980).

Hypo's precedent-citing arguments present opposing viewpoints of both sides in the argument: plaintiff and defendant. They are called "3-Ply Arguments" because they step through three plies, or turns, of an argument citing a precedent. In each 3-Ply Argument, Hypo makes a point for one side, drawing the analogy between the problem and the precedent, responds on behalf of the opponent by distinguishing the cited case and citing other precedents as counterexamples to it, and finally rebutting the response by, for example, distinguishing the counterexample.

> **3-Ply Argument for *Amexxco* Case**
>
> $\Longrightarrow$ Point for Plaintiff as Side 1:
>
> Where: Plaintiff and defendant entered into a nondisclosure agreement.
> Even though: Employee defendant was sole developer of plaintiff's product.

Plaintiff should win a claim for Trade Secrets Misappropriation.

Cite: Structural Dynamics Research Corp. v. Engineering Mechanics Research Corp., 401 F. Supp. 1102 (E.D. Mich. 1975).

$\Longleftarrow$ Response for Defendant as Side 2:

Structural Dynamics Research Corp. v. Engineering Mechanics Research Corp. is distinguishable because:

In Structural Dynamics, defendant received something of value for entering into the agreement. Not so in Amexxco.

In Structural Dynamics, plaintiff's former employee brought product development information to defendant. Not so in Amexxco.

In Structural Dynamics, the nondisclosure agreement specifically referred to plaintiff's product. Not so in Amexxco.

$\Longrightarrow$ Rebuttal for Plaintiff as Side 1: None.

3-Ply Argument for *Amexxco* Case

$\Longrightarrow$ Point for Defendant as Side 1:

Where: Employee defendant was sole developer of plaintiff's product.

Even though: Plaintiff and defendant entered into a nondisclosure agreement. Plaintiff adopted security measures.

Defendant should win a claim for Trade Secrets Misappropriation.

Cite: Amoco Production Co. v. Lindley, 609 P.2d 733 (Okla. 1980).

$\Longleftarrow$ Response for Plaintiff as Side 2: None.

$\Longrightarrow$ Rebuttal for Defendant as Side 1: None.

Hypo also suggests hypothetical variations of the problem situation that would help or hurt the associate's side.

Suggested Hypotheticals for *Amexxco* Case

Plaintiff's position would be strengthened in following situations:

Suppose:

Defendant's access to plaintiff's product information saved it time or expense. Plaintiff's former employee brought product development information to defendant.

Cf. Analogic Corp. v. Data Translation, Inc., 358 N.E.2d 804 (S. J. C. Mass. 1976)

Defendant's access to plaintiff's product information saved it time or expense. Defendant paid plaintiff's former employee to switch employment. Plaintiff's former employee brought product development information to defendant.
Cf. Space Aero Products Co. v. R. E. Darling Co., 208 A.2d 74 (Ct. App. Md. 1965)

Defendant's access to plaintiff's product information saved it time or expense. Defendant paid plaintiff's former employee to switch employment.
Cf. Telex Corp. v. IBM Corp., 510 F.2d 894 (10 Cir. 1975)

Plaintiff's former employee brought product development information to defendant.
Cf. Structural Dynamics Research Corp. v. Engineering Mechanics Research Corp., 401 F. Supp. 1102 (E.D. Mich. 1975)

The kind of output that Hypo generates—citations, arguments, and suggested hypotheticals—would have been extremely useful in preparing the associate's memorandum. For example, the 3-Ply Arguments would warn the associate of a good case for his opponent: the *Amoco* case that is exactly on point to his problem.

None of the other search methods can tailor the selections of relevant cases to the specific facts of the problem situation or explain their utility by illustrating how they can be employed in arguments about the problem. Using any of them, the associate would have to decide how the cases retrieved can be used in arguments about a particular fact situation, whether the opponent might have more persuasive cases to cite, and whether additional but as yet unknown facts in his client's situation might seriously affect the argument. Moreover, in order to use the other methods, he must perform a legal analysis of his fact situation and anticipate what he is looking for before he can find it. With Hypo, the program performs the analysis.

Alas, the story does not have a happy ending. Since the associate's firm did not have Hypo, he was late for the opera. His future father-in-law was so incensed that the wedding was postponed. Although the associate never found the *Amoco* case, Amexxco's house counsel did (her office had Hypo), and she decided that she no longer needed the services of a high-priced New York law firm. The firm thus lost a valuable corporate client. Although the associate never became a partner, he is considering returning to graduate school. Computer science, maybe?

3 Introduction to Hypo and Its Adversarial Reasoning Process

The Hypo computer program assists attorneys in evaluating disputes about trade secrets law. For each side, Hypo generates the best arguments, citing the most relevant legal cases in its database, and poses hypotheticals to show how to strengthen or weaken a side's argument.

Hypo is a case-based reasoning program. It employs actual legal cases in its database to analyze problem disputes. Given a description of a legal dispute, the program compares the problem to relevant cases, selects the most analogous cases, and cites them in arguments. It draws simple factual analogies between the problem and precedents, distinguishes precedents, cites counterexamples, and poses hypothetical variations of the problem to spur an attorney to focus on important additional facts that would strengthen or weaken the arguments. In short, Hypo symbolically compares and contrasts the problem situation and cases in its case database.

Hypo is also an adversarial reasoner. It makes competing arguments on how to decide a new problem. Instead of presenting the one "right" answer for how the case should be decided, it presents competing reasonable answers, citing the best cases for each side and showing the responses to those arguments.

The main inputs to the program are problem situations describing legal disputes. An attorney or assistant types in a description of the problem situation at the computer keyboard. Since the Hypo program does not have the ability to understand English, the user must input the problem situation in a specially designed language for representing legal disputes. The program has a menu-driven editing environment to guide the input process.

Hypo's primary outputs are a summary of the best cases for each side to cite, arguments citing each side's best cases and illustrating how to respond to them on behalf of the opponent, and hypotheticals showing how the problem situation could be modified to strengthen or weaken a side's argument.

Between inputs and outputs Hypo symbolically compares the problem dispute to cases in its Case Knowledge Base (CKB) in order to select the most analogous cases for each side. Hypo's process of reasoning adversarially with cases comprises the following general steps:

1. Analyze the problem situation and retrieve prior cases that share some important similarities with the problem.

2. Select the precedents most similar to the problem. (These precedents may have contradictory outcomes.)

3. For each of the most similar precedents, justify deciding the problem situation like the precedent by drawing an analogy emphasizing the similarities between them. (Justifications conflict where competing analogies may be drawn to prior cases with opposite outcomes.)

4. Attack conflicting justifications by distinguishing the associated precedent, citing other precedents as counterexamples, or posing hypotheticals.

5. Decide the problem situation, to the extent possible, by evaluating the best precedent-citing arguments pro and con alternative decisions and explain the decision by comparing the arguments and precedents.

This process, called the adversarial case-based reasoning process, tracks how attorneys argue with precedents. It deals with such concepts of vital interest to attorneys as relevant similarities and differences among cases, selecting the cases most relevantly similar to a problem, distinguishing precedents, and posing counterexamples and hypotheticals.

In order for Hypo to reason adversarially with cases, these legal concepts have been defined computationally; that is, they have been defined so that the program can compute them. Although Hypo's computational definitions of these legal concepts do not capture all aspects of the ways in which attorneys argue with legal precedents, they do capture an important subset. The computational definitions are good enough to enable Hypo to generate outputs that are legally reasonable and useful.

In Hypo, the legal concepts of relevant similarities and differences, most relevant cases, distinguishing, and counterexamples are defined in terms of factors. Factors are a kind of expert knowledge of the commonly observed collections of facts that tend to strengthen or weaken a plaintiff's argument in favor of a legal claim.

Each kind of legal claim has its own set of factors. Authors of legal treatises and law review articles regularly identify factors to look for in assessing the strength or weakness of a party's position and often footnote cases that exemplify the factors. The factors that affect trade secrets misappropriation claims have been gleaned from legal treatises and law review articles. The drafters of the Restatement (appendix B), for example, employed factors to supplement their definition of trade secrets. An example of a factor that affects a claim for trade secret misappropriation is the extent to which a plaintiff has taken security measures to protect its secret; the more security measures that were taken, the better is the plaintiff's argument. Another factor involves disclosing the secret. The fewer outsiders to whom the plaintiff has disclosed the secret, the better the case is for the plaintiff.

One can think of examples of factors for almost any legal claim. The plaintiff in a medical malpractice suit is helped to the extent that a physician failed to take steps to warn the patient of the consequences of a proposed course of treatment. In a suit for breach of contract, the alleged breacher is helped to the extent that it received nothing of value (no consideration) in exchange for entering into the contract. In a prosecution for murder, the defendant who asserts self-defense is hurt to the extent that time has passed between the threat and his response.

Factors have magnitudes to reflect the fact that a particular case may be a more or less extreme example of the factor. Disclosure to one hundred outsiders is worse for the trade secrets plaintiff than disclosure to six outsiders. No warning at all is worse for the physician than providing a written description of the possible consequences. Nothing of value received in the exchange is worse for the contract claim plaintiff than receipt of a peppercorn. Two days between threat and response is worse for the criminal defendant than two minutes.

The magnitude of a factor should be distinguished from its weight. A factor's weight is some kind of measure of the support it lends to a conclusion that the plaintiff should win a claim. While attorneys probably will agree that for any given kind of claim, factors can be identified, they will disagree how much weight the various factors have.

Hypo's model of legal analysis involves factors. When an expert attorney analyzes a problem, it is assumed that he or she determines which legal claims may apply to the case and identifies the factors in the case that favor or hurt the plaintiff on each of those claims. A judge's task is to assign an outcome to a problem, that is, to decide that plaintiff has won or failed to win a particular legal claim. The task of an attorney is to persuade the judge what outcome to assign. As legal experts, attorneys know for a given kind of claim the factors that apply, as well as the side that the factors favor, and they emphasize those factors, and precedents exemplifying the factors, in their arguments to the judge.

Hypo performs a legal analysis of a problem situation in much the same way. In Hypo, factors are represented with Dimensions. A Dimension is a general framework for recording information about a factor for the program to manipulate. Hypo has a library of Dimensions for the claim of trade secrets misappropriation, each associated with a factor that identifies a common strength or weakness in a trade secrets claim. Each Dimension has a set of prerequisites used to test if the factor applies to a case and a range of values over which the magnitude of the factor in a particular case may vary.

In Hypo, a precedent is treated as a historical collection of factors, each with a particular magnitude, to which some authoritative decision-maker, the judge, has assigned an outcome, either in favor of or against the plaintiff with respect to a legal claim. A problem situation, after Hypo analyzes it, is also treated as a collection of factors but one whose outcome has not yet been decided.

In problem disputes as in precedents, the factors generally conflict. Some of the factors favor the plaintiff on a particular claim, and others favor the defendant. The question for the judge, and for attorneys who try to influence the judge, is how to resolve the conflicts among the factors found in a case.

In general, in the legal domain, there is no one answer to the question of how to resolve the competing factors in a particular case. The law has no analytic model or procedure for resolving the competing factors, no weighting scheme or function that yields the "right answer" through some deductive or mathematical process. Instead judges expect an attorney to make a reasonable argument citing cases that justifies a resolution of the conflict favorable to the client. Since there are two sides to the argument, the legal experts usually come up with conflicting reasonable arguments.

Precedents are used to support arguments about how to resolve conflicting factors in a current problem. Since the precedent is a collection of factors to which some judge has assigned an outcome, the precedent may be cited by an advocate to support the assertion that the conflict among the same factors in the current dispute should be resolved in just the same way.

That attorneys use precedents to justify a resolution of conflicting factors in a current dispute is a simplifying assumption that has been made in designing Hypo. Attorneys, of course, make other uses of precedents— for example, in building more theoretical analogies between cases. Hypo cannot draw those kinds of analogies. Although Hypo draws only simple factual analogies in terms of shared and unshared factors, its model of arguing with precedents is good enough to generate intelligent, helpful outputs.

The Venn diagrams shown in figure 3.1 illustrate how Hypo uses factors. For a particular kind of legal claim, Hypo represents the important factors that favor an outcome for or against a side. Figure 3.1a shows two kinds of claims; claim 1 might be a trade secrets claim and claim 2 a copyright claim. For claim 1, the figure indicates all of the important factors that favor a positive outcome for a side (+) and those that favor a negative outcome (−). In other words, some of the factors favor a positive outcome for plaintiff on a trade secrets claim (+), and some favor a negative outcome for plaintiff (−), that is, favor a decision for defendant on the claim. Claim 2, a copyrights claim, would involve different (although possibly related) factors.

A problem is treated as a collection of usually competing factors. Figure 3.1b shows a problem P and its set of competing factors. Although deciding problem P's outcome, $O(P)$, entails resolving the competing factors, the question is how. Since the law usually has no analytic model or procedure for resolving the conflict, attorneys argue with precedents. An adversary hopes to find a precedent that has the same set of conflicting factors as in the problem situation so that he or she may argue that the same outcome should be assigned to the problem as in the precedent. In figure 3.1c, case A can be cited in an argument that problem P should have a positive outcome for claim 1 because case A had a positive outcome, $O(A) = +$, and shared some of the same factors with the problem.

Hypo's definitions of relevant similarities and differences among cases are based on this idea that precedents are used to justify the resolution of competing factors. The set of relevant similarities between two cases is the set of factors that the two cases share. The set of relevant differences between two cases contains factors not shared in the cases that favor opposite outcomes and differences in the magnitudes of shared factors.

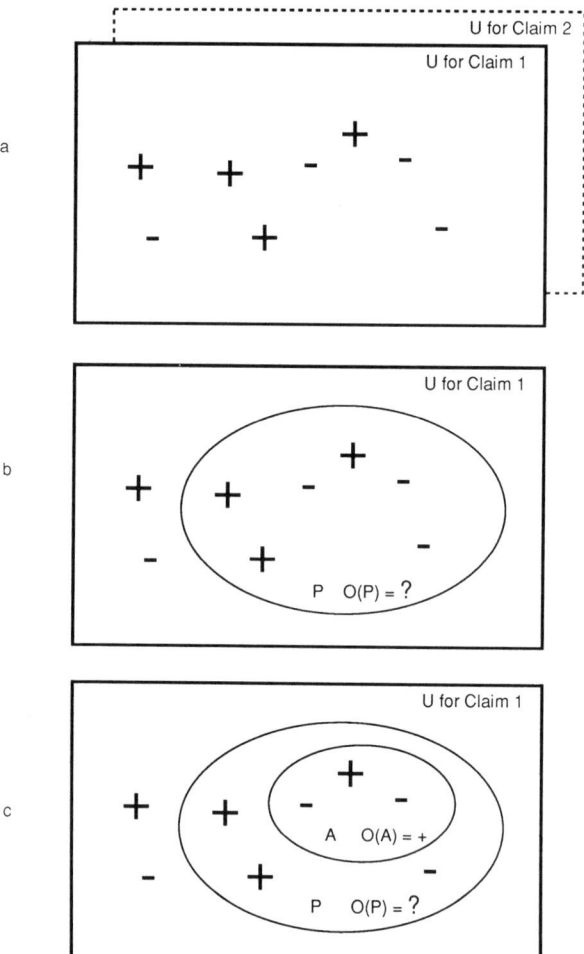

Figure 3.1
Precedents Resolve Competing Factors. *a*, Some factors favor a positive outcome
(+) for plaintiffs on Claim 1, and some favor a negative outcome (−). Claim 2 may
involve other factors. *b*, A problem P is a collection of competing factors. *c*, Case A
is on point to P because they share factors. Case A has a positive outcome
($O(A) = +$) and can be cited for a positive outcome in P. The unshared negative
(−) factor distinguishes A from P. It favors a negative outcome in P. The unshared
positive factors are not distinctions. They favor a positive outcome in P.

Hypo treats the shared factors as relevant similarities that justify treating the new problem like the old case. The old case was decided because, or in spite, of the factors that applied to it. Some of those factors also apply to the new problem and justify the same outcome. Similarly the relevant differences are reasons that the two cases should be decided differently. The unshared factors make a side's position stronger in one case than in the other and thus may cause the case to be a weaker justification in a legal argument. In figure 3.1c, for example, case A is relevantly similar to the problem P because of the factors it shares with P. In this instance, case A has one relevant difference from P: the negative factor that applies to P but not to A. If one were citing case A in an argument for a positive outcome in P, one would emphasize the shared factors. The opponent would emphasize the unshared negative factor as a relevant difference. That is what Hypo does when it cites a case in a 3-Ply Argument and responds for the opponent by distinguishing the case.

The important legal concepts of a case's being on point, most on point, a best case for a side to cite, or a counterexample to another case are also defined in terms of factors. In Hypo, a past case is on point with respect to a problem if it is relevantly similar, that is, shares at least one factor with the problem situation. One precedent is more on point with respect to a problem than another precedent if its set of relevant similarities (that is, its set of shared factors) includes that of the other precedent as a proper subset. Cases that are most on point are the most relevantly similar of all the cases in the CKB; there is no case in the CKB whose set of relevant similarities includes that of a most-on-point case. Hypo may cite a case as a precedent in an argument on behalf of a side if the case is on point and at least one of the shared factors favors that side. With Hypo, as in law, the more on point a case is, the better it is to cite it in an argument. For example, in figure 3.1c case A is on point with respect to problem P because it is relevantly similar. In figure 3.2, case B is more on point than case C because case B has every factor that case C shares with problem P and shares other factors with P that case C does not. In other words, case C's set of factors shared with P is a subset of those of case B.

Hypo is programmed to look for cases to cite as counterexamples in response to an argument citing a precedent. Hypo's various kinds of counterexamples are also defined in terms of factors. In figure 3.2, if

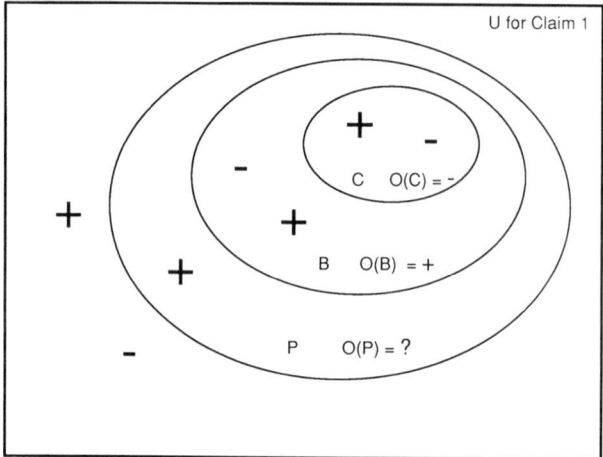

Figure 3.2
Defining Relative Similarity of Cases in Terms of Factors

an arguer cited case C on behalf of a negative outcome in the problem situation, an opponent could cite case B as a counterexample. In a sense, case B trumps case C, it has the same factors in common with P that case C does and then some and had the opposite outcome.

Since Hypo represents the context in which a precedent is used in a legal argument, it can also determine the differences among cases that are salient in a particular context. For instance, in figure 3.3, the question is whether case D is relevantly similar to problem P. Although case D shares some factors with problem P, there is one unshared factor. Does that mean that the case is not relevantly similar? It is a hard question to answer, especially if, as is usually the case in law, there is no analytic theory of a domain to resort to. By taking into account the context of how a case is to be used in an argument, however, some intelligent assessments of similarity can still be made. For example, if case D is to be cited in support of an argument that P should have a positive outcome, then the negative unshared factor does not matter; in fact, it even helps the argument. Its presence in case D implies that the shared factors so strongly favored a positive outcome that they overcame the negative factor, an obstacle not even presented in problem P. This kind of information can also be used to select among cases. Case D is a better

Introduction to Hypo and Its Adversarial Reasoning Process

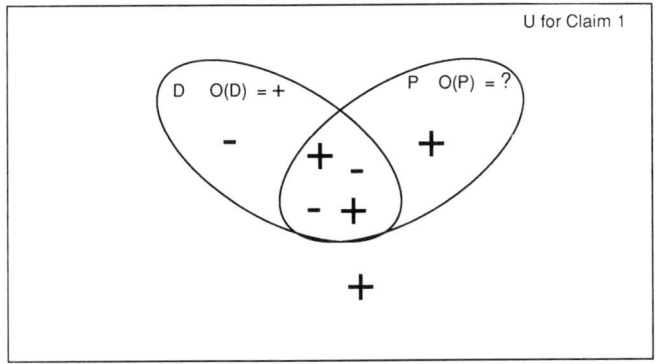

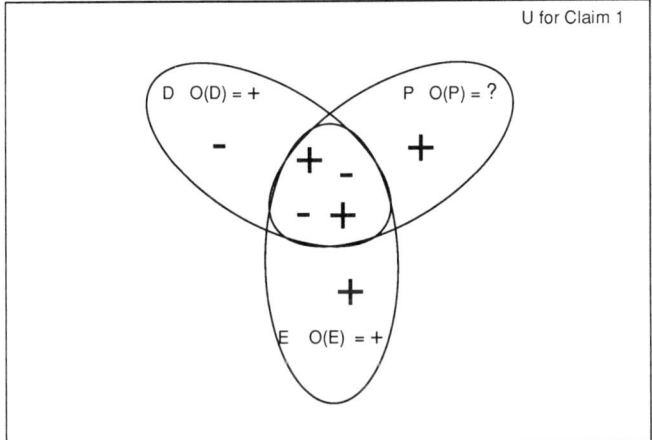

Figure 3.3
Reasoning about Significance of Differences

case to cite on behalf of a positive outcome than case E because of E's unshared positive factor.

These examples illustrate the kind of reasoning that Hypo performs with cases and, in particular, how Hypo symbolically compares cases. In performing each step of its adversarial case-based reasoning process, Hypo is comparing or modifying cases in terms of factors as represented by its Dimensions.

In step 1 of its adversarial case-based reasoning process, Hypo analyzes a problem by determining what factors (as represented by Dimensions) apply. Using the factors as an index into the cases in the CKB, Hypo retrieves any case sharing a factor with the problem. These cases are relevantly similar. Hypo selects the most similar precedents in step 2. It orders the on-point cases according to the inclusiveness of their sets of factors to find those with the greatest overlaps of factors shared with the problem. In steps 3 through 5, Hypo draws analogies between the problem and a most-on-point precedent by reciting the factors that they share. It distinguishes a precedent by focusing on relevant differences, the unshared factors. The various kinds of counterexamples that Hypo cites in response to a precedent are defined in terms of overlaps of factors or differences in factor magnitudes. Similarly, Hypo hypothetically modifies the problem situation by adding, subtracting, or exaggerating factors.

4 The Hypo Program: An Overview

This chapter presents an overview of the Hypo program and how it represents and applies legal case precedents and hypothetical cases to assist an attorney in evaluating and making arguments about disputes involving trade secrets law. The Hypo program's key elements include its

- Case Knowledge Base (CKB), a structured database of actual legal cases,

- Dimension Index, an indexing scheme employing Dimensions for retrieval of relevant precedents from the CKB,

- Dimensional Analysis, methods for analyzing a problem (referred to as the current fact situation, or cfs) and retrieving relevant cases from the CKB,

- Case Positioning, methods for positioning the problem situation with respect to relevant precedent cases in the CKB and finding the most-on-point cases,

- Symbolic Case Comparison, methods for comparing and contrasting cases (e.g., citing, distinguishing, finding counterexamples),

- Hypotheticals, methods for perturbing the current fact situation to generate hypotheticals that test the strength of an argument as new damaging facts come to light and existing favorable facts are discredited,

- 3-Ply Arguments, methods for generating 3-Ply Arguments to dry run and debug a legal argument and to characterize the strength of available precedents using citation labels in a manner familiar to attorneys,

- Explanation, a framework for explaining a decision and its alternatives by citing precedents as examples, critically comparing the precedents' strengths using 3-Ply Arguments, and posing hypothetical variations of the current fact situation and precedents to demonstrate critical features that, if different, would lead to different conclusions.

4.1 Hypo's Reasoning Process

Basically Hypo takes as its input a fact situation describing a trade secrets dispute and generates an output consisting of a Citation Summary, 3-Ply Arguments, and Suggested Hypotheticals. The outputs show the best precedents to cite for each side on the claim, how those cases may be cited in legal points, how an opponent would respond to each point, and how a point or response could be strengthened by the addition or subtraction of crucial facts.

Hypo's reasoning process for generating the outputs corresponds closely to the adversarial case-based reasoning process described in chapter 3 that follows these basic steps:

1. Analyze the current fact situation Dimensionally.
2. Retrieve relevant precedent cases from the CKB.
3. Position the cfs with respect to retrieved cases.
4. Compare cases and select best precedents.
5. Generate 3-Ply Arguments for the cfs citing precedents.
6. Heuristically (hypothetically) modify the cfs.
7. Generate 3-Ply Arguments for selected hypotheticals.
8. Explain by illustrating arguments and comparing arguments for the cfs and selected hypotheticals.

4.2 Knowledge Sources in Hypo

Hypo employs four knowledge sources to perform the reasoning process: (1) Case Representation Language, (2) Case Knowledge Base, (3) Dimensions, and (4) Argument Evaluation Criteria.

Hypo's Case Representation Language is a frame-based language for representing the facts of a case and certain aspects of the legal decision. The language has two tiers: Legal Case Frames and Factual Predicates.

Legal Case Frames are the basic language for representing cases in Hypo. Actual legal cases in the CKB, current fact situations presented by an attorney as inputs, and hypothetical cases posed by Hypo are expressed in Legal Case Frames. Each such case has the following:

- A top-level Legal Case Frame for representing information about the case, including its name, citation information, the parties to the dispute and their roles as plaintiff or defendant, what claims were raised, and how the case was decided. For current fact situations entered by the user and hypotheticals generated by Hypo, the top-level frame will be mostly blank, reflecting the fact that those cases have not actually been decided by a court.

- Underlying Legal Case Frames for representing the factual objects and relations that are important in trade secrets and related cases. The actors in the dispute are represented by frames for persons, corporations, and employees. Information related to the parties' products appears in frames for products, knowledge, products worked on by a particular employee, product similarities, breaches of security, and disclosure events. There are special frames for representing the relationship of being employed by some corporation and changing employment from one employer to another. Finally, there are Legal Case Frames for representing agreements, noncompetition covenants, nondisclosure agreements, promises and reliance. Appendix C contains a complete list of Legal Case Frames.

Factual Predicates are a second language for summarizing the facts of a case represented by the underlying Legal Case Frames. They are generalized factual statements that confirm whether certain legally significant relationships are true in the case (e.g., that a plaintiff's product information has been disclosed to some outsiders or that one of plaintiff's employees switched employers). Factual Predicates are used primarily in Dimensional analysis of a fact situation. A complete list of all of the Factual Predicates is shown in appendix D.

The CKB contains 30 actual and hypothetical legal cases. All of the cases are represented in Legal Case Frames and entail claims for trade secrets misappropriation, breach of nondisclosure or noncompetition agreements, or breach of other kinds of contracts. Appendix E lists all of the cases in the CKB.

Dimensions are the Hypo program's principal index to cases in the CKB. They are a knowledge representation construct for representing factors, stereotypical facts of legal cases important for the strength of a plaintiff's position on a particular kind of claim. Factors are a conceptual link between various clusters of operative facts that may appear in legal disputes and the legal conclusions that they support or undermine. Dimensions allow a computer program to reason with those links. Appendix F summarizes the thirteen Dimensions implemented for the trade secrets domain.

Each Dimension is structured to allow the program to determine whether the Dimension applies to a case and the Dimension's magnitude in the case. Each Dimension has

- prerequisites, lists of Factual Predicates that must be satisfied in a case for the Dimension to apply to the case;

- focal slots that single out the particular facts making a case more or less extreme along the Dimension; and

- range information that tells how a change in the focal slot value makes the case better or worse for the plaintiff along the Dimension.

Argument Evaluation Criteria allow Hypo to make simple comparisons of the relative strengths of case-based arguments in favor of or against the plaintiff by comparing the precedents that can be marshaled on either side. The criteria are listed in Appendix G. Although the criteria are not strong enough to determine a winner of a case (probably no criteria are strong enough for that), they are strong enough to select and order the precedents in terms of their utility in a legal argument. In evaluating competing arguments, Hypo determines whether any side can cite cases for which the opponent has no more similar cases to cite in response as counterexamples. If only one side can cite such cases, Hypo treats that side as having the stronger argument. If both sides can cite such cases, Hypo treats each side as having a strong argument and regards the dispute as a tie.

4.3 Hypo's Architecture

The Hypo program is divided into eight modules that use these knowledge sources in performing the program's basic processing steps:

1. The Case Analyzer. Performs a Dimensional analysis of a current fact situation to determine what cases are relevant to the situation.
2. The Case Positioner. Retrieves relevant cases from the CKB and organizes those cases according to how on point they are with respect to the current fact situation.
3. The Best Case Selector. Selects from the positioned relevant cases the most-on-point cases for the plaintiff and defendant, as well as cases that potentially are most on point.
4. The 3-Ply Arguer. Generates 3-Ply Arguments consisting of points, responses, and rebuttals using the most-on-point cases and cases selected by the attorney as examples and counterexamples in a legal argument.
5. The Hypo Generator. Generates hypothetical variants of the current fact situation to bolster points and responses or generate new ones.
6. The Explainer. Summarizes the cases that can be cited in favor of a position, characterizes how strongly they support the position, focuses the attorney's attention on the most significant cases and hypotheticals, including those that the user may wish to have Hypo analyze for the sake of comparison, and facilitates comparing arguments between cases and hypotheticals that Hypo has analyzed.
7. The Session Manager. Keeps track of current fact situations analyzed and hypotheticals generated in a session.
8. The Case Editor. Assists the attorney in inputting new fact situations, modifying existing fact situations, or permanently storing a fact situation in the CKB.

The flow of control in HYPO consists of a session of recursive runs through a basic processing loop. In the basic processing loop, a single current fact situation undergoes Dimensional analysis, positioning, best case selection, and argument generation. The basic processing loop is the main loop shown in figure 4.1, a schematic diagram of the flow of control through Hypo's modules. A session with Hypo consists of multiple recursions through the basic processing loop. On each recursion, the cfs may be the same fact situation, a hypothetical variant of a fact situation previously analyzed in the session, or a different case from the CKB.

The input to the basic loop is a current fact situation expressed in the Legal Case Frame language. The current fact situation describes a dispute between parties involving trade secret information or breaches of nondisclosure and noncompetition agreements. The flow of control and information through each basic loop in the session starts with the Session Manager through which the user selects the current fact situation. The cfs may be a case from the CKB, a new case entered by the user through the use of the menu-driven Case Editor, or a hypothetical variant of the cfs previously generated by Hypo in the session. The Session Manager creates a Case Analysis Record for the current fact situation. The *Case Analysis Record* is the basic data structure for storing information about the results of the analysis and interpretation of the current fact situation produced in the basic processing loop. The Session Manager keeps track of this and all other Case Analysis Records for a session.

Upon receiving a new current fact situation, the Case Analyzer Dimensionally analyzes it. The Analyzer determines what Factual Predicates are satisfied by the cfs and records that information in an Interpretation Frame, which is stored in the Case Analysis Record. An *Interpretation Frame* is the basic data structure for summarizing the values of all Factual Predicates for a particular case. Using the information contained in the Interpretation Frame, the Case Analyzer determines which Dimensions' prerequisites are satisfied by the cfs. A Dimension is applicable if all of its prerequisites (which are expressed in terms of lists of Factual Predicates) are satisfied. A Dimension is a *near miss* if all a Dimension's prerequisites are satisfied in a fact situation except those prerequisites associated with the Dimension's focal slots, the slots that locate the fact situation somewhere along the Dimension's range. The applicable and near-miss Dimensions are recorded in the appropriate slots of the Case Analysis Record.

Using the list of applicable and near-miss Dimensions in the Case Analysis Record, the Case Positioner retrieves any case in the CKB indexed by any of the applicable or nearly applicable Dimensions. These cases are, to a first approximation, all of the cases in the CKB that are relevant for the analysis of the current fact situation. The Case Positioner then organizes those cases in Claim Lattices. A *Claim Lattice* is the basic

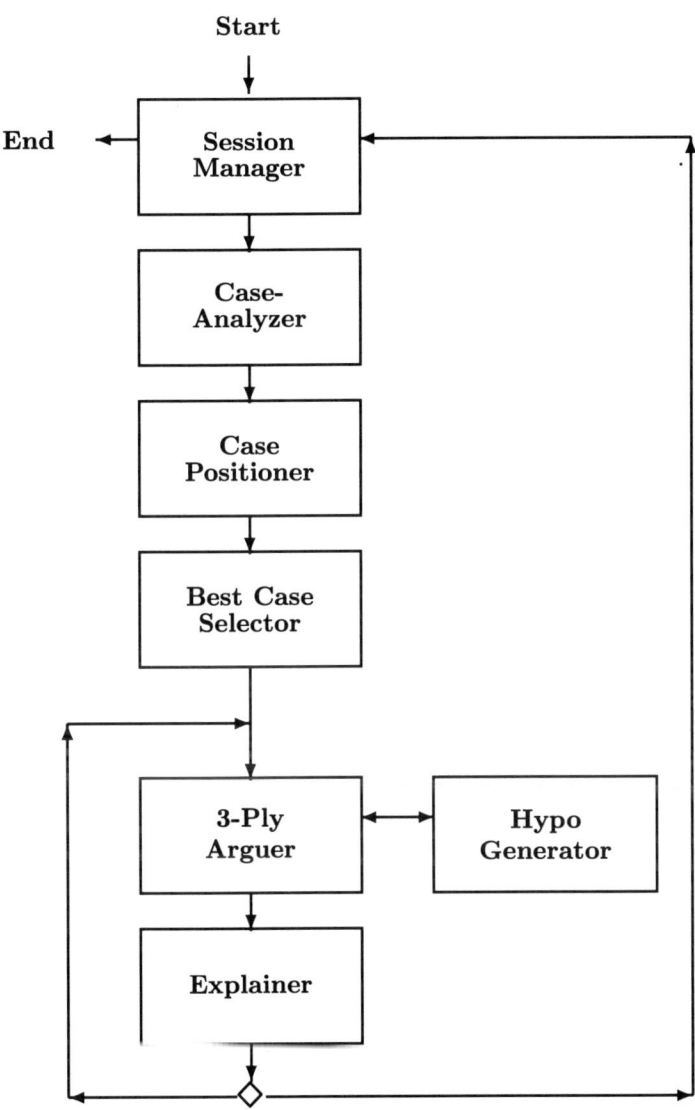

Figure 4.1
Basic Processing Loop

data structure for organizing the relevant cases according to how on point they are relative to the current fact situation—more specifically, how great the overlap is between Dimensions that apply to the case and those that apply or nearly apply to the cfs. Basically, the closer a case is to the root of the Claim Lattice, the more on point the case is to the cfs.

Once Claim Lattices are created, it is a simple matter for the Best Case Selector to choose the most-on-point cases. The *most-on-point* cases are the cases in the Claim Lattice that have the greatest overlap of applicable Dimensions with the cfs. The Best Case Selector sorts the most-on-point cases by the winner (the plaintiff or the defendant). Depending on who won, the most-on-point cases may be the best cases to cite in support of a particular side in the current fact situation or the most troublesome cases for that side. The Best Case Selector also selects potential most-on-point cases. *Potential most-on-point* cases have the greatest overlap of applicable and near-miss Dimensions with the cfs. Depending on who won a potential most-on-point case and its relative position with respect to existing most-on-point cases, it may be the basis of a useful hypothetical variant of the cfs. The most-on-point cases are also recorded in the appropriate slots of the Case Analysis Record.

Using the Claim Lattices and best case information, the 3-Ply Arguer generates Argument Records. An *Argument Record* is a blueprint for constructing a 3-Ply Argument. It is the basic data structure for recording information about how to

- cite a case in a legal point for a side in the cfs by drawing an analogy between the two,

- respond to that point on behalf of the opposing side by distinguishing the case and citing counterexamples, and

- pose hypothetical variations of the cfs that would strengthen the point or the response.

A 3-Ply Argument is constructed by presenting the information in an Argument Record in a 3-ply, turn-taking model of a (1) point for one side, (2) response to the point on behalf of the opposing side, and (3) rebuttal for the first side. Theoretically the exchange of point, response, and rebuttal could go on for many ply, but in legal practice, the sequences tend to be shallow; three ply is usually the limit.

The Explainer assembles the outputs for a cfs. It explains the strengths and weaknesses of a side's position by demonstrating the 3-Ply Arguments, summarizing the relevant cases' significance in a manner familiar to attorneys including applying "citation labels," posing hypotheticals to show how particular points or responses can be bolstered and how to make new points, and comparing 3-Ply Arguments for other hypotheticals and cases analyzed during the session.

For each claim, the Explainer automatically generates 3-Ply Arguments for all of the most-on-point cases that a side could cite in the first instance and for which the opponent cannot cite any counterexample that is more on point. The Explainer also allows the attorney to select cases with which Hypo makes 3-Ply Arguments.

The Explainer suggests hypothetical variations of the cfs that would strengthen or weaken a side's argument and offers to demonstrate the effect of the change on the argument. If the attorney chooses, the Explainer implements the change and generates new arguments for the hypothetical fact situation. The 3-Ply Arguer and the Hypo Generator work together to pose hypothetical variants of the cfs that could bolster certain points or responses or generate new points. The Hypo Generator uses specifications derived by the 3-Ply Arguer and a set of heuristics to generate legally relevant hypotheticals. The specifications tell the Hypo Generator, for example, to make a variant of the cfs that is more like a targeted potential most-on-point case. The hypothetical will become the subject of a subsequent recursive call through the basic processing loop. New 3-Ply Arguments are created that show how the target case can then be cited as a new point or counterexample.

5 Hypo in Action: An Extended Example

Hypo's knowledge sources, reasoning process, and flow of control are best explained in the context of an extended example. The example demonstrates the steps by which Hypo's modules analyze a problem situation and generate arguments and hypotheticals.

The sample problem situations discussed in this and the following chapters are based on the fact situations of actual legal cases. It is as if an attorney for one of the parties to the lawsuit were consulting Hypo for help in planning arguments to make in court. By using real cases, Hypo's arguments can be compared with those that lawyers and judges actually made in the opinions and briefs.

This extended example illustrates Hypo's reasoning process in a sequence of runs through the basic processing loop starting with a cfs based on *Crown v. Kawneer*, 335 F. Supp. 749-762 (N.D. Ill., 1971). The facts of the case as reported in the opinion are summarized in the squib set out below. A squib is a structured summary of a legal case much like case briefs prepared by law students. Like all of the other squibs in this book, this one was produced manually by an attorney familiar with the opinion of the case. As the squib shows, the court in *Crown* held for the defendant where the plaintiff had made disclosures of its alleged trade secret information through negotiations with the defendant and sales to third parties.

Squib for *Crown* Case

Title: Crown Industries, Inc. v. Kawneer Co.

Cite: 335 F. Supp. 749-762 (N.D. Ill.)

Date: June 29, 1971

Parties: Plaintiff, Crown; Defendant, Kawneer

Claim: Trade Secrets Misappropriation

Procedural Setting: Defendant moves to dismiss complaint after trial.

Decision: Judgment for Defendant dismissing complaint.

Facts: From 1962 to 1964, Crown developed a hydraulic power pack, PX-121, for automatic door openers. Crown complained that Kawneer Co. developed a competing product, PX-125, by misappropriating Plaintiff's trade secrets. Crown's power packs had been sold to and installed in five public retail establishments where the units were accessible for inspection. Crown made disclosures about the power pack to another third party, and in 1963 and 1965 a Crown employee made disclosures concerning the pack to Kawneer in connection with possible contract negotiations. None of the disclosees entered into any agreement with Crown to keep the information confidential or not to use the information. PX-121 did not have any unique features not generally known to the prior art. It took Kawneer six years to develop PX-125, from 1962 to 1968. When Kawneer developed the PX-125, it had access to Crown's disclosed information.

Issues:

(1) Did Plaintiff lose its trade secrets in the PX-121 by making public disclosures through its sale of the units and disclosures to a third party and to Defendant?

(2) Did Defendant breach a confidential relationship with Plaintiff regarding the disclosed information?

Holding:

(1) Held for Defendant: Yes.

(2) Held for Defendant: No. Defendant did not enter into a nondisclosure agreement with Plaintiff.

Cases cited: re (2): *Midland-Ross Corp. v. Sunbeam Equipment Co.*, 316 F. Supp. 171 (W.D. Pa 1970), affirmed, 435 F.2d 159 (3d Cir. 1970).

5.1 The Case Editor

The Case Editor allows the attorney to input a new fact situation or edit an existing one. The Editor presents a menu of Factual Predicates and allows the attorney to input values for them, such as a string indicating the name of an object representable with a Legal Case Frame, for example a party or a product, or some specific focal slot values. Given a Factual Predicate and the input value, Hypo has methods that find or instantiate the appropriate Legal Case Frames, set the values of the slots, and cross-reference them. The attorney can browse the Legal Case Frames in the Editor to fill in details. Alternatively, an attorney may begin with an existing fact situation already represented in Legal Case Frames and use the Editor to change names and facts to fit the new fact situation. The Editor also allows the attorney to store fact situations permanently in the CKB as new actual legal cases or interesting hypotheticals.

Here is how the *Crown* case looks as represented in the Legal Case Frame language. The top-level Legal Case Frame contains the following legal information:

Case: Crown Industries Inc. v. Kawneer Co.

SHORT TITLE: "Crown Industries"

CITATION: 335 F. Supp. 749 (N.D. Ill., 1971)

DATE: 1971

PARTIES:
Plaintiff Corporate-Party: Crown
Defendant Corporate-Party: Kawneer

DECISION FOR:
Corporate-Party: Kawneer

CLAIMS DECIDED:
Type-of-Claim: Trade-Secrets-Misappropriation
Won by: Corporate-Party: Kawneer

DIMENSIONS LIST:
Secrets-Voluntarily-Disclosed
Disclosure-In-Negotiations-With-Defendant

CASES CITED BY COURT: Midland-Ross Corp. v. Sunbeam Equipment Co.

The underlying Legal Case Frame representation of the facts of the *Crown* case comprises the objects representing the parties, products, and alleged trade secret information and disclosure. The Corporate-Party objects show the roles of the parties in the case (with Crown as plaintiff and Kawneer as defendant) and their relationship as producers of competing products (a slot value of "Nil" indicates that the facts of the case contain no information with which to fill the slot):

Corporate-Party: Crown

NAME: Crown

CASE: Crown Industries Inc. v. Kawneer Co.

CASE ROLE: Plaintiff

EMPLOYEE LIST: Nil

PRODUCT LIST: Product: PX-121

COMPETITOR'S PRODUCTS: Corporate-Party: Kawneer, Product: PX-125

Corporate-Party: Kawneer

NAME: Kawneer

CASE: Crown Industries Inc. v. Kawneer Co.

CASE ROLE: Defendant

EMPLOYEE LIST: Nil

PRODUCT LIST: Product: PX-125

COMPETITOR'S PRODUCTS: Corporate-Party: Crown, Product: PX-121

Crown's Product, PX-121, is a hydraulic power pack used for automatic door openers. It took Crown 72 months to develop the product, from 1962 through 1968:

Product: PX-121

NAME: PX-121

CASE: Crown Industries Inc. v. Kawneer Co.

A KIND OF: Hydraulic Power Pack

PRODUCT USED FOR: Automatic Door Openers

GENERAL PRODUCT MARKET: Building Owners

COMPETITOR'S PRODUCTS:
Corporate-Party: Kawneer Product: PX-125

DEVELOPER: Corporate-Party: Crown

EMPLOYEES WHO WORKED ON PROJECT: Nil

PROJECT DEVELOPMENT START: 1962

PROJECT DEVELOPMENT END: 1968

PROJECT DEVELOPMENT TIME: 72 months

EXPENDITURES MADE: Nil

KNOWLEDGE USED:
Knowledge: About-PX-121

SECURITY MEASURES LIST: Nil

SECURITY BREACH LIST: Nil

Defendant Kawneer's competing product, PX-125, is shown below:

Product: PX-125

NAME: PX-125

CASE: Crown Industries Inc. v. Kawneer Co.

A KIND OF: Hydraulic Power Pack

PRODUCT USED FOR: Automatic Door Openers

GENERAL PRODUCT MARKET: Building Owners

COMPETITOR'S PRODUCTS:
Corporate-Party: Crown Product: PX-121

DEVELOPER: Corporate-Party: Kawneer

EMPLOYEES WHO WORKED ON PROJECT: Nil

PROJECT DEVELOPMENT START: Nil

PROJECT DEVELOPMENT END: Nil

PROJECT DEVELOPMENT TIME: Nil

EXPENDITURES MADE: Nil

KNOWLEDGE USED:
Knowledge: About-PX-121

SECURITY MEASURES LIST: Nil

SECURITY BREACH LIST: Nil

Both products were developed using the same product development information associated with PX-121. That information is represented in an instance of Knowledge called "About-PX-121." The case frame shows that the information is technical information, was disclosed to seven persons, and none of the disclosures was subject to restriction on further disclosures:

Knowledge: About-PX-121

NAME: About-PX-121

CASE: Crown Industries Inc. v. Kawneer Co.

KNOWLEDGE ABOUT: Product: PX-121

KIND OF KNOWLEDGE: Technical

PARTIES WITH ACCESS TO KNOWLEDGE:
Corporate-Party: Crown
Corporate-Party: Kawneer

SPECIFIC DISCLOSURE EVENTS:
Disclosure-Event: Crown-Discloses-To-Kawneer

NUMBER OF DISCLOSEES: 7

PERCENTAGE OF DISCLOSEES RESTRICTED: 0.0

GENERALLY KNOWN IN INDUSTRY: Nil

The case included information about a specific Disclosure-Event where the knowledge was disclosed by plaintiff Crown to defendant Kawneer in contract negotiations:

Disclosure-Event: Crown-Discloses-To-Kawneer

NAME: Crown-Discloses-To-Kawneer

CASE: Crown Industries Inc. v. Kawneer Co.

INFO DISCLOSED: Knowledge: About-PX-121

DISCLOSER: Corporate-Party: Crown

DISCLOSEE: Corporate-Party: Kawneer

HOW DISCLOSURES MADE: Negotiation

NONDISCLOSURE AGREEMENTS: None

As these examples indicate, the Legal Case Frames are nested. A particular instantiated case frame, such as Corporate-Party, will refer by pointer to another frame like a Product, which in turn may refer by pointer to yet another object, like an instance of Knowledge.

In this example, the *Crown* case is the cfs. When the *Crown* case is inputted to the Case Analyzer for analysis, it is represented in Legal Case Frames as shown above. It also happens that the *Crown* case is already in the CKB. For purposes of the example, Hypo reanalyzed the *Crown* case as if it had never seen it before. In making the analysis and generating the arguments and hypotheticals reported in this example, Hypo did not use any of the information contained in the top-level Legal Case Frame of the *Crown* case, including its listings of who won the case, what claims were involved, and the applicable Dimensions that index the case in the CKB. Hypo used only the facts of the case as represented in the underlying Legal Case Frames.

5.2 The Session Manager

The Session Manager starts a cfs down the path through the basic control loop. The Session Manager maintains a master list of all Case Analysis Records generated during a single session (the Session Master List). As the cfs proceeds through the loop the results of the actions of the Case Analyzer, Case Positioner, Best Case Selector, and 3-Ply Arguer are stored in the Case Analysis Record for the cfs.

At the start, the slots of the Case Analysis Record for the *Crown* case are still empty. There are slots for

- The Interpretation Frame: a frame setting forth values for Factual Predicates;

- The Applicable Dimensions: a list of all Dimensions whose prerequisites are satisfied;

- The Near-Miss Dimensions: a list of all Dimensions whose prerequisites are satisfied except triggering prerequisites;

- The Excluded Dimensions: a list of all Dimensions with any negated prerequisites;

- Possible claims: a list of Claim Lattices for all claims for which related Dimensions apply or are near misses;

- The Most-on-point cases: a list of most-on-point cases sorted by claim and side (plaintiff or defendant);

- Potential most-on-point cases: a list of potential most-on-point cases sorted by claim and side;

- The Best cases: a list of most-on-point cases that are the best cases for each side to cite;

- Points: a list of all Argument Records for generating 3-Ply Arguments for the case.

5.3 The Case Analyzer

The Case Analyzer performs a Dimensional analysis of the cfs. The input to the module is the cfs represented in the Legal Case Frame representation language and a blank Case Analysis Record. The output is a partially filled in Case Analysis Record containing the satisfied Factual Predicates and applicable and near-miss Dimensions.

The Dimensional analysis process has the following steps:

1. Prepare a blank Interpretation Frame for the cfs and put it in the Case Analysis Record.

2. For each Factual Predicate in Hypo, test the cfs's Legal Case Frames for the value of the Factual Predicate and store it in the Interpretation Frame.

3. Obtain a list of all Dimensions in Hypo. For each Dimension, determine if it is applicable or a near miss with respect to the cfs. That is, do the following: Get the Dimension's lists of prerequisites and focal slot prerequisites from the Dimension's prerequisites slots. From the Interpretation Frame, generate a list of satisfied, unknown and negated Factual Predicates in the cfs. Compare the Dimension's prerequisites with the satisfied, unknown, and negated Factual Predicates. The Dimension is applicable if and only if none of its prerequisites is unknown or negated. The Dimension is a near miss if and only if the only unsatisfied prerequisites are focal slot prerequisites. If the Dimension applies or is a near miss, store it in the appropriate slot of the Case Analysis Record.

The Interpretation Frame stores the values of the Factual Predicates for a cfs. Each of the Interpretation Frame's slots corresponds to a single Factual Predicate. Hypo infers whether a Factual Predicate is satisfied by using a retrieval method associated with the predicate. The retrieval method tests information about the case contained in the Legal Case Frames. Having tested the information contained in the underlying Legal Case Frames for *Crown*, the Analyzer produces a completed Interpretation Frame:

Interpretation Frame after Dimensional Analysis

INTERPRETATION FRAME: Crown Industries Inc. v. Kawneer Co.

THERE IS A CORPORATE PLAINTIFF:
Corporate-Party: Crown

PLAINTIFF MAKES A PRODUCT: Product: PX-121

PLAINTIFF HAS PRODUCT INFORMATION:
Knowledge: About-PX-121

THERE IS A CORPORATE DEFENDANT:
Corporate-Party: Kawneer

DEFENDANT MAKES A PRODUCT: Product: PX-125

PLAINTIFF AND DEFENDANT COMPETE: Affirmative

PLAINTIFF'S AND DEFENDANT'S PRODUCTS COMPETE: Affirmative

THERE IS AN EMPLOYEE DEFENDANT: Nil

...

PLAINTIFF MADE SOME DISCLOSURES TO OUTSIDERS: Affirmative

DISCLOSURES TO OUTSIDERS WERE SUBJECT TO RESTRICTION: Negative

DEFENDANT SAVED PRODUCT DEVELOPMENT EXPENSE RELATIVE TO PLAINTIFF: Nil

PLAINTIFF ADOPTED SECURITY MEASURES: Nil

PLAINTIFF DISCLOSED PRODUCT INFORMATION TO DEFENDANT IN NEGOTIATIONS:
Disclosure-Event: Crown-Discloses-To-Kawneer

DEFENDANT HAD ACCESS TO PLAINTIFF'S PRODUCT INFORMATION VIA COMMON EMPLOYEE OR NEGOTIATIONS:
Disclosure-Event: Crown-Discloses-To-Kawneer

DEFENDANT OR EMPLOYEE ENTERED INTO NONDISCLOSURE AGREEMENT WITH PLAINTIFF: Nil

The Interpretation Frame shows the values of all of the Factual Predicates for the *Crown* cfs. The Factual Predicates correspond to the slots of the Interpretation Frame. The Case Analyzer filled in the value of each slot automatically using the Factual Predicate's retrieval method—a procedure for testing the underlying case frames to determine whether the predicate is satisfied. For instance, the Factual Predicate "Plaintiff made some disclosures to outsiders" has a procedure that tests for a nonzero number in the NUMBER OF DISCLOSEES slot of the development information associated with plaintiff's product, Knowledge: About-PX-121. Note that that instance of Knowledge is the value of the Interpretation Frame slot associated with the Factual Predicate "Plaintiff has product information" whose retrieval method filled it in earlier. Similarly, the Factual Predicate "Plaintiff disclosed product information to defendant in negotiations" checks the Disclosure-Event Crown-Discloses-To-Kawneer, whose slot HOW DISCLOSURES MADE indicates that the disclosure was made in negotiations.

By reciting the Factual Predicates and their values in the order presented in the Interpretation Frame, one can almost generate a narrative summary of the case. In *Crown*, there is a plaintiff corporation, Crown, that makes a product, PX-121, for which there is product development information. A defendant corporation, Kawneer, makes product PX-125. The corporations compete with respect to the products. Plaintiff made some disclosures of the information to outsiders, and there are no restrictions with respect to those disclosures. Plaintiff disclosed the information to the defendant in negotiations.

Having summarized the facts in the form of the Interpretation Frame, the Case Analyzer knows what Factual Predicates are satisfied and determines which Dimensions' prerequisites, expressed in terms of Factual Predicates, are satisfied or nearly so. Those results are recorded in the Case Analysis Record as shown below. Two Dimensions apply to the *Crown*, case and five Dimensions are near misses:

Case Analysis Record (CAR) after Dimensional Analysis

CAR: Crown Industries Inc. v. Kawneer Co.

APPLICABLE DIMENSIONS:
Secrets-Disclosed-Outsiders
Disclosures-In-Negotiations-With-Defendant

NEAR-MISS DIMENSIONS:
Outsider-Disclosures-Restricted
Competitive-Advantage-Gained
Vertical-Knowledge
Security-Measures-Adopted
Nondisclosure-Agreement-Re-Defendant-Access

The Dimension *Secrets-Disclosed-Outsiders* applies to the *Crown* case because all of its prerequisites, which are expressed as a list of Factual Predicates, are satisfied. The Dimension's prerequisites include: "There is a corporate plaintiff," "There is a corporate defendant," "Plaintiff makes a product," "Plaintiff and defendant compete," "Plaintiff has product information," and "Plaintiff made some disclosures to outsiders." As the Interpretation Frame for the *Crown* case indicates, all of these prerequisite Factual Predicates are satisfied. If all had been satisfied except "Plaintiff made some disclosures to outsiders," the *Secrets-Disclosed-Outsiders* Dimension's focal slot prerequisite, then the Dimension would only be a near miss. If the plaintiff had no product information, the Dimension would not apply at all to the case. The *Outsider-Disclosures-Restricted* dimension is a near miss because its focal slot prerequisite "Disclosures to outsiders were subject to restrictions" is the only prerequisite not satisfied.

5.4 The Case Positioner

The Case Positioner takes those applicable and near-miss Dimensions, retrieves all of the cases in the CKB indexed by any one of them, and constructs Claim Lattices in order to position the cfs relative to the relevant cases. For each applicable or near-miss Dimension listed in the Case Analysis Record, the Positioner retrieves all cases indexed by the Dimension. A case is indexed by a Dimension if the top-level case frame's list of Dimensions contains a pointer to that Dimension.

The Positioner builds two kinds of Claim Lattices for any claim for which there are relevant cases:

1. A regular Claim Lattice for cases indexed by Dimensions that apply to the cfs

2. An extended Claim Lattice for cases indexed by Dimensions that apply or are near misses with respect to the cfs

A Claim Lattice is a directed acyclic graph, each of whose nodes consists of pointers to parent and children nodes, a list of Dimensions, and a list of cases. Each Claim Lattice has a maximal root node whose list of Dimensions (the root's Dimension list) contains all of the Dimensions that apply to the cfs and whose list of cases contains at least the cfs. Each node contains all cases in the CKB such that the intersections of the root's Dimension list and the lists of Dimensions applicable to each case in the node are the same. As such, each node defines an equivalency class of cases that are equally on point with respect to the current fact situation.

An *extended Claim Lattice* is the same as a regular Claim Lattice except that its root's Dimension list also contains Dimensions that are near misses for the cfs. In either kind of Claim Lattice, the Dimension list of each node other than the root contains only Dimensions that are applicable to all of the cases in that node.

The ordering scheme of the Claim Lattice, the relative inclusiveness of the Dimension lists of each node with respect to the root's Dimension list, is Hypo's primary measure of a case's on pointness to the current fact situation. The closer a node is to the root, the more on point are the node's cases.

For the *Crown* case fact situation, the Case Positioner generates the regular Claim Lattice shown in Figure 5.1. The root node represents the *Crown* case fact situation and its two applicable Dimensions. Successor nodes contain the six pro-plaintiff (π) or pro-defendant (δ) cases, involving trade secrets misappropriation claims, that are on point to the cfs. The lists of Dimensions in the successor nodes are Dimensions that apply to the cases in the node and that are shared with the cfs's applicable Dimensions as recorded in the root's Dimension list. The Claim Lattice organizes the six cases according to the collections of Dimensions shared with the fact situation. The *Speedry, Space Aero*, and *Automated Systems* cases share one Dimension with the fact situation, *Disclosures-In-Negotiations-With-Defendant*. The *Yokana, Midland-Ross*, and *Data*

Hypo in Action 57

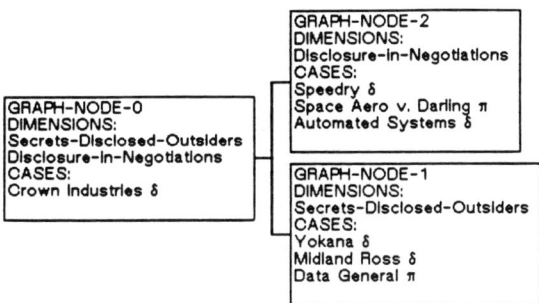

Figure 5.1
Claim Lattice for the *Crown* Example

General cases share another Dimension with the fact situation, *Secrets-Disclosed-Outsiders*.

The extended Claim Lattice shows a variety of cases that are relevant to the fact situation under a broader definition. Figures 5.2 and 5.3 show the overall shape and some detail of the more complex extended Claim Lattice. In the extended Claim Lattice, the root node contains not only Dimensions that apply to the fact situation but also Dimensions that are a near miss with respect to the problem situation. These Dimensions are marked with an asterisk ("*"). As shown in figure 5.3, the *Space Aero* case has three Dimensions that either apply or are near misses with respect to the fact situation. The Dimension *Disclosures-In-Negotiations-With-Defendant* applies to both the *Space Aero* case and the fact situation, while Dimensions *Security-Measures-Adopted* and *Competitive-Advantage-Gained* apply to the *Space Aero* case but are near misses with respect to the fact situation. If the latter two Dimensions applied to the fact situation, the *Space Aero* case would become more on point and a better case to cite on behalf of the plaintiff.

5.5 The Best Case Selector

The Best Case Selector selects the most-on-point cases for each side (plaintiff and defendant) on each claim and stores them in the Case Analysis Record. The selector searches the Claim Lattice until it finds the most-on-point cases. By virtue of the Claim Lattice's ordering scheme, the nodes containing most-on-point cases are closer to the root. Leaf

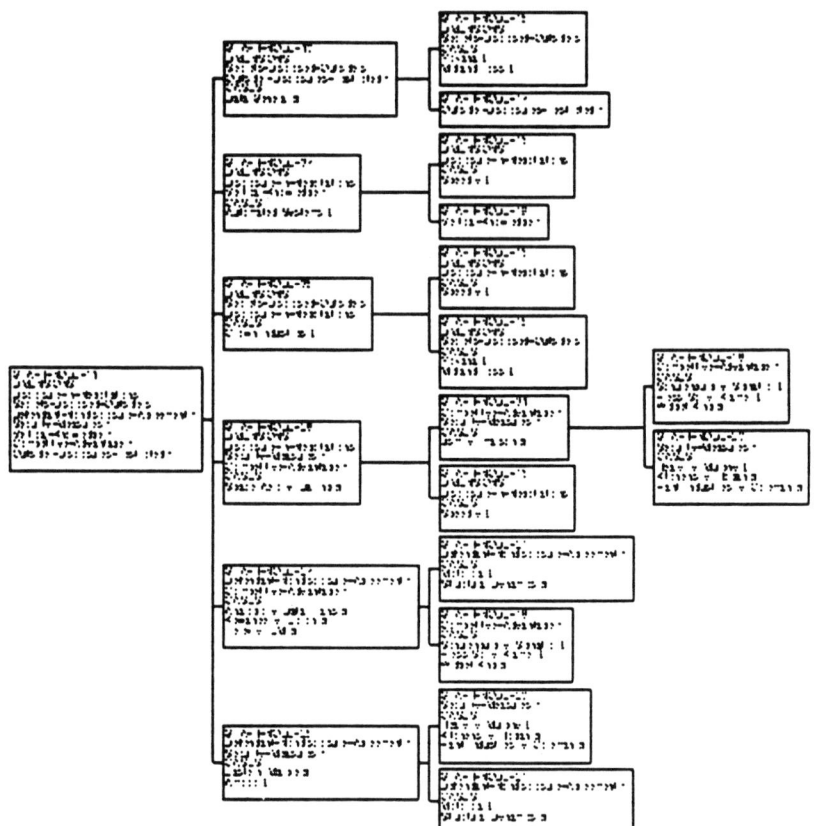

Figure 5.2
Overall Shape of Extended Claim Lattice for the *Crown* Example

Hypo in Action

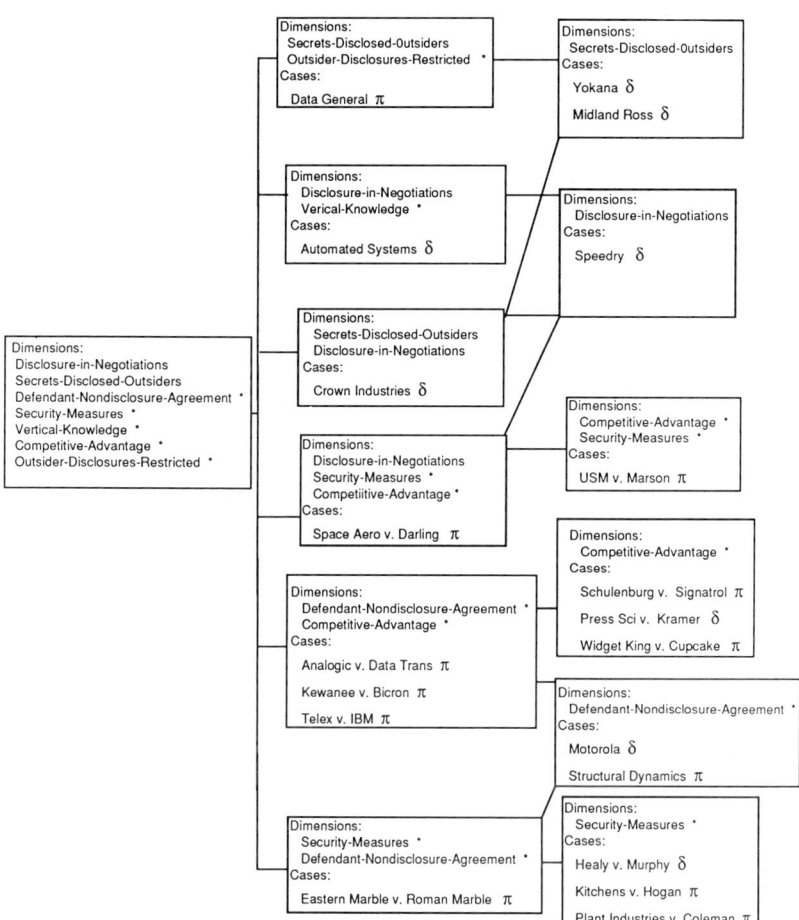

Figure 5.3
Detail of Extended Claim Lattice for the *Crown* Example

nodes contain least on point cases. Each major branch of the lattice that contains most-on-point cases represents one way of arguing about the cfs. Most-on-point cases can be used in the arguments to respond to points citing cases from successor nodes.

The Selector performs a depth-first search through the Claim Lattice to find most-on-point cases for each side. The search descends each branch until it finds a node containing cases citable for a side or until a terminal node is reached. By virtue of the Claim Lattice's ordering scheme, the first citable cases encountered in a node are the most-on-point cases on that branch; they have the greatest set of Dimensions in common with those applicable to the cfs. A node is deemed to contain cases citable for a side if and only if (1) the node contains cases that held for the side and (2) the node's Dimension list contains at least one Dimension applicable to the cfs. A similar algorithm is used to select the most-on-point near-miss cases but from the extended Claim Lattice. The significance of these near-miss cases is that if the cfs were modified so that all of the near-miss Dimensions applied, these cases would then be most on point.

The Best Case Selector also filters the best cases to cite from among the most-on-point cases. Best cases to cite are those most-on-point cases that are *citable in the first instance*. They must share with the cfs at least one dimension that favors the side who won the case. These cases make more convincing points that the same side that won the case should win the cfs. One may draw a more convincing analogy based on the shared pro-side dimensions. The remaining most-on-point cases may still be useful as counterexamples.

For the *Crown* case, the Best Case Selector selects the most-on-point and best cases to cite from the Claim Lattice of figure 5.1. The most-on-point near-miss cases are taken from the extended Claim Lattice of figures 5.2 and 5.3. The results of the selection are stored in the Case Analysis Record as shown below:

The Case Analysis Record after Best Case Selection

MOST-ON-POINT CASES FOR TRADE SECRETS MISAPPROPRIATION CLAIM:
Plaintiff:
Data General Corp. v. Digital Computer Controls Inc.
Space Aero Products Co. v. R. E. Darling Co.

Defendant:
Midland-Ross Corp. v. Sunbeam Equipment Corp.
Midland-Ross Corp. v. Yokana
Automated-Systems v. Service-Bureau
Speedry Chemical Products, Inc. v. Carter's Ink Company

MOST-ON-POINT NEAR-MISS CASES FOR TRADE SECRETS MISAPPROPRIATION CLAIM:
Plaintiff:
Eastern Marble Products Corp. v. Roman Marble, Inc.
Telex Corp. v. IBM Corp. (1)
Kewanee Oil Co. v. Bicron Corp.
Analogic Corp. v. Data Translation, Inc.
Space Aero Products Co. v. R. E. Darling Co.
Data General Corp. v. Digital Computer Controls Inc.

Defendant:
Automated-Systems v. Service-Bureau

BEST CASES TO CITE FOR TRADE SECRETS MISAPPROPRIATION CLAIM:
Plaintiff:
None

Defendant:
Midland-Ross Corp. v. Sunbeam Equipment Corp.
Midland-Ross Corp. v. Yokana
Automated-Systems v. Service-Bureau
Speedry Chemical Products, Inc. v. Carter's Ink Company

Both *Midland-Ross* cases are best cases for the defendant to cite because they are most-on-point and each has in common with the cfs at least one dimension that favors the defendant (namely *Secrets-Disclosed-Outsiders.*) By contrast, neither *Data General* nor *Space Aero* were selected as best cases for plaintiff to cite even though they are both plaintiff's most-on-point cases. Since neither case shares any dimension with the cfs that favors the plaintiff, the cases are not citable in the first instance. The Dimensions *Secrets-Disclosed-Outsiders* and *Disclosures-In-Negotiations-With-Defendant* generally favor the defendant in trade secrets misappropriation cases. It would not make a very good argument for plaintiff to cite *Data General* as justifying a decision for plaintiff where the only similarity between the precedent and the fact situation is that the plaintiff disclosed its secrets to outsiders since that dimension represents one of defendant's strengths. On the other hand, if the defendant argues that it should win because of plaintiff's disclosures, it would be strategically sound for plaintiff to cite *Data General* as a counterexample, a case where a plaintiff won despite its disclosures to outsiders.

The Best Case Selector ignored one case in the *Crown* Claim Lattice, figure 5.1, even though that case shares both of the cfs's Dimensions. That case is the CKB version of *Crown Industries*, and it appears in the root node. (See the reference to the "Crown Industries" case under "CASES:" in the root node of figure 5.1.) This simply indicates that the Case Positioner successfully retrieved the real *Crown* case from the CKB and classified it as most on point to its own fact situation, confirmation that the Positioner is correctly assessing on pointness (a case is most on point to itself). Hypo analyzed the fact situation of *Crown* as if it were newly introduced to the program and not in the CKB. The Best Case Selector's algorithms ignore the real *Crown* case to avoid citing the case as authority for a legal point about itself.

5.6 The 3-Ply Arguer

The 3-Ply Arguer is responsible for generating arguments about the cfs. The inputs to the Arguer are the Case Analysis Record for the cfs, complete with all of the pro or con most-on-point cases and best cases to cite, Claim Lattices, and results of the Dimensional analysis. The outputs are 3-Ply Arguments and suggestions of hypotheticals that would improve a point or response in the argument.

A *3-Ply Argument* consists of

1. a point on behalf of the plaintiff or defendant as Side 1 consisting of a legal conclusion that Side 1 in a fact situation should win a particular claim, a justification for the legal conclusion in the form of a citation to a prior legal case, and a rationale for the

justification in the form of an analogy between the fact situation and the cited case;

2. a response on behalf of the opponent as Side 2 consisting of some combination of distinguishing the fact situation from the cited case on behalf of Side 2 and citing counterexamples to the cited case; and

3. a rebuttal on behalf of Side 1, consisting of a response to any of the counterexamples cited in the response.

The primary data structure of the 3-Ply Arguer is the Argument Record, which is a blueprint for generating a 3-Ply Argument and identifies useful hypotheticals. An Argument Record's slots contain such information as the following:

- Cfs: a pointer to the current fact situation argued about

- Side 1: Side 1 is the side on behalf of whom a legal point is made (plaintiff or defendant).

- Cited case: a pointer to the case cited

- Claim: a pointer to the type of claim for which the point is made. The default is the type of claim raised in the cited case

- Shared Dimensions: a list of Dimensions shared by the cfs and cited case. These represent the factors shared by the cfs and cited case and are the basis of a factual analogy between them.

- Distinctions for Side 2: a list of ways in which the cfs is stronger for Side 2 (the opponent of Side 1) relative to the cited case. These distinctions between the cfs and cited case can be used to respond to the cited case.

- Counterexamples: a list of cases that held for Side 2 and can be cited in response to the cited case. There are four kinds of counterexamples, each focusing on counteracting a different aspect of the cited case.

- Hypotheticals: a list of targets for hypothetical variations of the cfs that would bolster either side's position in an argument on the claim

The 3-Ply Arguer's basic functions are to generate Argument Records, 3-Ply Arguments, and specifications for hypotheticals.

The Arguer automatically generates an Argument Record for every best case to cite for either side and for every case that can be cited as either of two types of counterexample (trumping or boundary) in response to such a case. It does this for each claim for which either side has a best case to cite. The Arguer creates Argument Records for counterexamples in order to generate a 3-Ply Argument rebuttal to a response that cites the counterexample. The Arguer also creates Argument Records for any case selected manually by the user. It stores all of the Argument Records in the Case Analysis Record. It generates 3-Ply Arguments and specifications for hypos as called upon by the Explainer.

The 3-Ply Arguer creates five Argument Records with respect to the *Crown* cfs, one for each of the four best cases to cite and a fifth for a counterexample. In other words, Argument Records are created for the *Midland-Ross Corp. v. Sunbeam Equipment Corp.*, *Midland-Ross Corp. v. Yokana, Automated Systems* and *Speedry* cases, all of which are best cases to cite for the defendant. (There are no best cases to cite for plaintiff.) A fifth Argument Record is generated for the *Data General* case which is cited as a boundary counterexample to the *Midland-Ross* cases.

Here we focus on two of the records: one for the *Midland-Ross v. Sunbeam* case, one of the defendant's best cases, and the other for the *Data General* case, which may be cited as a counterexample to *Midland-Ross*.

Argument Record 0

CURRENT FACT SITUATION:
Crown Industries Inc. v. Kawneer Co.

SIDE 1: Defendant

CLAIM: Type-of-Claim: Trade-Secrets-Misappropriation

CITED CASE:
Midland-Ross Corp. v. Sunbeam Equipment Corp.

SHARED DIMENSIONS:
Secrets-Disclosed-Outsiders

DISTINCTIONS FOR SIDE 2:
Distinction 1:

Crown Industries Inc. v. Kawneer Co. is stronger for plaintiff than Midland-Ross Corp. v. Sunbeam Equipment Corp. along *Secrets-Disclosed-Outsiders* because 7 disclosures are fewer than 97 disclosures.

MORE-ON-POINT COUNTEREXAMPLES: None

AS-ON-POINT COUNTEREXAMPLES:
Data General Corp. v. Digital Computer Controls Inc.

POTENTIALLY MORE-ON-POINT COUNTEREXAMPLES:
Data General Corp. v. Digital Computer Controls Inc.

BOUNDARY COUNTEREXAMPLES:
Data General Corp. v. Digital Computer Controls Inc. along *Secrets-Disclosed-Outsiders*

HYPOTHETICALS FOR SIDE 1: None

HYPOTHETICALS FOR SIDE 2:
Data General Corp. v. Digital Computer Controls Inc.

RESPONSIVE ARGUMENT RECORDS: Argument Record 1

Argument Record 1

CURRENT FACT SITUATION:
Crown Industries Inc. v. Kawneer Co.

SIDE 1: Plaintiff

CLAIM: Type-of-Claim: Trade-Secrets-Misappropriation

CITED CASE:
Data General Corp. v. Digital Computer Controls Inc.

SHARED DIMENSIONS:
Secrets-Disclosed-Outsiders

DISTINCTIONS FOR SIDE 2:
Distinction 1: Crown Industries Inc. v. Kawneer Co. is weaker for plaintiff on *Disclosure-In-Negotiations-With-Defendant*
Distinction 2: Data General Corp. v. Digital Computer Controls Inc. is stronger for plaintiff on *Outsider-Disclosures-Restricted*

MORE-ON-POINT COUNTEREXAMPLES: None

AS-ON-POINT COUNTEREXAMPLES:
Midland-Ross Corp. v. Yokana
Midland-Ross Corp. v. Sunbeam Equipment Corp.

POTENTIALLY MORE-ON-POINT COUNTEREXAMPLES: None

BOUNDARY COUNTEREXAMPLES: None

HYPOTHETICALS FOR SIDE 1: None

HYPOTHETICALS FOR SIDE 2: None

RESPONSIVE ARGUMENT RECORDS: None

In filling out an Argument Record, the Arguer gathers three types of information: (1) similarities for drawing an analogy between the cfs and cited case, (2) differences for distinguishing the cfs from the cited case, and (3) counterexamples for citing in response to the cited case.

The similarities between the cfs and the cited case are the Dimensions that apply to both representing factors they have in common. These are the cases' shared factual strengths and weaknesses of the plaintiff's claim, in essence, the reason why the cfs should be decided like the cited case. The Arguer stores this information in the Argument Record's SHARED DIMENSIONS slot. The slot contains the intersection of the set of Dimensions that apply to the cfs, taken from the cfs's Case Analysis Record, and the set of Dimensions that index the cited case, taken from the cited case's top-level Legal Case Frame. When the Arguer makes a point about the cfs citing this case, it draws the analogy by reciting this information. The SHARED DIMENSIONS slot of Argument Record 0, for example, contains a pointer to the *Secrets-Disclosed-Outsider* Dimension which the Midland-Ross case shares with the *Crown* cfs.

The Arguer recognizes two kinds of relevant differences, or distinctions, between the cfs and the cited case which involve certain (1) differences in position along shared Dimensions and (2) differences in position along unshared Dimensions.

The Arguer uses these differences to distinguish the cited case from the cfs. They represent factual differences that make the cfs stronger for Side 2 than the cited case and justify deciding the cfs for Side 2, not for Side 1 as was done in the cited case.

The Arguer has a procedure for computing distinctions along shared Dimensions that takes advantage of specialized comparison information contained in a Dimension. Each Dimension has information for comparing cases' focal slot values and determining which side any difference favors. That information includes a comparison type appropriate to the range of values a case may have along a Dimension. Dimensions have five different types of focal slot ranges including binary, partially ordered sets of objects, ordered sets, intervals and number lines. There are five comparison types to accomodate the ranges including comparing some versus none, more versus less, relative position in an ordered set, numerically greater than versus less than, and a computed type for special comparison computations. Associated with each comparison type is a method that specifies

- how to find (or derive) the corresponding cfs and cited focal slot values for comparison,
- the kind of computation needed to compare the values (defined in terms of operations like set inclusion, greater than, less than, not empty),
- how to interpret that comparison in the light of the direction that would favor the plaintiff (e.g., whether a greater value is better for plaintiff, worse, or the same).

Using an appropriate comparison method, the Arguer compares the cfs and cited case along the shared Dimension. If the difference along the Dimension favors Side 2, the difference is treated as a distinction. For example, in Argument Record 0, the *Crown* fact situation and the *Midland-Ross* case were compared along the Dimension they share, *Secrets-Disclosed-Outsiders*, where the former was found to involve fewer disclosures. Since fewer disclosures to outsiders are better for the plaintiff (information which is represented as part of the Dimension), the Arguer treats this difference as a distinction and notes it in the DISTINCTIONS FOR SIDE 2 slot.

The Arguer's procedure for computing distinctions based on unshared Dimensions is to screen the set of unshared Dimensions (computed as the set difference of the Dimensions that apply to only one of the cfs or cited case and the shared Dimensions) to determine which side each one favors. Dimensions are grouped according to which side they favor. For each unshared Dimension, if its application only to the cfs favors Side 2 (or if its application only to the cited case favors Side 1), it is treated as a distinction. For example, in Argument Record 1, the DISTINCTIONS FOR SIDE 2 slot shows two distinctions based on unshared Dimensions. The *Disclosure-In-Negotiations-With-Defendant* Dimension favors defendant and applies only to the *Crown* case. The *Outsider-Disclosures-Restricted* Dimension favors plaintiff and applies only to the *Data General* case. Both distinctions make *Data General* a stronger case for the plaintiff than *Crown*.

Counterexamples are cases that share some or all of the same strengths and weaknesses with the fact situation as the cited case but in which the opponent nevertheless won the claim. Counterexamples are cited in response to a cited case. Hypo has four types of counterexamples: more on point (or trumping), potentially more on point, as on point or partial, and boundary.

A *more-on-point* or *trumping* counterexample is a case that held for Side 2 on the claim such that the set of Dimensions shared by the cited case and cfs is a proper subset of the Dimensions shared by the counterexample and the cfs. Thus, a trumping counterexample has more (in the set inclusion sense) important strengths and weaknesses in common with the fact situation than the cited case. It presents a closer analogy to the cited case and therefore is preferable as an authority. For each most-on-point case that held for Side 2 listed in the Case Analysis Record for the cfs, the Arguer compares the most-on-point case to the cited case for on pointness relative to the cfs. If the most-on-point case is more on point than the cited case, it is a more-on-point counterexample. With respect to Argument Record 0, for example, the Arguer compared the cited case, *Midland-Ross*, to each of the two most-on-point cases that held for the plaintiff, *Data General* and *Space Aero*. It checked whether the set of Dimensions that *Midland-Ross* shared with the cfs were a proper subset of the Dimensions shared by either *Data General* or *Space Aero* and the cfs. Since the answer was negative, neither case was more on point than *Midland-Ross*. The Arguer could find no more-on-point counterexamples.

A potentially more-on-point counterexample is a case that held for Side 2 that would be more on point than the cited case if the fact situation had some extra facts. It is important because it suggests a hypothetical variant of the fact situation in which the potential counterexample would be an actual counterexample more on point than the cited case. In other words, it suggests a possible way of bolstering Side 2's response to the point. A similar procedure is used to collect potential more-on-point counterexamples except that the cited case is compared to the potential most-on-point cases favoring Side 2 listed in the cfs's Case Analysis Record. Such a case is a counterexample only if the near-miss Dimensions would help Side 2 if they applied. When filling out Argument Record 0, the Arguer compared the cited case, *Midland-Ross* to all of the pro-plaintiff most-on-point near-miss cases listed in the Case Analysis Record. *Data General* was selected as a potentially more-on-point counterexample to *Midland-Ross* because, if *Crown*'s near-miss Dimensions applied to *Crown*, *Data General* would be more on point than *Midland-Ross*. In other words, the Dimensions shared by *Midland-Ross* and *Crown* are a subset of those shared by *Data General* and the set of *Crown*'s applicable and near-miss Dimensions. To put it in in terms of the extended Claim Lattice of figure 5.3, *Data General* is closer to the root node than *Midland-Ross*.

An *as-on-point* or *partial* counterexample is a case that held for Side 2 that has exactly the same set of Dimensions in common with the cfs as the cited case or some nonempty subset of that set. A counterexample is as-on-point as the cited case if it has exactly the same set of Dimensions in common with the cfs that the cited case does. A partial counterexample is less on point than the cited case; it shares with the cfs only a nonempty subset of the Dimensions that the cited case shares with the cfs. An as-on-point counterexample has utility in an argument because it calls into question the reliability of the cited case. It implies that the shared collection of Dimensions does not always lead to the same result as in the cited case. A partial counterexample has much less force in an argument because, by definition, the cited case is a trumping counterexample to a partial counterexample. The Arguer looks for as-on-point counterexamples but ignores partial ones. The procedure is the same as for finding trumping counterexamples. In Argument Record 0, the *Data General* case was selected as a counterexample as-on-point as *Midland-Ross*, because it was one of the pro-plaintiff most-on-point cases in the Case Analysis Record, and had exactly the same set of Dimensions in common with the cfs as *Midland-Ross* (i.e., the set of *Secrets-Disclosed-Outsiders*.)

A *boundary* counterexample is a case that held for Side 2 even though it is much weaker for Side 2 than the cited case. This kind of counterexample shows how much worse the situation could be for Side 2 in the fact situation without necessarily causing Side 1 to win. The procedure for finding boundary counterexamples is to find cases that held for Side 2 despite the fact that they are weaker for Side 2 along a shared Dimension. Only Dimensions whose ranges are number lines, ordered sets of more than 2 members, or partially ordered sets are checked for boundary counterexamples. In Argument Record 0, the Arguer checked the shared Dimension, *Secrets-Disclosed-Outsiders*, and found one case, *Data General*, where the plaintiff won despite the fact that the case was weaker for the plaintiff along that Dimension than the cited case, *Midland-Ross*. *Data General* involved disclosures to 6,000 outsiders versus the *Midland-Ross* case's 97. Consequently, the Arguer lists *Data General* as a boundary counterexample.

Using an Argument Record as a blueprint, the Arguer can generate a 3-Ply Argument in a straightforward way. The Arguer makes a point by citing the Argument Record's cited case on behalf of Side 1 and draws the analogy to the cfs by reciting the facts associated with the Argument Record's shared Dimensions. The Arguer makes a response on behalf of Side 2 consisting of distinctions and counterexamples. It recites Side 2's distinctions from the Argument Record and cites each more-on-point or boundary counterexample in the Argument Record. The Arguer makes a rebuttal on behalf of Side 1 by responding to any cases cited in the response. For each potentially more-on-point counterexample in the Argument Record, the Arguer appends a note to the 3-Ply Argument offering to pose a hypothetical variant of the cfs to show how to bolster the response.

Using the information in Argument Records 0 and 1, the Arguer generates 3-Ply Argument [1] for the *Crown* cfs:

> $\Longrightarrow$ Point For Defendant as Side 1:
>
> Where: Plaintiff disclosed its product information to outsiders. Defendant should win a claim for Trade Secrets Misappropriation.
>
> Cite: Midland-Ross Corp. v. Sunbeam Equipment Corp. 316 F. Supp. 171 (W.D. Pa., 1970).
>
> $\Longleftarrow$ Response for Plaintiff as Side 2:
>
> Midland-Ross Corp. v. Sunbeam Equipment Corp. is distinguishable because: In Midland-Ross, plaintiff disclosed its product in-

formation to more outsiders than in Crown Industries

Counterexamples:

Data General Corp. v. Digital Computer Controls Inc. 357 A.2d 105 (Del. Ch. 1975), held for plaintiff even though in Data General plaintiff disclosed its product information to more outsiders than in Midland-Ross Corp. v. Sunbeam Equipment Corp.

⟹ Rebuttal for Defendant as Side 1:

Data General Corp. v. Digital Computer Controls Inc. is distinguishable because: In Crown Industries, Plaintiff disclosed its product information in negotiations with defendant. Not so in Data General. In Data General, plaintiff's disclosures to outsiders were restricted. Not so in Crown Industries.

Note:

Plaintiff's response would be strengthened if: Plaintiff's disclosures to outsiders were restricted. Cf. Data General Corp. v. Digital Computer Controls Inc. 357 A.2d 105 (Del. Ch. 1975)

Argument [1] shows the basic components of a typical 3-Ply Argument: a Point for Side 1 (in this case, the defendant), a Response for Side 2 (the plaintiff), a Rebuttal for Side 1, and a suggested hypothetical to bolster the Response.

Like all of Hypo's legal points, the Point in [1]: states a legal conclusion that Side 1 should win on a particular claim (here, trade secrets misappropriation); cites an authority for the conclusion, here the *Midland-Ross* case; and provides a rationale, consisting of the analogous facts that the cfs and cited case both involved a disclosure of the product development information to outsiders.

As is typical, the Response in [1] consists of a combination of distinguishing the cited case and citing counterexamples. Here Side 2's distinction points out that the *Crown* case is stronger for it, the plaintiff, than *Midland-Ross* because there were disclosures to fewer outsiders. Note how the counterexample citing the *Data General* case (a boundary counterexample) follows up on the distinction and drives it home. It says, in effect, "Even if there were many more disclosures to outsiders, as many as in *Data General*, plaintiff should still win." (In the absence of *Data General*, another useful boundary counterexample would have been a case that had as many disclosures as the *Crown* case but held for the plaintiff.)

In the Rebuttal in [1], the 3-Ply Arguer distinguishes the counterexample from Side 1's viewpoint, pointing out that *Data General* should not be followed because the plaintiff's position in the *Crown* case is so much weaker: the outsiders were not restricted from making further disclosures, and the plaintiff had disclosed the secret to the defendant in negotiations.

The last part of the 3-Ply Argument consists of a suggestion of how the response could be strengthened. It poses a hypothetical modification of the cfs, which, if true, would make the noted case into a trumping counterexample. In [1], the Note points out that if the disclosures to outsiders were restricted, plaintiff could cite the *Data General* case as a trumping counterexample.

All of the information for generating Argument [1] comes from Argument Records 0 and 1. The claim, cited case, shared Dimensions, distinctions and boundary counterexample come from the corresponding slots of Argument Record 0. The presence of a potentially more-on-point counterexample in Argument Record 0 prompts the suggested hypothetical. The rebuttal distinctions were generated from Argument Record 1, where the cited case is *Data General* and the distinctions are differences between it and the *Crown* cfs. Since *Data General* could be cited as a boundary counterexample to *Midland-Ross*, the Arguer automatically generated Argument Record 1 and listed it as responsive to Argument Record 0.

The language of the 3-Ply Arguments is generated by combining pieces of "canned" text. Each of Hypo's thirteen Dimensions has an associated phrase for asserting that the factor associated with the Dimension applies to a case. Since the similarities and differences among cases and counterexamples are composed of lists of Dimensions, the program simply combines the associated phrases.

For completeness, the remaining three Argument Records for the *Crown* cfs are presented below. Argument Records 2, 3 and 4 deal respectively with cited cases *Midland-Ross v. Yokana*, *Automated Systems* and *Speedry*.

Argument Record 2

CURRENT FACT SITUATION:
Crown Industries Inc. v. Kawneer Co.

SIDE 1: Defendant

CLAIM: Type-of-Claim: Trade-Secrets-Misappropriation

CITED CASE:
Midland-Ross Corp. v. Yokana

SHARED DIMENSIONS:
Secrets-Disclosed-Outsiders

DISTINCTIONS FOR SIDE 2:
Distinction 1:
Crown Industries Inc. v. Kawneer Co. is stronger for plaintiff than Midland-Ross Corp. v. Yokana along *Secrets-Disclosed-Outsiders* because 7 disclosures are fewer than 100 disclosures.

MORE-ON-POINT COUNTEREXAMPLES: None

AS-ON-POINT COUNTEREXAMPLES:
Data General Corp. v. Digital Computer Controls Inc.

POTENTIALLY MORE-ON-POINT COUNTEREXAMPLES:
Data General Corp. v. Digital Computer Controls Inc.

BOUNDARY COUNTEREXAMPLES:
Data General Corp. v. Digital Computer Controls Inc.
along *Secrets-Disclosed-Outsiders*

HYPOTHETICALS FOR SIDE 1: None

HYPOTHETICALS FOR SIDE 2:
Data General Corp. v. Digital Computer Controls Inc.

RESPONSIVE ARGUMENT RECORDS: Argument Record 1

Argument Record 3

CURRENT FACT SITUATION:
Crown Industries Inc. v. Kawneer Co.

SIDE 1: Defendant

CLAIM: Type-of-Claim: Trade-Secrets-Misappropriation

CITED CASE:
Automated-Systems v. Service-Bureau

SHARED DIMENSIONS:
Disclosures-In-Negotiations-With-Defendant

DISTINCTIONS FOR SIDE 2:
Distinction 1:
Automated-Systems v. Service-Bureau is weaker for plaintiff on *Vertical-Knowledge*

MORE-ON-POINT COUNTEREXAMPLES: None

AS-ON-POINT COUNTEREXAMPLES: None

POTENTIALLY MORE-ON-POINT COUNTEREXAMPLES: None

BOUNDARY COUNTEREXAMPLES: None

HYPOTHETICALS FOR SIDE 1: None

HYPOTHETICALS FOR SIDE 2: None

RESPONSIVE ARGUMENT RECORDS: None

Argument Record 4

CURRENT FACT SITUATION:
Crown Industries Inc. v. Kawneer Co.

SIDE 1: Defendant

CLAIM: Type-Of-Claim: Trade-Secrets-Misappropriation

CITED CASE:
Speedry Chemical Products, Inc. v. Carter's Ink Company

SHARED DIMENSIONS:
Disclosures-In-Negotiations-With-Defendant

DISTINCTIONS FOR SIDE 2: None

MORE-ON-POINT COUNTEREXAMPLES: None

AS-ON-POINT COUNTEREXAMPLES: None

POTENTIALLY MORE-ON-POINT COUNTEREXAMPLES:
Space Aero Products Co. v. R.E. Darling Co.

BOUNDARY COUNTEREXAMPLES: None

HYPOTHETICALS FOR SIDE 1: None

HYPOTHETICALS FOR SIDE 2:
Space Aero Products Co. v. R. E. Darling Co.

RESPONSIVE ARGUMENT RECORDS: None

5.7 The Explainer

The Explainer assembles the outputs for a cfs. It has access to all of the Argument Records for the cfs listed in the Case Analysis Record. It calls upon the 3-Ply Arguer and the Hypo Generator in producing four kinds of outputs: Citation Summary, 3-Ply Arguments, Suggested Hypotheticals to Consider, and Comparisons of Points.

The Citation Summary characterizes the respective strengths of the competing sides' arguments and lists all of each side's best cases to cite for which there are no trumping counterexamples. Each side can use these cases to make points for which the opponent has no trumping counterexamples ("nontrumped" points.) The Explainer generates the list by screening the Argument Records associated with the best cases to cite listed in the Case Analysis Record. If the Argument Record shows that there are no more-on-point counterexamples, the case is included in the Citation Summary. The Explainer generates a Citation Summary for each claim for which either side can make a nontrumped point. Here is the citation summary that the Explainer generated for the *Crown* case.

3-Ply Arguments for Best Cases to Cite on Claim of Trade Secrets Misappropriation in Fact Situation of Crown Industries:

On a claim for Trade Secrets Misappropriation, Defendant can make a stronger argument. Defendant can cite the following cases for which there are no more-on-point counterexamples:

Speedry Chemical Products, Inc. v. Carter's Ink Company 306 F.2d 328 (2d Cir., 1962)

Automated-Systems v. Service-Bureau 401 F.2d 619 (10 Cir., 1968)

Midland-Ross Corp. v. Yokana 293 F.2d 411 (3 Cir. 1961)

Midland-Ross Corp. v. Sunbeam Equipment Corp. 316 F. Supp. 171 (W.D. Pa., 1970)

The Explainer assesses the relative strengths of each side's argument by comparing each side's ability to make nontrumped points. If either side has a monopoly on nontrumped points, its position is significantly stronger. If both can make nontrumped points, each has strong positions. The Explainer treats the arguments as tied regardless of the number of nontrumped points each side could make. In the example, defendant Kawneer has the stronger argument because it can make some nontrumped points and plaintiff Crown can make none. If both sides could have made some nontrumped points, the Explainer would have stated that both sides can make strong arguments and listed the corresponding nontrumped best cases to cite for each side.

Next, the Explainer outputs a 3-Ply Argument for each of the nontrumped best cases listed in the Citation Summary. The Explainer calls upon the 3-Ply Arguer to generate each 3-Ply Argument from the information contained in the corresponding Argument Records. In the *Crown* example, 3-Ply Arguments are generated for [1] *Midland-Ross v. Sunbeam Equipment*, [2] *Midland-Ross v. Yokana*, [3] *Automated Systems* and [4] *Speedry* cases, all of which are the defendant's best cases to cite and none of which have trumping counterexamples. (Plaintiff had no best cases to cite.) Argument [1] is shown above. Arguments [2], [3] and [4] are shown below.

3-Ply Argument in *Crown*: [2]

$\Longrightarrow$ Point for Defendant as Side 1:

Where: Plaintiff disclosed its product information to outsiders. Defendant should win a claim for Trade Secrets Misappropriation.

Cite: Midland-Ross Corp. v. Yokana 293 F.2d 411 (3 Cir. 1961).

$\Longleftarrow$ Response for Plaintiff as Side 2:

Midland-Ross Corp. v. Yokana is distinguishable because:
In Yokana, plaintiff disclosed its product information to more outsiders than in Crown Industries

Counterexamples:

Data General Corp. v. Digital Computer Controls Inc. 357 A.2d 105 (Del. Ch. 1975), held for plaintiff even though in Data General plaintiff disclosed its product information to more outsiders than in Midland-Ross Corp. v. Yokana.

⟹ Rebuttal for Defendant as Side 1:

Data General Corp. v. Digital Computer Controls Inc. is distinguishable because: In Crown Industries, Plaintiff disclosed its product information in negotiations with defendant. Not so in Data General. In Data General, plaintiff's disclosures to outsiders were restricted. Not so in Crown Industries.

Note:
Plaintiff's response would be strengthened if: Plaintiff's disclosures to outsiders were restricted. Cf. Data General Corp. v. Digital Computer Controls Inc. 357 A.2d 105 (Del. Ch. 1975)

Argument [2] is nearly identical to Argument [1] because the cases cited, *Midland-Ross v. Sunbeam* and *Midland-Ross v. Yokana*, are nearly identical. Note that in the Claim Lattices, these two cases are treated in the same equivalence class. One goal for improving Hypo's output is to treat nearly identical cases in the same 3-Ply Arguments.

3-Ply Argument in *Crown*: [3]

⟹ Point for Defendant as Side 1:

Where: Plaintiff disclosed its product information in negotiations with defendant.

Defendant should win a claim for Trade Secrets Misappropriation.

Cite: Automated-Systems v. Service-Bureau 401 F.2d 619 (10 Cir., 1968).

⟸ Response for Plaintiff as Side 2:

Automated-Systems v. Service-Bureau is distinguishable because: In Automated Systems, plaintiff's product information was about customer business relations. Not so in Crown Industries.

⟹ Rebuttal for Defendant as Side 1: None.

Argument [3] shows a comparison with the *Automated Systems* case, which the defendant can use to take advantage of the fact that in *Crown*, the plaintiff disclosed its product information directly to the defendant in negotiations. The distinction points out that in *Automated Systems*, the alleged secret information was of a special type arguably not protected in trade secrets law. Thus, *Automated Systems* is weaker for plaintiff and should not be followed, or so the response goes. In [3], the response did not cite a counterexample, so there is no rebuttal.

3-Ply Argument in *Crown*: [4]

$\Longrightarrow$ Point for Defendant as Side 1:

Where: Plaintiff disclosed its product information in negotiations with defendant.

Defendant should win a claim for Trade Secrets Misappropriation.

Cite: Speedry Chemical Products, Inc. v. Carter's Ink Company 306 F.2d 328 (2d Cir., 1962).

$\Longleftarrow$ Response for Plaintiff as Side 2: None.

$\Longrightarrow$ Rebuttal for Defendant as Side 1: None.

Note:
Plaintiff's response would be strengthened if: Defendant's access to plaintiff's product information saved it time or expense. Plaintiff adopted security measures. Cf. Space Aero Products Co. v. R.E. Darling Co. 208 A.2d 74 (Ct. App. Md., 1965)

Argument [4] shows a comparison with the *Speedry* case which held for defendant where the plaintiff disclosed the information to the defendant. From the plaintiff's point of view, *Speedry* is not relevantly distinguishable from *Crown*, and there are no trumping or as-on-point counterexamples to cite for Side 2. Nevertheless, the Explainer makes a useful suggestion for the attorney. If one could show that the defendant saved development time and expense or adopted security measures, the cfs would be more like *Space Aero*, which held for plaintiff although the plaintiff disclosed its information to defendant in negotiations. In that event, *Space Aero* would be a trumping counterexample citable in response to the *Speedry* case.

The Explainer suggests hypothetical modifications that would help either the plaintiff or the defendant on the claim. The suggested hypotheticals are the basis for interesting "what ifs" that illustrate how to bolster particular points and responses or how to make new points. Where possible, it lists the hypothetical at the end of the specific 3-Ply Argument that the hypothetical would affect. Examples of this are the notes appended to Arguments [1] and [4] above citing the *Data General* and *Space Aero* cases. The appended notes suggest a hypothetical modification in the context of the specific arguments where their potential significance would be most apparent—as counterexamples to be used to trump specific points.

The Explainer also outputs a general list of suggested hypotheticals each of which would serve as the basis of a possible point for a side given appropriate additional facts. Here is the Explainer's general list of hypotheticals for the *Crown* case:

Hypotheticals to Consider on Claim of Trade Secrets Misappropriation in Fact Situation of Crown Industries:

Plaintiff's position would be strengthened in following situations:

Suppose:

Plaintiff and defendant entered into a nondisclosure agreement. Plaintiff adopted security measures. Cf. Eastern Marble Products Corp. v. Roman Marble, Inc. 364 N.E.2d 799 (Mass. 1977)

Defendant's access to plaintiff's product information saved it time or expense. Plaintiff and defendant entered into a nondisclosure agreement. Cf. Telex Corp. v. IBM Corp. (1) 510 F.2d 894 (10 Cir., 1975)

Plaintiff and defendant entered into a nondisclosure agreement. Defendant's access to plaintiff's product information saved it time or expense. Cf. Kewanee Oil Co. v. Bicron Corp. 416 U.S. 470, 94 S. Ct. 1879, 40 L. Ed. 2d 315 (1974)

Defendant's access to plaintiff's product information saved it time or expense. Plaintiff and defendant entered into a nondisclosure agreement. Cf. Analogic Corp. v. Data Translation, Inc. 358 N.E.2d 804 (S.J.C. Mass., 1976)

Defendant's access to plaintiff's product information saved it time or expense. Plaintiff adopted security measures. Cf. Space Aero Products Co. v. R.E. Darling Co. 208 A.2d 74 (Ct. App. Md., 1965)

Plaintiff's disclosures to outsiders were restricted. Cf. Data General Corp. v. Digital Computer Controls Inc. 357 A.2d 105 (Del. Ch. 1975)

Defendant's position would be strengthened in following situations:

Suppose:

Plaintiff's product information was about customer business relations. Cf. Automated-Systems v. Service-Bureau 401 F.2d 619 (10 Cir., 1968)

The Explainer determines that there are interesting hypotheticals to suggest by checking for the following:

- Potentially more-on-point counterexamples in an Argument Record. These target cases make hypotheticals that show how to bolster a side's response.

- Distinctions in an Argument Record. By posing a hypothetical eliminating the distinctions, a side's point can be bolstered.

- Most-on-point near-miss cases in the Case Analysis Record. These target cases make hypotheticals that show how to make new points. For example, each of the suggested hypotheticals listed above corresponds to a most-on-point near-miss case listed in the Case Analysis Record for the *Crown* cfs.

Where possible, the Explainer characterizes the cited case with citation labels that indicate the degree of support that cases lend to a legal conclusion. The Explainer's citation labels come from the *Blue Book* [BlueBook 1986], a standard legal reference work familiar to attorneys. For example, the "Cf." citation label in Argument [1] instructs the attorney to compare *Data General* with the cfs and *Midland-Ross*. The Explainer could also use "contra" labels to introduce the trumping counterexamples in the 3-Ply Arguments. The Explainer has computational definitions of each of the labels in terms of the existence of distinctions, trumping counterexamples and other information in the Argument Records.

The Explainer enables the user to compare the strength of a side's position in the current cfs with that in any of the suggested hypothetical variants. If the user selects a suggested hypothetical, the Explainer does the following:

- It calls the 3-Ply Arguer and Hypo Generator to generate a hypothetical case consisting of a variant of the current cfs.

- It recursively calls the basic processing loop to analyze and generate Argument Records for the hypothetical variant. The variant becomes a new cfs with its own Case Analysis Record.

- It compares the arguments for the hypothetical with those for the original cfs, as recorded in the Argument Records. It compares the sides' relative positions in the hypothetical and the original fact situation to see if any new nontrumped points are gained (or sometimes lost). It also replays a previously made point in the context of the new hypothetical and compares the responses to the cited case to see what new responses are available.

To illustrate the process, suppose that the attorney instructed Hypo to generate a hypothetical variant for the *Crown* fact situation based on the *Data General* case as suggested by the Explainer in Argument [1]. The Hypo Generator creates a variant called "Crown Industries Inc. v. Kawneer Co.—4," which is just like the *Crown* case except that (1) all of the disclosures are subject to restriction, as in *Data General*, and (2) all of the object names are changed by adding a version number ("4"). The Explainer then replays, in the context of version 4, the point in Argument [1] (citing the *Midland-Ross* case), generating a new 3-Ply Argument [5]. The result is shown in the following example of Hypo's output:

> **Comparing an Argument in *Crown* with *Crown Version 4***
>
> On a claim for Trade Secrets Misappropriation, the Defendant in Crown Industries Inc. v. Kawneer Co.—4 can make a stronger response to a point citing Midland-Ross Corp. v. Sunbeam Equipment Corp. than in Crown Industries Inc. v. Kawneer Co. because it can cite the following additional more-on-point counterexamples: Data General Corp. v. Digital Computer Controls Inc. 357 A.2d 105 (Dcl. Ch. 1075)
>
> Compare the following arguments:
>
> This is the point in Crown Industries Inc. v. Kawneer Co. (i.e., Argument [1])
>
> $\Longrightarrow$ Point For Defendant As Side 1:
>
> Where: Plaintiff disclosed its product information to outsiders. Defendant should win a claim for Trade Secrets Misappropriation.

Cite: Midland-Ross Corp. v. Sunbeam Equipment Corp. 316 F. Supp. 171 (W.D. Pa., 1970).

⇐ Response for Plaintiff as Side 2:

Midland-Ross Corp. v. Sunbeam Equipment Corp. is distinguishable because: In Midland-Ross, plaintiff disclosed its product information to more outsiders than in Crown Industries

Counterexamples:

Data General Corp. v. Digital Computer Controls Inc. 357 A.2d 105 (Del. Ch. 1975), held for plaintiff even though in Data General plaintiff disclosed its product information to more outsiders than in Midland-Ross Corp. v. Sunbeam Equipment Corp.

⟹ Rebuttal for Defendant as Side 1:

Data General Corp. v. Digital Computer Controls Inc. is distinguishable because: In Crown Industries, Plaintiff disclosed its product information in negotiations with defendant. Not so in Data General. In Data General, plaintiff's disclosures to outsiders were restricted. Not so in Crown Industries.

Note:

Plaintiff's response would be strengthened if: Plaintiff's disclosures to outsiders were restricted. Cf. Data General Corp. v. Digital Computer Controls Inc. 357 A.2d 105 (Del. Ch. 1975)

This is the point in Crown Industries Inc. v. Kawneer Co.—4 Argument [5]

⟹ Point for Defendant as Side 1:

Where: Plaintiff disclosed its product information to outsiders.

Defendant should win a claim for Trade Secrets Misappropriation.

Cite: Midland-Ross Corp. v. Sunbeam Equipment Corp. 316 F. Supp. 171 (W.D. Pa., 1970).

⇐ Response for Plaintiff as Side 2:

Midland-Ross Corp. v. Sunbeam Equipment Corp. is distinguishable because:

In Midland-Ross, plaintiff disclosed its product information to more outsiders than in Crown Industries—4

Counterexamples:

Data General Corp. v. Digital Computer Controls Inc. 357 A.2d 105 (Del. Ch. 1975), is more on point and held for Plaintiff where it was also the case that: Plaintiff's disclosures to outsiders were restricted.

Data General Corp. v. Digital Computer Controls Inc. 357 A.2d 105 (Del. Ch. 1975), held for Plaintiff even though in Data General plaintiff disclosed its product information to more outsiders than in Midland-Ross Corp. v. Sunbeam Equipment Corp.

$\Longrightarrow$ Rebuttal for Defendant as Side 1: Data General Corp. v. Digital Computer Controls Inc. is distinguishable because: In Crown Industries, Plaintiff disclosed its product information in negotiations with defendant. Not so in Data General.

Comparing Argument [1] and the new 3-Ply Argument [5], Hypo concluded that the plaintiff's response is strengthened by virtue of the fact that *Data General* could be cited as a trumping counterexample. Note the differences in Side 2's responses in [1] and [5] where *Data General* has been promoted to a trumping counterexample. Also, the defendant's rebuttal in [5] is weaker because *Data General* is less distinguishable from the cfs.

The Explainer's Citation Summary for Version 4 of the *Crown* case is also shown below. As a comparison to the original Citation Summary will show, Hypo has revised its assessment of the relative strengths of the parties on a trade secrets claim. Now plaintiff, as well as defendant, can cite nontrumped points, a definite improvement in plaintiff's argument position.

Citation Summary for Version 4 of *Crown*

3-Ply Arguments for Best Cases to Cite on Claim of Trade Secrets Misappropriation in Fact Situation of Crown Industries—4:

On a claim for Trade Secrets Misappropriation, both sides can make a strong argument.

Plaintiff can cite the following cases for which there are no more-on-point counterexamples:

Data General Corp. v. Digital Computer Controls Inc. 357 A.2d 105 (Del. Ch. 1975)

Defendant can cite the following cases for which there are no more-on-point counterexamples:

Speedry Chemical Products, Inc. v. Carter's Ink Company 306 F.2d 328 (2d Cir., 1962)

Automated-Systems v. Service-Bureau 401 F.2d 619 (10 Cir., 1968)

Keeping track of the old and new cfs's, and the before and after arguments is the responsibility of the Session Manager. For bookkeeping purposes, the Manager employs the Session Master List and the Comparison Lists in each of the Argument Records. The Comparison List associates the Argument Records with target cases that lead to new responses or points.

The replay of a 3-Ply Argument and the new Citation Summary reveal how the hypothetical variation supports new or changed points and responses. The before and after views of the argument explain the hypothetical's significance to the user. By guiding the user to contrast the fact situation to neighboring cases and hypothetical variants of the fact situation, the Explainer interrogates the user about possibly important facts and leads the user to augment the description of the fact situation. The posed hypotheticals, motivated by potentially significant cases that may affect the balance of the argument, prompt the user to identify useful or potentially dangerous facts about which he or she may not have been aware.

5.8 The Hypo Generator

The Hypo Generator computes the hypothetical variations of the cfs used by the Explainer to demonstrate how points or responses can be strengthened or weakened. The hypotheticals are copies of the cfs that are stronger or weaker for a particular side. The modifications involve adding, changing, or removing facts with respect to the cfs copy such that new Dimensions apply, old Dimensions no longer apply, or the position along a Dimension changes. The modifications change the configuration of the Claim Lattice and the strength of a side's argument.

A specification for a hypothetical consists of a seed case (the case a copy of which will be modified hypothetically), a target case (the case, if any, relative to which the copy of the seed case is to be modified), and a list of changes. Each change consists of a Dimension along which to change the copy of the seed case, whether the change is to favor plaintiff or defendant, and whether the target value should be the same as or greater than that in the target or an extreme value along the Dimension.

When the user authorizes the Explainer to run a hypothetical, the Explainer determines from the context which cases to use as the seed case and target case. Typically the seed case is the cfs, and the target cases are potential counterexamples or potential most-on-point cases as revealed in Argument Records or the Case Analysis Record of the cfs. The Explainer calls upon the 3-Ply Arguer to specify a list of changes. If the hypothetical is posed to bolster a response, for instance, the Arguer fills out the change list from information contained in the associated Argument Record. The Arguer directs changes along each of the Dimensions that the potential counterexample shares, and the cited case does not share, with the cfs's list of applicable and near-miss Dimensions. The direction of the change is to favor Side 2, and the target values are those of the targeted potential counterexample.

Given a specification, the steps for generating a hypothetical are the following:

1. Make a copy of the seed case. The copy is identical to the seed case except that the names of Legal Case Frame instances are modified to avoid obliterating the seed case.

2. Implement changes on change list using five heuristics and special modification methods associated with the Dimensions

The five heuristics for modifying cases hypothetically are

(H1) make a near-miss Dimension apply,

(H2) strengthen or weaken a case along an applicable Dimension,

(H3) move case along a related Dimension,

(H4) make case extreme along a Dimension,

(H5) make case into a near-win given a target.

The heuristics use special modification methods similar to the Dimensions' comparison methods. Like the comparison methods, the modification methods are associated with the Dimensions' particular comparison types. Instead of simply comparing focal slot values of one case to another case, however, these methods change the values. The modification methods can make a near-miss Dimension apply or make an applicable Dimension into a near miss by adding or deleting Legal Case Frame facts associated with Factual Predicates or change the values in a case of a Dimension's focal slot.

The move from the *Crown* fact situation to *Crown Version 4*, for example, involved H1. A change was made so that the seven disclosures to outsiders in *Crown* became subject to confidentiality restrictions. As a result of the change, the near-miss Dimension *Outsider-Disclosures-Restricted* became applicable.

Placing the Hypo Generator under the control of the Explainer and 3-Ply Arguer helps to ensure that the hypotheticals are significant and helpful in the context of the argument. The Explainer and Arguer use the context of a particular argument to create specifications for meaningful hypotheticals.

6 The Case Knowledge Base

Hypo's arsenal of cases for making legal arguments is its CKB. The cases in the CKB are represented and organized to make retrieval of relevant cases as straightforward a task as possible. This chapter describes the content and organization of Hypo's CKB and explains the aspects of a legal precedent represented in Hypo.

6.1 Legal Case Frames

Legal Case Frames are used to represent all legal disputes in Hypo, including actual legal cases in Hypo's CKB, as well as current fact situations presented by the attorney to Hypo through the Case Editor and hypothetical cases generated by the Hypo Generator. Legal Case Frames summarize much of the same information about a legal case that lawyers or law students record in squib summaries. A squib, or case brief, is a schematic summary of the important facts and legal conclusions of a case as set forth in the opinion of the court. Law students make squibs to help them remember cases to cite in examinations and oral arguments in class. Similarly, Legal Case Frames are a schematic summary of a case that record enough information about a case to enable the 3-Ply Arguer to cite them in arguments. Like squibs, Legal Case Frames record the following information about a case:

- Title (e.g., *USM Corp. v. Marson Fastener Corp.*)

- Citation to the case, including the location of the published opinion, the court that decided the case, and the date of the decision

- Parties, including identifying the plaintiffs and defendants

- Legal claims asserted by the plaintiff (e.g., trade secrets misappropriation or breach of contract)

- Winner of the decision on each claim (plaintiff or defendant)

- A partial representation of the legal issues implicit in the court's decision

- Important cases cited, distinguished, or overturned by the court

- Selected facts of the case

Each legal case represented in Hypo has a top-level and various underlying Legal Case Frames. The top-level Legal Case Frame records various legal information like title, citation, parties, claims, overall decision, and holdings on individual claims. It also summarizes the factors that applied in the case by virtue of its list of the Dimensions that index the case in the CKB. Underlying Legal Case Frames represent the facts of the case. There are nested frames to represent the important objects, participants, and selected relationships in the case. A complete listing of types of Legal Case Frames may be found in appendix C.

The components of Legal Case Frames are illustrated here in the context of two cases. The *USM* case demonstrates the Legal Case Frames for representing a simple trade secrets disputes. The *Amexxco* case illustrates the case frames designed especially to represent a standard scenario often found in trade secrets cases in which an employee conveys plaintiff's secrets to defendant.

Squib for *USM* Case

Title: *USM Corp. v. Marson Fastener Corp.*

Cite: 379 Mass. 90 (Supreme Judicial Court)

Date: August 29, 1979

Parties: Plaintiff: USM Corp.; Defendant: Marson

Claim: Trade Secrets Misappropriation

Procedural Setting: Plaintiff appeals from judgment affirming master's report and dismissing complaint.

Decision: For Plaintiff reversing dismissal.

Facts: From 1954 to 1959, USM began to develop a machine ("USM machine") to produce blind rivets (fasteners insertable from only one end of the material to be fastened). The information associated with developing the machine was not generally known. Marson hired someone to construct a machine similar to that of USM using blueprints supplied by Marson. USM took the following steps to protect the information: (1) employees were required to sign nondisclosure agreements; (2) excluded general public from production areas. However, USM: (a) did not stamp drawings "confidential"; (b) did not direct employees that drawings were secret; (c) allowed escorted tours by distributors, including defendants. The secrets were not easily discernable by inspection of the machine. The defendant produced its product in less time than it took the plaintiff. The plaintiff's product took 60 months to produce while defendant's took only 36 months.

Issues: Did USM Corp. take sufficient reasonable steps to preserve the secrecy of the information embodied in the USM machine?

Holding: Yes, for Plaintiff: "We do not require the possessor of a trade secret to take heroic measures to preserve its secrecy."

Cases cited by court: *Eastern Marble Prods. Corp. v. Roman Marble, Inc.*, 372 Mass. 835 (1977); Distinguished *J. T. Healy & Son v. James A. Murphy & Son*, 357 Mass. 728 (1970).

As the squib indicates, the court decided the trade secrets claim in favor of the plaintiff, *USM*, and focused on the security measures the plaintiff took in protecting its secret. The top-level case frame for *USM* is shown in figure 6.1. With the assistance of the Case Editor, a case entry person has filled in the legal information called for, including the name of the case, the citation and date, the parties, the claims, the party that won each claim, and selected important cases cited by the court. Hypo fills in the DIMENSIONS LIST slot.

The underlying case frames represent the facts of the dispute. For each party, the case enterer fills in a Corporate-Party frame, shown in figure 6.2. There are two corporate parties—the plaintiff, USM Corp., and the defendant, Marson—and each makes a product. Their respective products are shown in the Product frames of figures 6.3 and 6.4. The fact that the products compete with one another is recorded in the Corpororate-Parties' and Products' COMPETITORS PRODUCTS slots. USM's Product also indicates the knowledge used to develop it, information that is represented by the Knowledge case frame, About-USM-Machine, shown in figure 6.5.

As the Knowledge case frame indicates, there is no information in the case about whether the information was disclosed to outsiders or to the other party in the case. That is represented by a "Nil" in the PARTIES WITH ACCESS and NUMBER OF DISCLOSEES slots. The knowledge is not generally known in the industry, however.

USM's Product also indicates the steps that the plaintiff took to protect security of the product. The SECURITY MEASURES LIST slot in-

Case: USM Corp. v. Marson Fastener Corp.

SHORT TITLE: "USM v. Marson"

CITATION: 379 Mass. 90

DATE: August 29, 1979

PARTIES:
Plaintiff Corporate-Party: USM
Defendant Corporate-Party: Marson

DECISION FOR: Plaintiff Corporate-Party: USM

CLAIMS DECIDED: Type-of-Claim: Trade-Secrets-Misappropriation
Won by: Plaintiff Corporate-Party: USM

DIMENSIONS LIST:
Competitive-Advantage-Gained
Security-Measures-Adopted

CASES CITED:
Eastern Marble v. Roman Marble
Healy v. Murphy

Figure 6.1
Top-Level Case Frame for *USM Corp. v. Marson*

Corporate-Party: USM

NAME: USM

CASE: USM Corp. v. Marson Fastener Corp.

CASE ROLE: Plaintiff

EMPLOYEE LIST: Nil

PRODUCT LIST: Product: USM-Machine

COMPETITOR'S PRODUCTS:
Corporate-Party: Marson
Product: Marson-Machine

Corporate-Party: Marson

NAME: Marson

CASE: USM Corp. v. Marson Fastener Corp.

CASE ROLE: Defendant

EMPLOYEE LIST: Nil

PRODUCT LIST: Product: Marson-Machine

COMPETITOR'S PRODUCTS:
Corporate-Party: USM
Product: USM-Machine

Figure 6.2
Case Frames for Parties in *USM Corp.*

Product: USM-Machine

NAME: USM-Machine

CASE: USM Corp. v. Marson Fastener Corp.

A KIND OF: Blind Rivet Machine

PRODUCT USED FOR: Rivet Manufacture

GENERAL PRODUCT MARKET: Rivet Buyers

COMPETITORS PRODUCTS:
Corporate-Party: Marson Marson-Machine

DEVELOPER: USM

EMPLOYEES WHO WORKED ON PROJECT: Nil

PROJECT DEVELOPMENT START: 1954

PROJECT DEVELOPMENT END: 1959

PROJECT DEVELOPMENT TIME: 60 (months)

EXPENDITURES MADE: Nil

KNOWLEDGE USED:
Knowledge: About-USM-Machine

SECURITY MEASURES LIST:
Minimal Measures
Access to Premises Controlled
Restrictions on Entry by Visitors
Employee Nondisclosure Agreements

SECURITY BREACH LIST: Nil

Figure 6.3
Case Frame for Plaintiff's Product in *USM*

Product: Marson-Machine

NAME: Marson-Machine

CASE: USM Corp. v. Marson Fastener Corp.

A KIND OF: Blind Rivet Machine

PRODUCT USED FOR: Rivet Manufacture

GENERAL PRODUCT MARKET: Rivet Buyers

COMPETITORS PRODUCTS:
Corporate-Party: USM USM-Machine

DEVELOPER: Marson

PROJECT DEVELOPMENT START: 1961

PROJECT DEVELOPMENT END: 1964

PROJECT DEVELOPMENT TIME: 36 (months)

EXPENDITURES MADE: Nil

Figure 6.4
Case Frames for Defendant's Product in *USM*

Knowledge: About-USM-Machine

CASE: USM Corp. v. Marson Fastener Corp.

KNOWLEDGE ABOUT: USM-machine

KIND OF KNOWLEDGE: Technical

PARTIES WITH ACCESS: Nil

OTHER PERSONS WITH ACCESS: Nil

SPECIFIC DISCLOSURE EVENTS: Nil

NUMBER OF DISCLOSEES: Nil

PERCENT OF DISCLOSURES RESTRICTED: Nil

GENERALLY KNOWN IN INDUSTRY: Negative

Figure 6.5
Case Frame for Plaintiff's Knowledge in *USM*

dicates that the plaintiff took the following steps: minimal measures, access to premises controlled, restrictions on entry by visitors, and employee nondisclosure agreements. There are four other possible security steps represented in Hypo that the plaintiff did not take: product marked confidential, restrictions on entry by employees, employee trade secret program exists, and restrictions on hardcopy release. The complete list of possible security measures is defined by the range of the *Security-Measures-Adopted* dimension. See appendix F.

In the squib, it appears that defendant Marson developed its product in substantially less time than the plaintiff took (36 months versus 60 months). Both USM's and Marson's Products' slots for PROJECT DEVELOPMENT START, END, and PROJECT DEVELOPMENT END indicate how many months it took for each party to produce its product. From this information, the program can compute Marson's savings in product development time relative to that of USM (36/60). Since there is no information about the plaintiff's product development expenses (the EXPENDITURES MADE slots' values are Nil), the program cannot compute Marson's savings in product development cost, if any.

As the *USM* frames illustrate, Legal Case Frames are nested. The top-level frame points to an instance of a Corporate-Party frame, which points to a Product instance, which in turn points to an instance of Knowledge. Each instantiated case frame also contains a back pointer to the top-level Legal Case Frame.

A number of the cases in the CKB involve the "common employee scenario" where an employee brought confidential information from the plaintiff to the defendant. An employee was involved in the *Amexxco* fact situation described in chapter 2, which involved a former employee who brought secrets he developed himself to a competing employer. Figures 6.6 through 6.12 show the Legal Case Frames for various employment, relations such as Employee, Employment, and Employment Change, as well as a Nondisclosure Agreement. The Employee frame in figure 6.6 shows that G. Whiz was employed by both Amexxco and Exxssinc, the two corporate parties in the suit. The dates of employment in figures 6.7 and 6.8 show that G. Whiz started working for Amexxco in 1980 and then left to work for Exxssinc in 1987. While employed by Amexxco, he worked on the Dipper product. While at Exxssinc, he worked on Exxssinc's competing system. The two Product-Worked-On frames in figures 6.9 and 6.10 indicate that G. Whiz used the same in-

Employee-Party : Gwhiz
NAME: GWhiz
CASE: Amexxco Production Co. v. Gwhiz
CASE ROLE: Defendant
EMPLOYMENTS:
Employment: Of-Gwhiz-By-Amexxco
Employment: Of-Gwhiz-By-Exxssinc
EMPLOYERS:
Corporate-Party: Amexxco
Coroporate-Pary: Exxssinc

Figure 6.6
Case Frame for Representing Employee in *Amexxco*

formation, Knowledge: About-Dipper, on each product and that he was the sole developer of the Dipper product. The frame representing the Employment Change, figure 6.11, indicates that there is no information in the case that G. Whiz received anything of value for switching employers or that he brought any records, devices, or code with him. Note that each slot contains a "Nil," indicating an absence of information. Finally, the nondisclosure agreement in figure 6.12 between G. Whiz and Amexxco indicates that both sides received some consideration and that the agreement did not specifically refer to the Dipper product.

Hypo uses information contained in the underlying frames to compare a case to other cases in the CKB. For example, using the information described, Hypo can compare the *USM* case to other cases in terms of the defendants' savings in product development time and in plaintiffs' security measures taken. Such comparisons among cases are important. The fact that a defendant saved development time or expense has been cited in other cases as a factor that strengthens the plaintiff's position in a trade secrets misappropriation claim. Similarly the fact that a plaintiff has taken measures to secure confidential information has been treated as a factor that strengthens its claim. In Hypo, these and other factors important for the claim of trade secrets misappropriation claims have been represented as Dimensions. The two factors referred to above are represented by the *Competitive-Advantage-Gained*

Employment: Of-Gwhiz-By-Amexxco

CASE: Amexxco Production Co. v. Gwhiz

EMPLOYEE: Employee-Party: Gwhiz

EMPLOYER: Corporate-Party: Amexxco

STARTING DATE: 1980

ENDING DATE: 1987

THERE IS COVENANT NOT TO COMPETE: Nil

THERE IS CHANGE OF EMPLOYERS:
Employment-Change: Of-Gwhiz-From-Amexxco-To-Exxssinc

PRODUCT WORKED ON:
Product-Worked-On: Work-On-Dipper

Figure 6.7
Case Frame for Representing Employment in *Amexxco*

Employment: Of-Gwhiz-By-Exxssinc

CASE: Amexxco Production Co. v. Gwhiz

EMPLOYEE: Employee-Party: Gwhiz

EMPLOYER: Corporate-Party: Exxssinc

STARTING DATE: 1987

ENDING DATE: Nil

THERE IS COVENANT NOT TO COMPETE: Nil

THERE IS CHANGE OF EMPLOYERS:
Employment-Change: Of-Gwhiz-From-Amexxco-To-Exxssinc

PRODUCT WORKED ON:
Product-Worked-On: Work-On-Exxssinc-System

Figure 6.8
Case Frame for Representing Employment in *Amexxco*

Product-Worked-On: Work-On-Dipper

CASE: Amexxco Production Co. v. Gwhiz

PRODUCT: Product: Dipper

EMPLOYMENT: Employment: Of-Gwhiz-By-Amexxco

KNOWLEDGE EMPLOYED: Knowledge: About-Dipper

EMPLOYEE ROLE IN PRODUCT DEVELOPMENT: Sole Developer

Figure 6.9
Case Frame for Representing Product Worked On in *Amexxco*

Product-Worked-On: Work-On-Exxssinc-System

CASE: Amexxco Production Co. v. Gwhiz

PRODUCT: Product: Exxssinc-System

EMPLOYMENT: Employment: Of-Gwhiz-By-Exxssinc

KNOWLEDGE EMPLOYED: Knowledge: About-Dipper

Figure 6.10
Case Frame for Representing Product Worked On in *Amexxco*

Employment-Change: Of-Gwhiz-From-Amexxco-To-Exxssinc

CASE: Amexxco Production Co. v. Gwhiz

FORMER EMPLOYER: Corporate-Party: Amexxco

FORMER EMPLOYMENT: Employment: Of-Gwhiz-By-Amexxco

VALUE RECEIVED TO MAKE CHANGE: Nil

RECORDS, DEVICES, CODE BROUGHT BY EMPLOYEE: Nil

Figure 6.11
Case Frame for Representing Change Of Employment in *Amexxco*

Nondisclosure Agreement: Between-Gwhiz-And-Amexxco-2

CASE: Amexxco Production Co. v. Gwhiz

DISCLOSER: Corporate-Party: Amexxco

DISCLOSEE: Employee-Party: Gwhiz

CONSIDERATION RECEIVED BY PARTY:
Corporate-Party: Amexxco got promise
Employee-Party: Gwhiz got employment

DID AGREEMENT REFER TO PRODUCT: Negative

DURATION OF PROHIBITION: Nil

EXPRESS OR IMPLIED: Express

DATE ENTERED: Nil

Figure 6.12
Case Frame for Representing Nondisclosure Agreement in *Amexxco*

and *Security-Measures-Taken* Dimensions.

Dimensions facilitate making these kinds of comparisons among cases. The underlying Legal Case Frames and their slots have been selected and designed to facilitate determining the Dimensions that apply to a case and comparing a case to other cases along Dimensions.

6.2 Factual Predicates

Factual Predicates are a more abstract language for summarizing the facts of a case as represented by the underlying case frames. They assist in determining the Dimensions that apply to a case and locating the crucial information for comparing cases along Dimensions.

Factual predicates represent the components of various stereotypical fact situations, or scenarios, that arise in trade secrets and related cases. These more complex factual scenarios involve collections of case frame objects and relationships. For example, a common scenario involves a common employee, one who formerly worked for plaintiff on a particular product and subsequently worked for the defendant on a competing product. The Factual Predicates "Employee switched from working for plaintiff to working for defendant" and "Employee received something of value to switch employment" capture this information. Other scenarios include plaintiff's voluntarily having disclosed the "secret" information to the defendant, perhaps in connection with negotiations to enter into a sales or other agreement with the defendant. "Plaintiff disclosed product information to defendant in negotiations" corresponds to this scenario.

In addition to representing scenarios, Factual Predicates generalize collections of other Factual Predicates. For example, the Factual Predicate "Defendant had access to plaintiff's product information by common employee or negotiations" represents the fact that defendant had access to confidential product information by negotiations or the common employee scenario.

Other Factual Predicates characterize information crucial for making comparisons among cases along Dimensions. For example, the Factual Predicate "Plaintiff made some disclosures to outsiders" contains information for comparing a case to other cases in terms of the number of outside disclosures. The Factual Predicate "Plaintiff adopted security measures" contains data for comparing a case to other cases in terms of the extent of security measures taken.

Factual Predicates are used primarily in the process by which Hypo infers from the underlying case frames the Dimensions that apply. In analyzing a case, the Case Analyzer generates a summary in terms of Factual Predicates. The summary is contained in an Interpretation Frame (part of the Case Analysis Record described in chapter 4). Each slot of the Interpretation Frame corresponds to a different Factual Predicate. Factual Predicates are not predicates in the Boolean sense. They may have the following values: nil (indicating no information), negative (indicating false), affirmative (indicating true) or a specific instantiated underlying case frame or case frame slot value that stands for an affirmative answer and provides additional information.

Determining whether a case evinces a Factual Predicate requires checking for a number of relationships involving a variety of participants, objects, and constraints, such as whether plaintiff and defendant did employ the same employee for subsequent periods or whether the employee worked on competing products. Each of these components may be associated with its own Factual Predicate in the Interpretation Frame or be inferred from the underlying case frames. Each Factual Predicate has an attached procedure called a retrieval method to perform these tests. Retrieval methods contain instructions of where to look in the Interpretation Frame or among the underlying case frames for the relevant information.

The following Interpretation Frame for the *USM* case summarizes the information contained in the underlying case frames:

Interpretation Frame

CASE: USM Corp. v. Marson Fastener Corp.

THERE IS A CORPORATE PLAINTIFF:
Corporate-Party: USM

PLAINTIFF MAKES A PRODUCT:
Product: USM-Machine

PLAINTIFF HAS PRODUCT INFORMATION:
Knowledge: About-USM-Machine

THERE IS A CORPORATE DEFENDANT:
Corporate-Party: Marson

DEFENDANT MAKES A PRODUCT:
Product: Marson-Machine

PLAINTIFF AND DEFENDANT COMPETE: True

PLAINTIFF'S AND DEFENDANT'S PRODUCTS COMPETE: True

THERE IS A DEFENDANT EMPLOYEE: Nil

PLAINTIFF MADE SOME DISCLOSURES TO OUTSIDERS: Nil

DEFENDANT SAVED PRODUCT DEVELOPMENT EXPENSE RELATIVE TO PLAINTIFF:
36 months versus 60 months

PLAINTIFF ADOPTED SECURITY MEASURES:
Minimal Measures
Access to Premises Controlled
Restrictions on Entry by Visitors
Employee Nondisclosure Agreements

PLAINTIFF DISCLOSED PRODUCT INFORMATION TO DEFENDANT IN NEGOTIATIONS: Nil

For each Factual Predicate, the Interpretation Frame shows whether it is satisfied in the *USM* case. When the Case Analyzer filled in the

Interpretation Frame slot for the Factual Predicate "Plaintiff adopted security measures," the corresponding retrieval method was called. The retrieval method checked the list of security measures in USM's product (figure 6.3). The retrieval method found USM's product in the "Plaintiff makes a product" slot of the Interpretation frame.

The common employee scenario calls into play another set of Factual Predicates. Illustrated below are the parts of the completed Interpretation Frame for *Amexxco* that deal with the employee scenario:

Excerpts from Interpretation Frame for *Amexxco*

CASE: Amexxco Production Co. v. Gwhiz

THERE IS A CORPORATE PLAINTIFF:
Corporate-Party: Amexxco

THERE IS A CORPORATE DEFENDANT:
Corporate-Party: Exxssinc

THERE IS AN EMPLOYEE DEFENDANT:
Employee-Party: Gwhiz

EMPLOYEE WORKED FOR PLAINTIFF:
Employment: Of-Gwhiz-By-Amexxco

EMPLOYEE WORKED FOR DEFENDANT:
Employment: Of-Gwhiz-By-Exxssinc

EMPLOYEE WORKED FOR BOTH PLAINTIFF AND DEFENDANT: True

EMPLOYEE SWITCHED FROM WORKING FOR PLAINTIFF TO WORKING FOR DEFENDANT:
Employment Change: Of-Gwhiz-From-Amexxco-To-Exxssinc

EMPLOYEE RECEIVED SOMETHING OF VALUE TO SWITCH EMPLOYMENT: Nil

EMPLOYEE BROUGHT PLAINTIFF'S PRODUCT DEVELOPMENT TOOLS TO DEFENDANT: Nil

EMPLOYEE WORKED ON PLAINTIFF'S PRODUCT:
Product Worked On: Work-on-Dipper

DEFENDANT HAD ACCESS TO PLAINTIFF'S PRODUCT VIA EMPLOYEE:
Disclosure Event: Amexxco-Discloses-To-Exxssinc-Via-Gwhiz

DEFENDANT OR EMPLOYEE ENTERED INTO NONDISCLOSURE
AGREEMENT WITH PLAINTIFF:
Nondisclosure-Agreement: Between-Gwhiz-and-Amexxco-2

Basically the Interpretation Frame reports the facts that the employee switched from working for plaintiff to working for defendant and had worked on plaintiff's Dipper product and thus was a route by which defendant gained access to information about the product. It also reports that there was no information that the employee received something of value to switch or brought plaintiff's product development tools. The employee, however, had entered into a nondisclosure agreement with plaintiff.

As experience has shown, a case entry person or system user finds that the Factual Predicates are much easier to work with than the underlying case frames. The Case Editor has been designed to present a case enterer with a menu form patterned on a blank Interpretation Frame. The enterer can specify on the form the names of parties, products, knowledge, or agreements and lists of information that correspond to the values that the Factual Predicates should have in the case. Then the Editor processes the form, creating underlying case frames to embody or contain the inputted information, as well as a filled-in Interpretation Frame. This facility has been partially implemented.

6.3 Indexing a Case in the CKB

The CKB consists of 30 legal cases. Each case is represented in the Legal Case Frame language with a completely filled-in top-level frame and as many underlying frames as are necessary to represent the facts of the case. (Appendix E shows a complete listing of all of the cases in the CKB.)

The CKB is implemented as a list of pointers to the instantiated top-level frames of all the cases. The list of cases is one of the typed lists of the Global Catalog, which contains an association list of pointers to all of the instantiated frames in Hypo sorted by type. For example, there are typed lists for all Products, Disclosure-Events, Employees, Knowledge, Nondisclosure Agreements, and top-level Legal Case Frames (as well as all Case Analysis Records, Interpretation Frames, Argument Records, and so forth). One of these lists is the CKB, a list of pointers to the

The Case Knowledge Base 103

thirty top-level case frames corresponding to each legal case in the Hypo program.

A case is indexed in the CKB when its Dimensions List is filled in with a list of all of the Dimensions that apply to the case. This task is performed by the Case Analyzer. When a case is added to the CKB, the following occur: A case entry person uses the Case Editor to fill out the legal and factual information called for in the top-level and underlying Legal Case Frames (except the Dimensions List). The Case Analyzer Dimensionally analyzes the new case. It determines the Factual Predicates and the Dimensions that apply to the case. The Case Analyzer fills in the top-level Legal Case Frame's DIMENSIONS LIST with pointers to the applicable Dimensions.

Once the last step of the case entry process is complete, the case has been entered into the Dimensional Index, where it is indexed by its applicable Dimensions. For example, the *USM* case is indexed by its two applicable Dimensions: *Security-Measures-Adopted* and *Competitive-Advantage-Gained*. (The *USM* case's filled-in DIMENSIONS LIST is shown in figure 6.1.)

The Dimensional Index is the main route for accessing cases in the CKB. Hypo's Case Positioner uses the Dimensional Index to search for all cases in the CKB to which a particular Dimension applies. Typically the Dimensions of interest are those that have been found to apply to a current problem situation. When the Case Positioner retrieves all of the cases in the CKB to which a particular Dimension applies, it searches the typed list of top-level Legal Case Frames in the Global Catalog for any case frame whose Dimensions List contains a pointer to the Dimension.

When the Case Positioner searches for all cases in the CKB to which a particular Dimension applies, it is not necessary for each case to be reanalyzed. That analysis was done when each case was entered into the Dimensional Index and need not be repeated as long as the Dimensions and Factual Predicates known to the program have not been changed.

The Dimensional Index links a case to every other case in the CKB to which one or more of the Dimensions in its Dimensions List apply. For example, the Index links the *USM* case to each other case in the CKB indexed by either of its two Dimensions:

- *Security-Measures-Adopted* links it to the *Healy, Eastern Marble, Amoco, Kitchens, Plant Industries,* and *Space Aero* cases.

- *Competitive-Advantage-Gained* links it to the *Analogic, Schulenburg, Pressure Science, Kewanee, Widget King, Telex,* and *Space Aero* cases.

Beside the Dimensional Index, there are two other routes for accessing cases in the CKB: Global Catalog typed lists and cross-references in other cases. All cases in the CKB with a particular fact can be retrieved by searching the appropriate typed list of the Global Catalog. All of the case frames are cataloged in the Global Catalog according to their types (e.g., Case, Corporate-Party, Knowledge). Each case frame has a pointer to the top-level frame. A few examples of the kinds of queries that employ these hooks from the Global Catalog include the following:

- All cases in the CKB that involve trade secrets claims are retrieved by searching the typed list of case frames for those whose claims list contain such a claim. (One might also search for all cases, like the *USM* case, that deal with trade secrets misappropriation claims but do not involve nondisclosure agreements.)

- All cases involving a common employee are retrieved by searching the typed list for Employment-Changes.

- All cases involving computer-related products are retrieved by searching the Products typed list for all products with appropriate values in the A-KIND-OF slot.

- Similarly, retrieving a case by title or party is handled by searching the appropriate typed list in the Global Catalog for the case frame that lists the name of the case or party.

A third route for accessing cases in the CKB is by following links from one case to another. The links may be implicit links by shared indexing Dimensions or explicit cross-pointers from a case to other cases cited or distinguished in the opinion of the case. Each case frame contains a CASES CITED slot with references to major cases cited in the opinion of a case, some of them in Hypo's CKB. These links represent an alternative means of accessing relevant cases once an appropriate case has been found. Thus, the *USM* case may be accessed from any case, like the *Eastern Marble* case that cites it in its opinion as reflected in the CASES CITED slot. To date, Hypo does not make use of these explicit pointers.

6.4 Aspects of Legal Precedents Represented

Hypo's Case Representation Language records legal issues decided in a case in the following sense. A legal precedent is treated as a collection of factors. In general, those factors may conflict, some favoring the plaintiff's claim and others not. In deciding the case, the court assigns an outcome that resolves the conflict among the factors. That is what Hypo's Case Representation Language records in the top level Legal Case Frame. Specifically, it records claims that were involved in the case, side that won each claim (plaintiff or defendant), and dimensions that applied to the case. (The Dimensions listed in the top-level case frame's Dimensions List represent the factors that were present in the case).

With respect to the *USM* case, the top-level case frame shown in figure 6.1 contains, in essence, the following information about the legal issues in the case. The claims and Dimension List indicate that the court held for the plaintiff (USM) on a claim for trade secrets misappropriation because of, or in spite of, factors associated with the case's position along the *Competitive-Advantage-Gained* and *Security-Measures-Adopted* Dimensions. Given the information recorded in those Dimensions that they generally favor the plaintiff, Hypo treats the court's decision as in accord with those factors.

Hypo's Case Representation Language does not record the court's rationale for deciding the case. Neither does it break a claim down into elements or treat each separate element as a distinct legal issue, as a court might. Recording this kind of information would require a considerably more expressive language, complicate the computational process of reasoning with cases and make the human case enterer's task much more subjective. Courts are notorious for not making their rationales for decision very clear. They tend to cover the bases by adopting a variety of rationales. Much of legal scholarship is teasing apart the legal justifications that courts offer in opinions and getting down to what they must have meant.

Hypo's Case Representation Language minimizes subjectivity in entering cases. The enterer is required to determine from the opinion only the facts of the case. He or she is not required to make legal interpretations of the case. Though complicated enough a task, every law student becomes skilled at extracting the facts from an opinion.

7 A Dimensional Index

Dimensions constitute the primary index for retrieving relevant cases from the Case Knowledge Base. They are also instrumental for comparing cases, selecting the most relevant cases, citing them in legal arguments, and modifying them hypothetically. In this chapter, we examine the functions and structure of Dimensions in Hypo and describe the kind of reasoning supported by the Dimensional Index.

Dimensions encode knowledge of the features of a case that have relevance for arguing the legal merits of a claim. They represent factors that make a claim in a given fact situation stronger or weaker. If a Dimension applies to a fact situation, it means that the fact situation shares some factor in common with at least one case where a court decided the case because, or in spite, of the presence of that factor. That case can be cited in a legal argument that the fact situation should be decided in the same way.

7.1 The Primary Function of Dimensions

Computationally Dimensions allow Hypo to reason with relevant similarities and differences among precedents. In Hypo relevant similarities and differences are defined in terms of the factors present in a precedent that were important to the court's decision. If the precedent shares such a factor with a fact situation, that is a relevant similarity. A relevant difference is defined as (1) the presence in the fact situation or the precedent of additional, unshared factors that lead to a different outcome from the one argued for, or (2) a difference in the magnitude of a factor shared by the fact situation and the precedent that makes the former a weaker situation for the outcome argued for.

Dimensions are designed to enable a computer program to compare cases' similarities and differences symbolically. A Dimension's prerequisites allow Hypo to determine if a factor is present in a case. Cases can then be compared in terms of the collections of factors that apply to them using sets of Dimensions as illustrated in the Venn diagrams of chapter 3. A shared Dimension's focal slot and range information allow Hypo to compare the magnitudes of a factor in cases. Cases can also be compared in terms of where they sit along the shared Dimension, the measure of the Dimension's magnitude in each case. In both types of comparison, Hypo has a computational way of comparing the cases in terms of the relative strengths or weaknesses of the plaintiffs' legal positions in each.

Since Dimensions are instrumental in representing relevant similarities and differences, they are a natural choice for indexing precedents in the CKB. A case is relevant if it shares at least one Dimension with the cfs. By indexing cases according to Dimensions, the program can find all cases that share any Dimension that applies to the cfs.

7.2 Hypo's Dimensions

Hypo has thirteen implemented Dimensions. Appendix F contains a complete listing of implemented Dimensions that apply in cases involving claims for trade secrets misappropriation, breach of noncompetition/nondisclosure agreements, or breach of contract. For each Dimension, the listing shows its short name, the applicable claim, a generalized statement of the associated plaintiff's strength, and focal slot and range information.

Each of Hypo's Dimensions represents a tack for arguing about a legal claim. One way to argue about a trade secret misappropriation claim is to consider whether the plaintiff let the cat out of the bag by disclosing its supposed secrets to outsiders. From this viewpoint, the more disclosees there are, the worse off the plaintiff is with respect to claiming that his putative secret was misappropriated. Information for comparing trade secrets cases from this viewpoint is contained in the *Secrets-Disclosed-Outsiders* Dimension (figure 7.1). A second way to argue a trade secrets claim focuses on whether the plaintiff took adequate steps to protect its confidential information. The more kinds of precautions it took, the more it appears that the information was indeed a secret with commercial value. Cases can be compared in this regard using the information in the *Security-Measures* Dimension (figure 7.2). A third way of arguing checks how much of an unfair competitive advantage the defendant secured from its access to plaintiff's confidential information. The more development time and expense the defendant saved, the stronger is the plaintiff's position on a trade secrets claim. The *Competitive-Advantage* Dimension captures information for comparing cases along this line (figure 7.3).

Most of Hypo's Dimensions deal with the claim of Trade Secrets Misappropriation. Some deal with the claims of breach of nondisclosure/non-

A Dimensional Index

NAME: Secrets-Voluntarily-Disclosed

SHORT-TITLE: Secrets-Disclosed-Outsiders

CLAIMS: Trade Secrets Misappropriation

PREREQUISITES:
There is a corporate plaintiff
There is a corporate defendant
Plaintiff makes a product
Plaintiff and defendant compete
Plaintiff has product information
Plaintiff made some disclosures to outsiders

FOCAL SLOT PREREQUISITE:
Plaintiff made some disclosures to outsiders

FOCAL SLOT:
Plaintiff's Product: Number of disclosures

RANGE:
0 to 10,000,000

COMPARISON TYPE:
Greater-than versus Less-than

PRO-PLAINTIFF DIRECTION: Less-than

Figure 7.1
Secrets-Disclosed-Outsiders Dimension

NAME: Security-Measures-Adopted

SHORT-TITLE: Security-Measures

CLAIMS: Trade Secrets Misappropriation

PREREQUISITES:
There is a corporate plaintiff
There is a corporate defendant
Plaintiff makes a product
Plaintiff and defendant compete
Plaintiff has product information
Defendant makes a product
Plaintiff's and defendant's products compete
Plaintiff adopted security measures

FOCAL SLOT PREREQUISITE:
Plaintiff adopted security measures

FOCAL SLOT:
Plaintiff's Product: Security measures list

RANGE:
Minimal-Measures
Access to Premises Controlled
Restrictions on Entry by Visitors
Restrictions on Entry by Employees
Product Marked Confidential
Employee Trade Secret Program Exists
Restrictions on Hardcopy Release
Employee Nondisclosure Agreements

COMPARISON TYPE: More versus less

PRO-PLAINTIFF DIRECTION: More

Figure 7.2
Security-Measures Dimension

NAME: Competitive-Advantage-Gained

SHORT-TITLE: Competitive-Advantage

CLAIMS: Trade Secrets Misappropriation

PREREQUISITES:
There is a corporate plaintiff
There is a corporate defendant
Plaintiff makes a product
Defendant makes a product
Plaintiff's and defendant's products compete
Defendant saved product development expense relative to plaintiff

FOCAL SLOT PREREQUISITE:
Defendant saved product development expense relative to plaintiff

FOCAL SLOT:
Plaintiff's Product: Expenditures
Plaintiff's Product: Development time
Defendant's Product: Expenditures
Defendant's Product: Development time

RANGES:
$10,000 to $10,000,000
2 months to 60 months
1 to 99

COMPARISON TYPE: Computed

PRO-PLAINTIFF DIRECTION: Greater

Figure 7.3
Competitive-Advantage Dimension

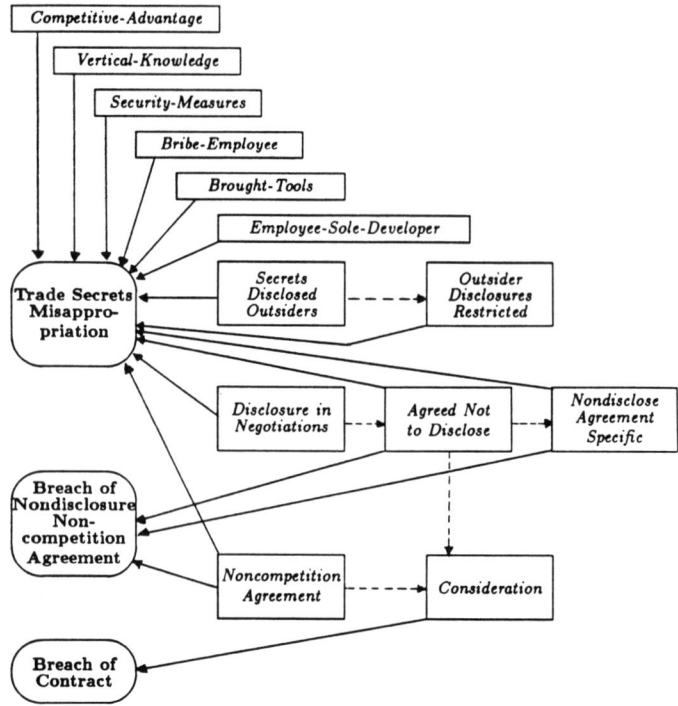

Figure 7.4
Relations among Claims and Dimensions

competition agreements and breach of contract in general. The relationships between Hypo's Dimensions and its claims is illustrated in figure 7.4. Each of the three root nodes (in ovals) represents a legal claim about which Hypo has some knowledge: trade secrets misappropriation, breach of nondisclosure/noncompetition agreements, and breach of contract. The rectangular nodes represent Dimensions. A solid arc upward from a Dimension to a claim node indicates that at least one case in the CKB involves that claim where the court decided the claim because, or in spite, of the factor associated with that Dimension.

Hypo's Dimensions are not definitional elements of a claim; they do not purport to specify necessary and sufficient conditions for determining the existence of a claim. Instead, they represent collections of facts that tend to strengthen or weaken an assertion that the claim applies to

A Dimensional Index   113

a fact situation. They abstract features of cases that are relevant to legal conclusions about a case without attempting to define necessary and sufficient conditions for those conclusions. Thus, adding the facts underlying the *Competitive-Advantage, Vertical-Knowledge* or *Security-Measures* dimensions to a case would affect the strength of a plaintiff's trade secret claim in the case. Similarly, changing the magnitude of those Dimensions in a case could affect the claim's strength.

Information for assessing the effect of such changes, whether they would strengthen or weaken the plaintiff's argument relative to other cases, is represented for each Dimension.

The Dimensions are grouped into those favoring the plaintiff generally and those favoring the defendant. The pro-plaintiff dimensions are the following:

- *Agreement-Supported-By-Consideration*
- *Common-Employee-Paid-To-Change-Employers*
- *Exists-Express-Noncompetition-Agreement*
- *Common-Employee-Transferred-Product-Tools*
- *Disclosures-Subject-To-Restriction*
- *Competitive-Advantage Gained*
- *Security-Measures-Adopted*
- *Nondisclosure-Agreement-Re-Defendant-Access*
- *Nondisclosure-Agreement-Specific*

The pro-defendant Dimensions are these:

- *Vertical-Knowledqe*
- *Secrets-Voluntarily-Disclosed*
- *Disclosure-In-Negotiations-With-Defendant*
- *Common-Employee-Sole-Developer*

Dimensions from the first group represent plaintiffs' strengths, those in the second group represent plaintiffs' weaknesses.

The effect of a change in the magnitude of a Dimension in a case is represented by the Dimension's focal slot and range information. Focal slots single out the particular facts making a case stronger or weaker along the Dimension. The range information tells how a change in the focal slot affects that strength. The range information includes the range of possible values of the focal slots and the direction in the range that strengthens the plaintiff's position along the Dimension. Hypo's Dimensions may have five different types of focal slot ranges including binary, partially ordered sets of objects, ordered sets, intervals and number lines. For examples, the *Noncompetition-Agreement* Dimension involves a binary range; the employee did or did not enter into a noncompetition agreement. The *Security-Measures* range comprises sets of security measures partially ordered in terms of set inclusion. Figure 7.2 shows all of the possible security precautions. *Secrets-Disclosed-Outsiders*, figure 7.1, has an interval range of from 0 to 10,000,000 disclosures. *Competitive-Advantage*, figure 7.3, involves cost savings from $10,000 to $10,000,000, time savings from 2 to 60 months, and relative savings from 1 to 99 percent.

If a Dimension's range is a continuous line with one ever-increasing end favoring a plaintiff and the other ever-decreasing end favoring a defendant, a question arises as to how to classify the Dimension. Is it generally pro-plaintiff or pro-defendant? For purposes of this classification, it is helpful to select a neutral point and treat the Dimension as two "rays," one that generally favors plaintiff and the other generally favoring the defendant. Selecting a neutral switch over point is usually a matter of common sense.

Some Dimensions are linked to more than one claim. In figure 7.4, *Agreed-Not-to-Disclose* and *Nondisclosure-Agreement-Specific* are linked both to the claims of trade secrets misappropriation and breach of nondisclosure or noncompetition agreements. This means that moving a case along such a Dimension may affect the strength of the plaintiff's position on either claim, sometimes in opposite directions (strengthening on one claim and weakening on the other). Making a nondisclosure agreement more specific, for example, not only helps the plaintiff's ability to enforce the agreement against a breaching employee but also improves its trade secrets claim because a specific agreement puts an employee on notice of the information that is to be treated as secret. Other Dimensions are linked only to one claim. Note that while *Agreed-Not-to-Disclose* is linked to the trade secrets claim, there is no arc linking *Consideration* to the trade secrets claim. That means that there is no case in which the lack of consideration for a nondisclosure agreement has been held to weaken a plaintiff's trade secrets claim. That remains an interesting legal possibility, however. If there were no better argument to make in a case, Hypo could take advantage of this information to suggest that the lack of consideration might also be treated as a weakness for a trade secrets claim.

The sources for Hypo's Dimensions are legal treatises and law review articles for trade secrets law. Various legal knowledge sources are implicitly organized by something like Dimensions. Legal treatises and law review articles commonly group together in footnotes cases that share some important factor. Within the footnote, the author includes, for comparison, cases that were won by defendants as well as plaintiffs and cases that show a range of magnitudes of the factor or a variety of additional counterveiling factors. The nature of the factual comparisons is usually evident from the author's comments or those of the cases reported.

7.3 A Dimension's Structure and Function

A Dimension's structure is designed to suit its function in three basic roles: (1) retrieving relevant cases, (2) symbolically comparing cases, (3) hypothetically modifying cases.

7.3.1 Retrieving Relevant Cases

Since cases are indexed by Dimensions, the major step in retrieving relevant cases is determining whether a Dimension applies to a fact situation. Each Dimension's prerequisites are conditions necessary for the Dimension to be said to apply to a fact situation. If the prerequisites are satisfied, it makes sense to compare the fact situation to other cases indexed by the Dimension.

The prerequisites are composed of Factual Predicates. Each Dimension's PREREQUISITES slot contains a list of Factual Predicates. For example, to paraphrase the prerequisites list of the *Security-Measures*

Dimension (figure 7.2), it requires that (1) there is a corporate plaintiff, (2) who makes a product, (3) about which there is product development information; (4) that there is a corporate defendant who makes a competing product; and (5) that there is information that plaintiff adopted some security measures to protect its product.

Factual Predicates are the second-tier language for summarizing the facts of a case represented by the underlying Legal Case Frames. They confirm whether legally significant relationships are true in the case. (Appendix D lists all of the Factual Predicates and the values that they may take.) Each Factual Predicate has an associated retrieval method—a function for determining whether the Factual Predicate is satisfied in the case. The Case Analyzer determines in one operation all of the Factual Predicates that are satisfied by the case and stores the results in the Interpretation Frame, each of whose slots corresponds to a Factual Predicate.

After the Interpretation Frame has been filled out, the Case Analyzer determines all of the Dimensions whose prerequisites are satisfied. For each Dimension, the Case Analyzer matches the prerequisites to the Factual Predicates as recorded in the Interpretation Frame. This matching process could be made more efficient by structuring the Factual Predicates and Dimensions' prerequisites to avoid duplication.

The process of determining applicable Dimensions can be illustrated in the context of the *USM* case. Figure 7.5 shows the completed Interpretation Frame, filled out as described in chapter 6. All of the Factual Predicates listed as prerequisites for the *Security-Measures* and for the *Competitive-Advantage* Dimensions are satisfied. The prerequisites for each of those Dimensions are shown in figures 7.2 and 7.3. By contrast, some of the prerequisites of the *Secrets-Disclosed-Outsiders* Dimension of figure 7.1 are not satisfied. Accordingly, the Case Analyzer records the applicable Dimensions in the Case Analysis Record. Figure 7.6 shows excerpts from a completed Case Analysis Record for the *USM* case. *Security-Measures* and *Competitive-Advantage* are the only Dimensions that apply to the *USM* case.

In order to index a case in the CKB, the Dimensions that apply to the case are added to the Dimensions List of the top-level Legal Case Frame. When the case's fact situation is first presented to Hypo, the Case Analyzer determines the applicable Dimensions and inserts them into the case's Dimensions List.

Interpretation Frame

CASE: USM Corp. v. Marson Fastener Corp.

THERE IS A CORPORATE PLAINTIFF:
Corporate-Party: USM

PLAINTIFF MAKES A PRODUCT:
Product: USM-Machine

PLAINTIFF HAS PRODUCT INFORMATION:
Knowledge: About-USM-Machine

THERE IS A CORPORATE DEFENDANT:
Corporate-Party: Marson

DEFENDANT MAKES A PRODUCT:
Product: Marson-Machine

PLAINTIFF AND DEFENDANT COMPETE: True

PLAINTIFF'S AND DEFENDANT'S PRODUCTS COMPETE: True

THERE IS A DEFENDANT EMPLOYEE: Nil

PLAINTIFF MADE SOME DISCLOSURES TO OUTSIDERS: Nil

DEFENDANT SAVED PRODUCT DEVELOPMENT EXPENSE RELATIVE TO PLAINTIFF:
36 months versus 60 months

PLAINTIFF ADOPTED SECURITY MEASURES:
Minimal Measures
Access to Premises Controlled
Restrictions on Entry by Visitors
Employee Nondisclosure Agreements

PLAINTIFF DISCLOSED PRODUCT INFORMATION TO DEFENDANT IN NEGOTIATIONS: Nil

Figure 7.5
Excerpts from Interpretation Frame for *USM* Case

Case Analysis Record
CASE: USM Corp. v. Marson Fastener Corp.
APPLICABLE DIMENSIONS:
Competitive-Advantage-Gained
Security-Measures-Adopted
NEAR-MISS DIMENSIONS:
Secrets-Disclosed-Outsiders
Vertical-Knowledge
Disclosure-In-Negotiations-With-Defendant

Figure 7.6
Excerpts from Case Analysis Record for *USM* Case

Once the Dimensions List is filled in, the case is indexed. Henceforth, the Case Analyzer can retrieve all of the cases in the CKB to which a Dimension applies simply by determining if that Dimension is contained in the case's Dimensions List. The Case Analyzer does not need to reanalyze the case to determine applicable Dimensions. For instance, when the *USM* case was first added to the CKB, the Case Analyzer determined that the two Dimensions applied to it, *Security-Measures* and *Competitive-Advantage*. Both were added to the top-level case frame Dimensions List. Henceforth the program can retrieve *USM* as relevant to any fact situation involving either Dimension.

7.3.2 Symbolically Comparing Cases

Any two cases to which a Dimension applies can be compared in terms of the relative values in each case of the Dimension's focal slots. This is what the 3-Ply Arguer does when it distinguishes a cited case from the cfs along a shared Dimension. The RANGE and PRO-PLAINTIFF DIRECTION slots of each Dimension contain information that help interpret the comparison. Associated with each range is information about the range's comparison type, possible values (and the appropriate units), and the direction in the range that favors the plaintiff.

The comparison type specifies the kind of ordering scheme that the range values represent and how to compare focal slot values along that range. In other words, it defines the "greater-than" relation to be used for that range. There are five comparison types: (1) binary (some versus none), (2) more versus less, (3) relative position in an ordered set (interval), (4) greater than versus less than, and (5) computed.

"Binary" indicates that the comparison involves only two values. Frequently the two values are "Some" and "None." "More versus Less" means that the more inclusive set of items from the possible values is treated as greater than its proper subset. For the "Interval" type, the range is treated as an ordered set. The left-most item is the minimal item; the item to the right on the range of values is greater than an item. "Greater-than versus Less-than" indicates that the values are to be compared as numbers. "Computed" is an ad hoc type allowing for special kinds of comparisons. For example, the Dimension *Noncompetition-Agreement* involves a binary comparison: the employee entered into a noncompetition agreement or did not. The Dimension *Security-Measures-Adopted* requires comparing "more versus less" security measures (e.g., taking minimal measures, restricting entry by visitors, and marking products confidential is more inclusive than just taking minimal measures. It is not more inclusive than taking minimal measures, having an employee trade secret program and obtaining employee nondisclosure agreements.) A "greater-than versus less-than" comparison is required for the Dimension *Secrets-Disclosed-Outsiders*, which compares numbers of disclosures. An example of a Dimension requiring a "computed" comparison is *Competitive-Advantage* in which the defendant's savings in development time or expense relative to the plaintiff's costs are computed, and those savings are compared to that in other cases.

Each comparison type has an associated method for retrieving the focal slot values from each case to be compared. The focal slot specifies a "path name" consisting of a list of object and slot names that lead from the Interpretation Frame to some slot value of an underlying Legal Case Frame.

The PRO-PLAINTIFF DIRECTION slot indicates whether being "greater-than" as defined by the comparison type favors the plaintiff or the defendant. For example, the PRO-PLAINTIFF DIRECTION for the *Security-Measures* Dimension is "more"; the more security measures were taken, the better is the case for plaintiff. Similarly, the greater are defendant's savings of time and money, the better is the case for plaintiff on the *Competitive-Advantage* Dimension. The more disclosures there are to outsiders, the worse it is for plaintiff on the *Secrets-Disclosed-Outsiders* Dimension.

The 3-Ply Arguer compares cases along shared Dimensions in distinguishing a cited case from the cfs. For an example of comparing cases along shared Dimensions, consider how Hypo compared the *USM* case to other cases along the *Security-Measures* and *Competitive-Advantage* Dimensions. The following excerpt from a 3-Ply Argument shows the result of Hypo's distinguishing the *USM* case, as cfs, from the *Healy* case. In the *Healy* case, the plaintiff took only minimal measures to protect its secret:

> ⟹ Point For Defendant as Side 1:
>
> Where: Even though: Plaintiff adopted security measures.
>
> Defendant should win a claim for Trade Secrets Misappropriation.
>
> Cite: Healy, Inc. v. Murphy, Inc. 357 Mass. 728 (1970).
>
> ⟸ Response for Plaintiff as Side 2:
>
> Healy, Inc. v. Murphy, Inc. is distinguishable because:
>
> In USM v. Marson, plaintiff adopted more security measures than in Healy v. Murphy. In USM v. Marson, defendant's access to plaintiff's product information saved it more time or expense than in Healy v. Murphy.

Hypo compared the *USM* case, as cfs, to the *Healy* case along the *Security-Measures* Dimension. The Dimension's focal slot values indicate the information in each case that is relevant for this comparison. The focal slot of the *Security-Measures* Dimension is the Security Measures List of the plaintiff's Product. The 3-Ply Arguer retrieved the focal slot value in each case from the cases' respective Interpretation Frames and then compared the security measures taken by plaintiff in each case. The result of the comparison was stored in the Argument Record and is shown below (paraphrased):

> Distinction 1, USM Corp. v. Marson Fastener Corp. is stronger for plaintiff than Healy, Inc. v. Murphy, Inc. along Dimension *Security-Measures-Adopted* because USM's security measures (minimal measures, access to premises controlled, restrictions on entry by visitors, and employee nondisclosure agreements) are more security measures than Healy's minimal measures.

In other words, the *USM* case was found to be stronger than the *Healy* case along the *Security-Measures* Dimension because plaintiff USM took more security measures.

In another 3-Ply Argument taken from Hypo's outputs for the *USM* case, Hypo compared the *USM* case, as cfs, to the *Telex* case along the *Competitive-Advantage-Gained* Dimension. Here is an excerpt from that argument:

> ⟹ Point for Plaintiff as Side 1:
>
> Where: Defendant's access to plaintiff's product information saved it time or expense.
>
> Plaintiff should win a claim for Trade Secrets Misappropriation.
>
> Cite: Telex Corp. v. IBM Corp. (1) 510 F.2d 894 (10 Cir., 1975).
>
> ⟸ Response for Defendant as Side 2:
> Telex Corp. v. IBM Corp. (1) is distinguishable because:
>
> In Telex v. IBM, defendant's access to plaintiff's product information saved it more time or expense than in USM v. Marson. In Telex v. IBM, plaintiff and defendant entered into a nondisclosure agreement. Not so in USM v. Marson. In Telex v. IBM, Defendant paid plaintiff's former employee to switch employment. Not so in USM v. Marson.

The *Competitive-Advantage-Gained* Dimension has "computed" type ranges. The comparison involves taking the difference of the respective product development times and expenditures made by plaintiff and defendant. A difference favoring plaintiff on both counts is treated as greater than a difference on only one count. In the Argument from the *USM* example, the 3-Ply Arguer compared *USM* to *Telex* along this Dimension in the process of distinguishing the latter. The result taken from the corresponding Argument Record is (paraphrased):

> Distinction 1, USM Corp. v. Marson Fastener Corp. is weaker for plaintiff than Telex Corp. v. IBM Corp. (1) along Dimension *Competitive-Advantage-Gained* because Marson saved 24 months while Telex saved $750,000 and 36 months.

In other words, the *USM* case is weaker than *Telex* because there was evidence as to a savings only of development time, not both time and money. An earlier version of the *Competitive-Advantage* Dimension also compared the relative amounts of time or money saved. Both kinds of comparisons are valid for distinguishing.

In selecting which precedents to cite for a side, Dimensions also play a major role. They not only enable Hypo to compare cases' on pointness by comparing the sets of Dimensions that each case shares with the cfs. They also allow Hypo to draw finer distinctions among cases to cite. They allow Hypo to determine if a case is "citable in the first instance" for a party in an argument, that is, whether the case is a good one to cite in a point for the side or whether it should be reserved as a counterexample to cite only if needed to respond to an opponent's point. For Hypo to select a case to cite in the first instance on behalf of a plaintiff, the case must share with the problem situation at least one pro-plaintiff Dimension. A case to cite on behalf of a defendant must share with the problem situation at least one pro-defendant Dimension. For example, the fact that plaintiffs in both the *USM* and *Eastern Marble* cases took some measures to protect security justifies citing the latter case in favor of USM Corp.'s trade secrets misappropriation claim. That is just what plaintiffs are supposed to do to keep their secrets confidential. By contrast, the fact that plaintiffs in both the *Crown* and *Data General* cases disclosed their secrets to outsiders is not a justification for citing the latter case in favor of Crown's trade secrets misappropriation, at least not in the first instance. Giving away their trade secrets is not what plaintiffs are supposed to do, although it is not always fatal to a plaintiff's claim. That is the significance of the *Data General* case. It is a good case for a plaintiff to cite as a counterexample to the proposition that a plaintiff who discloses its secrets always should lose a trade secrets misappropriation claim but not a good case to cite initially in a point justifying plaintiff's behavior.

7.3.3 Hypothetically Modifying Cases

A Dimension's structure plays a major role in enabling Hypo to identify and implement meaningful hypothetical changes to a case. Dimensions support two basic methods of modifying a case hypothetically: (1) Change the strength of a case along an applicable Dimension (making it extreme on the Dimension or changing it relative to the position of an actual case). (2) Make a near-miss Dimension apply to a case.

The first method involves the same information as comparing cases along a shared Dimension. The Dimension's range defines the extremes and the PRO-PLAINTIFF DIRECTION slot indicates the side that is favored by an extreme value. For example, the most extreme pro-defendant hypothetical along the *Secrets-Disclosed-Outsiders* Dimension, figure 7.1, would involve 10,000,000 disclosures. The most extreme pro-plaintiff version would involve 0 disclosures.

The second method employs the concept of a near-miss Dimension. A Dimension is a near miss with respect to a case if all of its prerequisites are satisfied except certain focal slot prerequisites. The focal slot prerequisites, the Factual Predicates associated with the Dimension's focal slots, contain the crucial information that places a case somewhere along the range of the Dimension. If the focal slot prerequisite is the only one missing, then the case is semantically close to other cases indexed by the Dimension, thus distinguishing the Dimension from other inapplicable ones.

Near-miss Dimensions indicate factors that the user should consider because they almost apply to the cfs and could make a difference if they did apply, especially if the Dimensions index cases that could then be cited for either side in the argument. Such cases would be legally significant if only the missing focal slot prerequisites were present. They make useful targets for hypothetical variations of the cfs to illustrate a factor's effect on an argument. The Case Positioner uses near-miss Dimensions in constructing extended Claim Lattices to locate these target cases. For example, the *Secrets-Disclosed-Outsiders* Dimension is a near miss with respect to the *USM* case. Note from the Interpretation Frame of figure 7.5 that the value of the focal slot prerequisite, "Plaintiff made some disclosures to outsiders," in the *USM* case is Nil, indicating that there is no information about disclosures to outsiders. All other prerequisites of the Dimension are satisfied. If there were information about whether the plaintiff USM Corp. disclosed its information to outsiders, then the *Secrets-Disclosed-Outsiders* Dimension would apply and the cases indexed by the Dimension, like the *Crown* case, would become more relevant and could be cited for the defendant.

A series of legal hypotheticals frequently show a kind of flip-flopping. Adding a fact may strengthen the hypothetical but often opens up new potential counterarguments. For example, adding the fact that a plaintiff made disclosures to outsiders helps the defendant on a trade secrets claim but opens the way for a hypothetical that strengthens plaintiff's claim where the disclosures are subject to restriction. Adding an agreement not to disclose helps the plaintiff but opens the way for a hypothetical where the agreement is not enforceable for lack of consideration.

Hypo's definition of near-miss Dimensions allows it to pose such flip-flopping series of hypotheticals. This can be illustrated in figure 7.4. A dashed arc downward from one Dimension to another indicates that the prerequisites of the lower Dimension are a subset of those of the upper Dimension such that if the upper Dimension applies to a case, the lower Dimension either applies or is a near miss. Thus, strengthening or weakening a claim by making the upper Dimension apply to a case paves the way for a complementary weakening or strengthening of the claim by making the lower Dimension also apply. For example, a case in which a trade secrets claim is weakened by introducing disclosures to outsiders (so that *Secrets-Disclosed-Outsiders* applies) can be strengthened by subjecting the disclosures to confidentiality restrictions (so that the near-miss Dimension *Outsider-Disclosures-Restricted* also applies). For another example, a case in which a claim for breach of a nondisclosure agreement is strengthened along *Agreed-Not-to-Disclose* can then be weakened along the *Consideration* Dimension if the employee failed to receive something of value for entering into the agreement.

By virtue of defining near misses in terms of focal slot prerequisites, Hypo has a semantic as opposed to a syntactic definition. It would, of course, be possible to define a near miss syntactically. For example, a syntactic near miss might be defined as a Dimension all but one of whose prerequisites is satisfied with no restriction on what the missing prerequisite could be. The Factual Predicates are not of uniform graininess, however. The focal slot prerequisites focus on details relative to the other predicates in the prerequisites list that establish broader relationships in the case, for example, whether there is a defendant with a competing product ("Plaintiff's and defendant's products compete") or whether the defendant had access to plaintiff's product information through plaintiff's former employee ("Defendant had access to plaintiff's product via employee"). The focal slot prerequisites tend to focus on missing details that are significant but only if the broader relationships are present in the case. Though more restrictive than a syntactically defined near miss, the semantic definition conveys greater assurance that the missing fact will be significant to the legal argument.

A compromise between a syntactic and semantic approach might be to start with one and switch to the other. The process of fact gathering would begin with a syntactic definition of near miss (even broader than the one suggested, for example, where the number of missing prerequisites may be greater than one) and then switch to more restrictive semantic definitions of near misses as the broad structure of the case becomes clear. Alternatively, the Factual Prerequisites could be given a more explicit structure to guide the initial fact-gathering process. Obtaining the right measure of flexibility is the problem. The program should not prevent the attorney from getting down to details quickly.

7.4 Advantages of Dimensions

Dimensions enable Hypo to draw inferences by comparing cases. As a knowledge representation tool, they offer the following advantages: reasoning within the index, model independence, minimized interpretation, and modularity.

Dimensions enable a program to perform a variety of reasoning within the index. Traditionally, case indexes support retrieving only relevant cases. Using Dimensions, Hypo can perform reasoning tasks well beyond those that one normally expects an index to support, such as interpreting precedents' significance as justifications in arguments, ordering precedents so that they may be compared and contrasted dynamically within the context of the current fact situation, and generating hypotheticals to explore neighboring fact situations.

Dimensions support inference even in a domain that lacks a strong causal model. High-level legal concepts lack definitions from which it can be inferred whether they apply to a given fact situation. For instance, there is no adequate description of the necessary and sufficient criteria of a valid trade secrets misappropriation claim. Dimensions bridge that gap by indexing positive and negative examples of the concept and providing a means for drawing conclusions about the applicability of the concept to a given fact situation from certain comparisons of it to those indexed examples. In other words, Dimensions link surface features of fact situations to ways of justifying legal conclusions about the fact situation even though the domain does not have a strong conceptual model of the linkage.

Dimensions cut down on the amount of interpretation needed by the person entering a case into the CKB. He or she need only record the court's decision with respect to plaintiff's claims and the facts reported by the court from which a case's position on various Dimensions can be inferred. Although that in itself is an interpretive task, it requires less interpretation than determining what issues the courts decided and what rationales they used in their decisions.

Dimensions accord a certain measure of modularity. As new Dimensions are added, inconsistency with existing Dimensions is not a problem. Three-Ply Arguments exploit conflicts among Dimensions by citing as counterexamples more-on-point cases that share additional, conflicting Dimensions with the cfs relative to some cited precedent.

Acquiring new Dimensions is not without costs, however. When a new Dimension is added, the question arises about whether it should apply to the cases already in the CKB. Usually new Factual Predicates and retrieval methods need to be defined to implement some of the new Dimension's prerequisites. If those retrieval methods operate on existing Legal Case Frame slots, whose values already have been filled in for the existing cases, then there is no problem. By reanalyzing the existing cases, Hypo can automatically determine if the new Dimension applies and update the Dimensional Index. If, however, new Legal Case Frames or slots have been added, a case entry person has to reread the opinions of existing cases to determine the values of the new slots in the old cases.

8 Basic Mechanisms of Case-Based Reasoning

An attorney evaluating and making arguments about a new fact situation using precedents and hypotheticals needs more than indexing and retrieval of relevant cases. Hypo must compare cases relative to the current fact situation and interpret those comparisons in terms of their significance in a legal argument.

In order to compare cases symbolically, Hypo performs operations that are basic to case-based reasoning: (1) ordering relevant cases and potentially relevant cases in terms of how analogous they are to the problem situation, (2) selecting the most analogous cases, (3) identifying configurations of counterexamples, (4) hypothetically modifying the problem situation to explore contingencies, and (5) comparing case-based analyses of different problem situations to explain differences. These basic operations allow a case-based reasoner to compare and contrast a problem situation with past experience and to take into account not only its similarities to past cases but also its differences.

Although the operations are general for case-based reasoning, the actual criteria for ordering, selecting, modifying, and comparing cases will reflect the domain-specific criteria of what constitutes relevancy and useful analogy. Hypo needs to classify and organize the cases in terms of their uses in a legal argument, specifically, whether they are any of the following:

- Citable in points. Which cases make strong legal points pro or con a plaintiff's claim in a fact situation?

- Citable in responses. Which cases make strong responses as counterexamples to cases cited in points?

- Potentially citable. Which cases could make strong points or responses given a slightly modified fact situation? How do hypothetical modifications of the fact situation affect the strength of existing points and responses for an argument as to this and other claims?

In order to make these determinations, Hypo compares cases in terms of four comparison metrics, drawn in part from its Argument Evaluation Criteria: on pointness, outcome, magnitudes of shared Dimensions, and potential relevance as a near miss.

Hypo's basic symbolic measure of useful legal analogy between a fact situation and a precedent is on pointness. A case is on point to the extent that a Dimension that applies to the case is applicable to the current fact situation. On pointness is measured in a Claim Lattice by the degree of overlap of Dimensions shared by a precedent and the fact situation relative to that of other precedents.

Outcome means who won the precedent: plaintiff or defendant. Precedents are compared in terms of whether they have the same or different outcomes. It is somewhat easier to determine a case's outcome in law than in other domains. First, who won a precedent is a matter of historical record. Second, subject to some qualification, there are only two possibilities: either the plaintiff won the case or did not. The qualification is that depending on the procedural context of the case, some outcomes are more determinative than others. A precedent that plaintiff won or lost after a full trial on the merits is a more authoritative determination of the issues than if it resolves only a preliminary motion. Hypo does not compare precedents' outcomes at that level. Third, the legal problem solver knows which side he or she represents (plaintiff or defendant), and in any event, when he or she switches hats to take a contrary viewpoint, there is only one other hat to try. In other case-based domains, determining the outcome of a case requires more interpretation, and there may be more than two sides to consider.

Magnitudes of shared Dimensions is another way of comparing cases. Precedents are compared in terms of their positions along shared Dimensions relative to each other and to the cfs. A case's position along the range of a Dimension is a measure of the magnitude of the strength of the plaintiff's legal position in terms of factors associated with the Dimension.

Potential relevance as a near miss is a different way to gauge useful analogy. Precedents that are nearly on point but for some crucial missing facts (cases indexed by Dimensions that are near misses with respect to the fact situation) are compared to see which ones would be more on point if certain small hypothetical changes were made to the cfs.

8.1 Ordering Analogous Cases

A case-based reasoner needs some mechanism for ranking the cases in terms of how analogous they are to the problem situation. The definition of relevant similarity will reflect the particular kind of problem-solving task performed by the case-based reasoner and the criteria for evaluating the solution. In Hypo, where the task is to make arguments and the criteria go to evaluating the strength of arguments, more analogous means more on point.

The Case Positioner employs Claim Lattices to order cases in terms of on pointness with respect to a given fact situation. There are two kinds of Claim Lattices, regular and extended, and they implement somewhat different senses of relative on pointness.

Case α is more on point than Case β if and only if the set of Dimensions β has in common with a reference set of Dimensions associated with the current fact situation are a proper subset of the set of α's applicable Dimensions shared with the reference set. In a regular Claim Lattice, the reference set is the set of Dimensions that apply to the cfs. In an extended Claim Lattice, the reference set is the set of Dimensions that apply to or are near misses for the cfs.

In constructing a Claim Lattice, the Positioner employs a partial ordering called *coverage*, which compares two lists to determine which covers a greater portion of a third reference list. To illustrate, if we consider each list to be a set, the coverage of lists A and B relative to reference list C is as follows. ($A \cap C$ means "intersection of sets A and C." $A \subset C$ means "A is a subset of C." $A \subseteq C$ means "A is a subset of or equal to C." The empty set is denoted by $\emptyset$.)

$A = B$ iff $(A \cap C) = (B \cap C)$ equal coverage

$A > B$ iff $(B \cap C) \subset (A \cap C)$ greater coverage

$A < B$ iff $(A \cap C) \subset (B \cap C)$ lesser coverage

A and B are disjoint iff $(A \cap C) \cap (B \cap C) = \emptyset$

A and B overlap iff $((A \cap C) \cap (B \cap C) \neq \emptyset) \wedge ((A \cap C) \nsubseteq (B \cap C)) \wedge ((B \cap C) \nsubseteq (A \cap C))$

The algorithm for entering a case into the Claim Lattice is shown below. The cases can be entered in any order. The algorithm assumes that the case has been placed in a graph node, which will be referred to as new-node. Initially, the only root in a list called new-roots is the Claim Lattice root containing the cfs. The metric for comparing nodes is coverage, as defined above.

1. Remove a root from new-roots and compare new-node and root for coverage. There are three cases:

    (a) If new-node = root, insert case from new-node into root.

    (b) If new-node < root, for each child of root, if new-node > child, put child into children of new-node, and remove child from children of root; if new-node is less than or equal to ("≤") or overlaps child, then push child onto new-roots. If there are no children of root that new-node is less than or equal to, add new-node as child of root.

    (c) If new-node overlaps root, for each child of root, if new-node > child, put child into new-node's children; if new-node overlaps child, push child onto new-roots.

2. If there are anymore roots in new-roots, go back to the first step.

Most-on-point cases for a side (plaintiff or defendant) are defined as those cases in the regular Claim Lattice that were won by that side and contained in the root or in nodes that are closer to the root than (or as close as) any case-containing node on that branch from the root.

The ordering scheme of Claim Lattices captures a symbolic sense of closeness to the cfs of cases in the CKB. The root of the Claim Lattice represents the cfs. The closer a case is to the root, the more on point it is, that is, the more legally important strengths and weaknesses it shares with the fact situation. As one moves along a branch to the leaf nodes, the cases are less analogous because they have less of an overlap of Dimensions with the cfs and therefore share fewer legally significant factors.

A simple Claim Lattice illustrates the definition of on pointness. Figure 8.1 shows the Claim Lattice for the *USM* fact situation of chapters 6 and 7. Each node of a Claim Lattice consists of a list of Dimensions and a list of cases. The root node's list of Dimensions is the reference list. The reference list of the regular Claim Lattice of figure 8.1 shows that, as determined by the Case Analyzer's Dimensional analysis, two Dimensions apply to the fact situation of the *USM* case: *Competitive-Advantage* and *Security-Measures*. The fact that the *Space Aero* case is in the root node's list of cases shows that it shares both of these Dimensions with the *USM* case and that it is the only case in the CKB that

Basic Mechanisms of Case-Based Reasoning

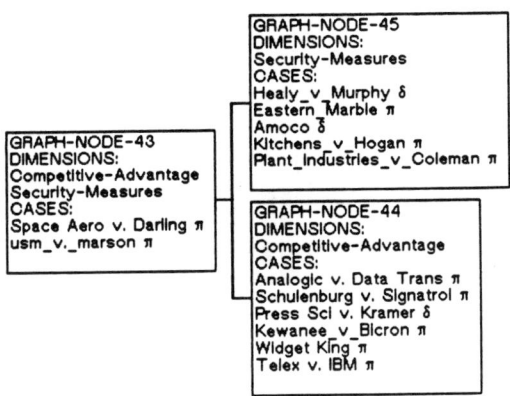

Figure 8.1
Claim Lattice for Trade Secrets Claim in *USM* Case

does so. *Space Aero* is the most-on-point case to *USM*. The list of cases also shows that plaintiff (π) won *Space Aero*.

The root node's case list also includes the *USM* case. In this example, the *USM* case appears in two roles: as the cfs and as a case in the CKB. The Case Analyzer independently analyzed the *USM* case as the cfs to determine its applicable Dimensions. Using the results of that analysis, the Case Positioner correctly retrieved the *USM* case from the CKB as a relevant precedent. That is why the case appears in the case list of some node of the Claim Lattice. The *USM* case appears in the root node's list of cases as a result of the Case Positioner's treating the case as most on point to itself, which, of course, it is.

Successor nodes in a Claim Lattice contain cases that are less on point. Together each of the other two nodes of figure 8.1 shows all of the cases in the CKB that are on point in that they share at least one Dimension in common with the *USM* case as cfs. There are five cases that share only the *Security-Measures* Dimension with the cfs and six cases that share only the *Competitive-Advantage* Dimension with the cfs. All eleven cases are less on point than the *Space Aero* case, which shares an inclusive set of those Dimensions with the cfs.

The Case Positioner constructs a somewhat more complicated regular Claim Lattice for the *Structural Dynamics* case, whose facts are as follows:

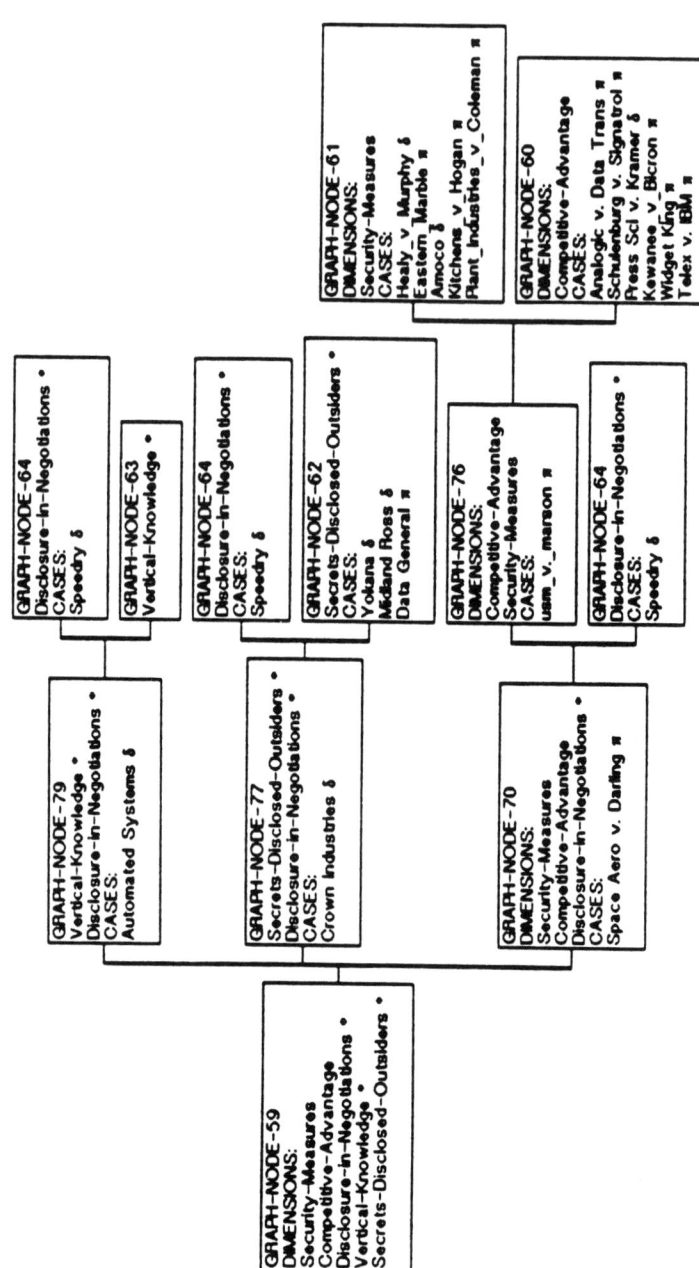

Figure 8.2
Extended Claim Lattice for Trade Secrets Claim in *USM* Case

MOST-ON-POINT CASES FOR TRADE SECRETS CLAIM:

PLAINTIFF:
Telex Corp. v. IBM Corp. (1)
Widget-King v. Cupcake
Kewanee Oil Co. v. Bicron Corp.
Schulenburg v. Signatrol, Inc.
Analogic Corp. v. Data Translation, Inc.
Plant Industries, Inc. v. Coleman
Peggy Lawton Kitchens, Inc. v. Hogan
Eastern Marble Products Corp. v. Roman Marble, Inc.
Space Aero Products Co. v. R. E. Darling Co.

DEFENDANT:
Pressure Science, Inc. v. Kramer
Amoco Production Co. v. Lindley
Healy, Inc. v. Murphy, Inc.

MOST-ON-POINT NEAR-MISS CASES FOR TRADE SECRETS CLAIM:

PLAINTIFF:

DEFENDANT:
Speedry Chemical Products, Inc. v. Carter's Ink Company
Crown Industries Inc. v. Kawneer Co.
Automated-Systems v. Service-Bureau

Figure 8.3
Most-On-Point Cases from Case Analysis Record for *USM* Case

BEST CASES TO CITE FOR TRADE SECRETS CLAIM:

PLAINTIFF:

Telex Corp. v. IBM Corp. (1)
Widget-King v. Cupcake
Kewanee Oil Co. v. Bicron Corp.
Schulenburg v. Signatrol, Inc.
Analogic Corp. v. Data Translation, Inc.
Plant Industries, Inc. v. Coleman
Peggy Lawton Kitchens, Inc. v. Hogan
Eastern Marble Products Corp. v. Roman Marble, Inc.
Space Aero Products Co. v. R. E. Darling Co.

DEFENDANT:

Figure 8.4
Best Cases to Cite from Case Analysis Record for *USM* Case

Squib for *Structural Dynamics* **Case**

Title: Structural Dynamics Research Corp. v. Engineering Mechanics Research Corporation

Cite: 401 F. Supp. 1102 (E.D. Mich. 1975)

Date: September 9, 1975

Parties: Plaintiff: SDRC; Defendant: EMRC, Kothawala, Surana

Claim: Trade Secrets Misappropriation, Breach of Nondisclosure Agreement

Procedural Setting:

Decision: Judgment for Plaintiff in amount of 15 percent on all sales by EMRC for a period of three years and $45,000 for a license fee.

Facts: In August 1972 SDRC began developing a computer program called NIESA to perform structural analysis using isoparametric or curved or irregularly shaped elements. SDRC began marketing its program in April 1974. SDRC employed Kothawala between August 1972 and December 1972 as a member of its technical staff. Surana worked for SDRC from February 1970 to January 1973 as a project leader in the computer operations department and as a member of the technical staff. Each signed an

Employee Patent and Confidential Information Agreement that stated, "At no time... subsequent to termination of such employment will Employee divulge to any person,... or use... any privileged or confidential information, trade secret or other proprietary information relating to the experimental and research work of the Corporation,... gained or developed by or otherwise discovered by Employee during his employment with the Company." Surana first generated the idea for the NIESA program. Kothawala had supervisory responsibility for the project. Together they were completely responsible for the development of the program. The court held that SDRC disclosed NIESA information to its largest shareholder and business partner and that SDRC did not take special security measures to protect the NIESA information.

The employee defendants were subsequently employed by EMRC, a company Kothawala founded when he left SDRC in January 1973. Kothawala is the president and sole shareholder of EMRC; Surana is its vice-president of engineering. In March 1973 EMRC began developing a computer program called NISA to perform structural analysis. EMRC began marketing the program in February 1974. The court held that defendants copied the NIESA code. The overall structure and organization of the code were similar; there were identical segments of code and identical errors; and the input data cards were the same. Defendants were found to possess internal SDRC documents pertaining to the NIESA program, including Surana's development notes. NISA and NIESA were functionally similar, but NISA has some additional capabilities. The court found that it would take a competitor three years to duplicate the NIESA program by independent research.

Issues:
(1) Did Defendants' development of NISA violate their nondisclosure agreement with Plaintiff regarding NIESA?
(2) Did Defendants' development of NISA misappropriate Plaintiff's trade secrets in NIESA?

Holding: (1) Held for Plaintiff: Yes; the agreement was broad enough to apply to their development work on NIESA. Court did not reach (2) in the light of holding on (1). Court said in dicta that absent express nondisclosure agreement, Defendants would have been free to use or disclose the NIESA information because they were the sole developers of the program.

The regular Claim Lattice for the *Structural Dynamics* case, shown in figure 8.5, shows two branches with conflicting most-on-point cases. Two cases from the CKB, *Amoco* and *Analogic*, each share a maximal (but different) set of Dimensions in common with the fact situation of *Structural Dynamics*. Note that the *Analogic* and *Amoco* cases had opposite outcomes, a fact that determines for which side they will be cited in arguments and whether they can be used as counterexamples to less-on-point cases. Every other relevant case from the CKB is less on point because it shares a set of Dimensions with the root node that is a proper subset of the corresponding sets for *Analogic* and *Amoco*. For example, the cases below the *Analogic* case in the Claim Lattice are less on point than *Analogic*. The cases below *Amoco* are less on point than *Amoco*. The *Structural Dynamics* case appears in the Claim Lattice in two roles: as the cfs and as a case retrieved from the CKB. As always, the analysis of the cfs was conducted independently of the fact that the case was in the CKB.

An extended Claim Lattice loosens the criteria for defining what counts as analogous to include cases potentially on point. The definition of relevance is relaxed by expanding the reference set to include Dimensions that are near misses as to the cfs. Figure 8.2 shows the extended Claim Lattice for the *USM* case. The asterisks following Dimensions in the Dimensions lists of the nodes of the extended Claim Lattice indicate that those Dimensions are near misses with respect to the cfs. (Those Dimensions are still applicable with respect to each of the cases in the particular node's case list.) Thus, in figure 8.2, the *Disclosure-in-Negotiations* Dimension is a near miss with respect to the cfs but applies

Basic Mechanisms of Case-Based Reasoning 137

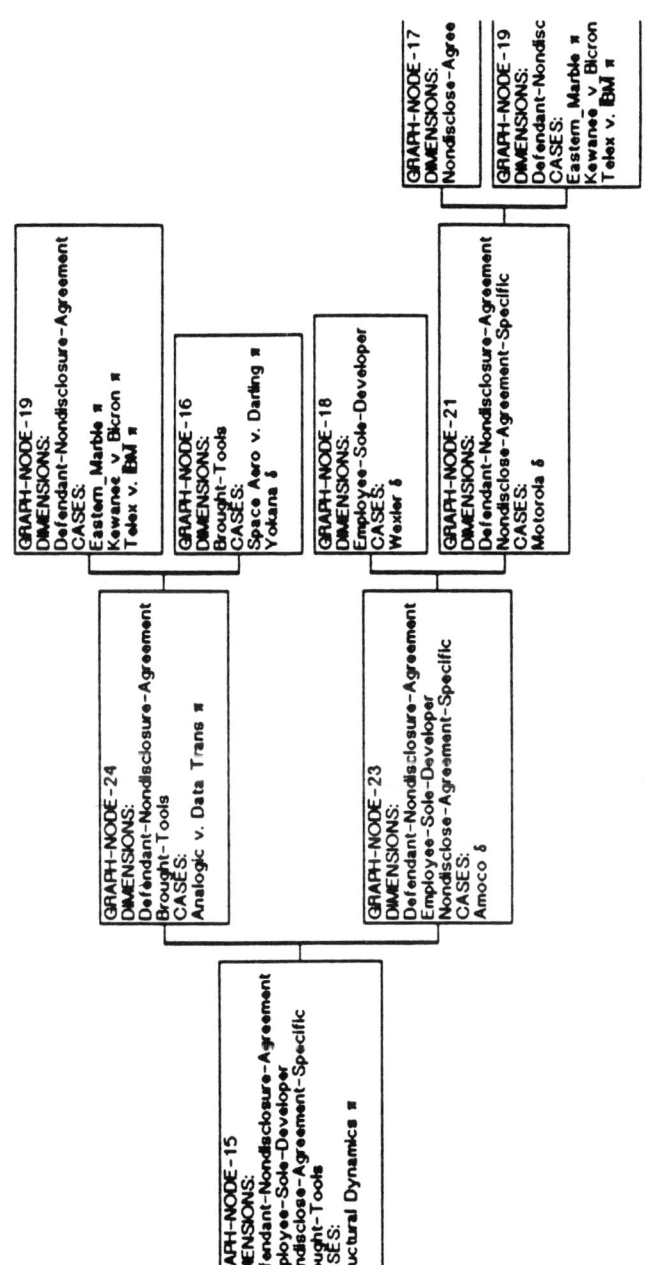

Figure 8.5
Claim Lattice for Trade Secrets Claim in *Structural Dynamics* Case

CASE: Structural Dynamics Research Corp. v. Engineering Mechanics Research Corp.

MOST-ON-POINT CASES FOR TRADE SECRETS CLAIM:
PLAINTIFF:
Analogic Corp. v. Data Translation, Inc.
DEFENDANT:
Amoco Production Co. v. Lindley

MOST-ON-POINT NEAR-MISS CASES FOR TRADE SECRETS CLAIM:
PLAINTIFF:
Eastern Marble Products Corp. v. Roman Marble, Inc.
Analogic Corp. v. Data Translation, Inc.
Space Aero Products Co. v. R.E. Darling Co.
Telex Corp. v. IBM Corp. (1)
DEFENDANT:
Crown Industries Inc. v. Kawneer Co.
Midland-Ross Corp. v. Yokana
Automated-Systems v. Service-Bureau
Midland-Ross Corp. v. Sunbeam Equipment Corp.

BEST CASES TO CITE FOR TRADE SECRETS CLAIM:
PLAINTIFF:
Analogic Corp. v. Data Translation, Inc.
DEFENDANT:
Amoco Production Co. v. Lindley

Figure 8.6
Excerpts from Case Analysis Record for *Structural Dynamics* Case

Basic Mechanisms of Case-Based Reasoning

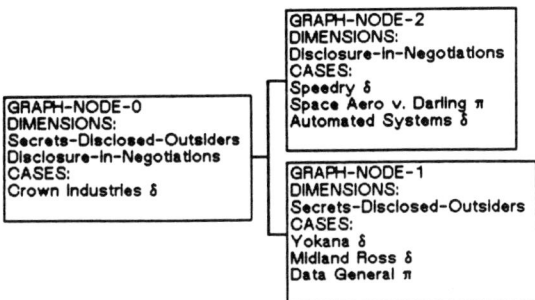

Figure 8.7
Claim Lattice for Trade Secrets Claim in *Crown* Case

to *Automated Systems*. Note that the extended lattice graphs a larger number of cases than and actually subsumes the regular Claim Lattice, reflecting the former's looser criteria for defining relevantly analogous.

An extended Claim Lattice shows cases that could strengthen a side's argument in a slightly different fact situation. This is illustrated in Hypo's analysis of the *Crown* case discussed in chapter 5. The Claim Lattice and excerpts from the extended Claim Lattice for the *Crown* case are shown in figures 8.7 and 8.8. Note the difference in positions of the *Data General* case in the two Claim Lattices. In the regular Claim Lattice (figure 8.7), pro-plaintiff *Data General* is treated as as on point as the pro-defendant *Midland Ross* and *Yokana* cases. In the extended Claim Lattice (figure 8.8), however, the *Data General* case is more on point (closer to the root, which is toward the bottom lower left of the figure out of view) than either of the other two cases. The significance of its position in the extended Claim Lattice is that if the cfs were modified so that the *Outsider-Disclosures-Restricted* Dimension applied, the *Data General* case would make a fine trumping counterexample to either the *Midland Ross* or *Yokana* cases with respect to which it would be more on point and have a contrary outcome. This counterexample would strengthen the plaintiff's position.

8.2 Selecting Most-Analogous Cases

Case-based reasoners need to select the cases most analogous to the cfs. Different domains and reasoning tasks require different definitions

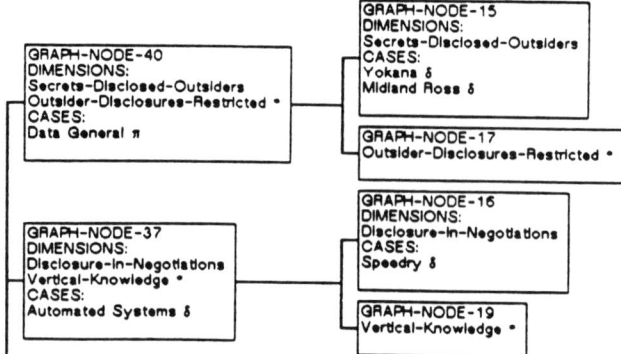

Figure 8.8
Excerpt of Extended Claim Lattice in *Crown*

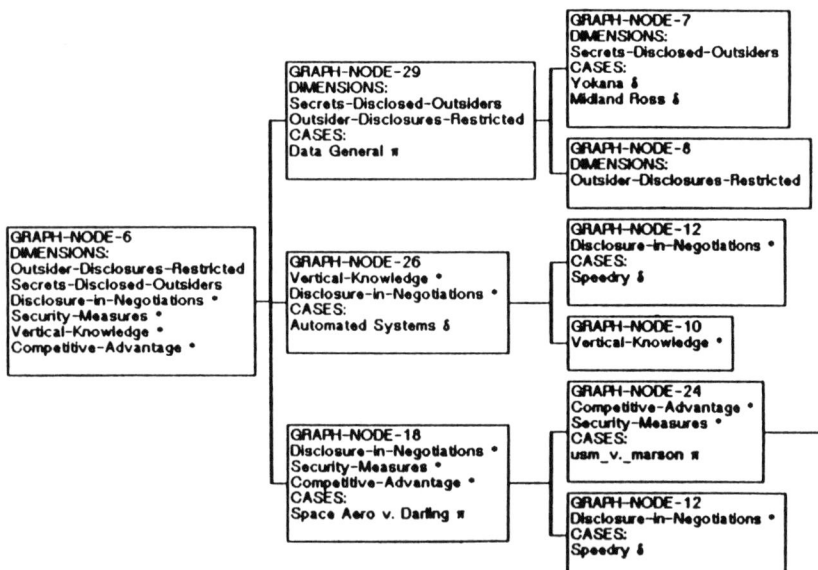

Figure 8.9
Extended Claim Lattice for Trade Secrets Claim in Variant of *Crown* Case Where Disclosures Are Restricted

Most-On-Point Cases for Trade Secrets Claim:
Plaintiff:
Data General Corp. v. Digital Computer Controls Inc.
Space Aero Products Co. v. R. E. Darling Co.
Defendant:
Midland-Ross Corp. v. Sunbeam Equipment Corp.
Midland-Ross Corp. v. Yokana
Automated-Systems v. Service-Bureau
Speedry Chemical Products, Inc. v. Carter's Ink Company

Most-On-Point Near-Miss Cases for Trade Secrets Claim:
Plaintiff:
Eastern Marble Products Corp. v. Roman Marble, Inc.
Telex Corp. v. IBM Corp. (1)
Kewanee Oil Co. v. Bicron Corp.
Analogic Corp. v. Data Translation, Inc.
Space Aero Products Co. v. R. E. Darling Co.
Data General Corp. v. Digital Computer Controls Inc.
Defendant:
Automated-Systems v. Service-Bureau

Best Cases to Cite on Trade Secrets Claim:
Plaintiff:
Defendant:
Midland-Ross Corp. v. Sunbeam Equipment Corp.
Midland-Ross Corp. v. Yokana
Automated-Systems v. Service-Bureau
Speedry Chemical Products, Inc. v. Carter's Ink Company

Figure 8.10
Excerpts from Case Analysis Record for *Crown* Case

of most analogous cases. There are a couple of important considerations that apply across domains and tasks.

First, there may be more than one most analogous case. In some domains like law, the evaluation criteria are not so well defined that it can be determined always or even often what the one best case is. There may also be a variety of definitions of most analogous, each serving a somewhat different function. Thus, it may be useful for purposes of decision making or explanation to define "most analogous" less restrictively to yield a larger set of alternatives.

Second, the most analogous cases may lead to conflicting answers. In law, there usually are good cases on both sides of an argument, each with a claim to being the most analogous.

Third, comparing and contrasting the conflicting most analogous cases in a symbolic way can help educate the decision maker. She or he sees the alternative ways of answering a question and is better prepared to make a wise decision. She or he also sees how small changes in the problem could lead to different results. The law's adversarial system institutionalizes this approach to decision making.

Hypo's methods of selecting and using most-analogous cases have been designed with these considerations in mind. Hypo's Case Positioner uses Claim Lattices to select three kinds of most-analogous precedents, each useful for somewhat different functions: most-on-point cases, best cases to cite, and most-on-point near-miss cases.

The most-on-point cases for a side have already been defined. They are selected from a regular Claim Lattice. The best cases for a side to cite are a subset of the most-on-point cases.

The best cases to cite for a side are defined as those cases that are most on point for that side and citable for that side in the first instance.

A precedent is citable in the first instance for a side on a claim if and only if the court held for that side on the claim and the precedent shares at least one applicable Dimension favoring the side.

The best cases to cite make the most convincing points in favor of a side's position on a claim. They not only share the most factors with the fact situation of any other case holding for that side, but at least some of the factors represent strengths of the side's position. By contrast, most-on-point cases may not make convincing points if cited in the first instance since they do not necessarily share any Dimension with the fact situation that favors the side for whom the case is cited. Nevertheless,

Basic Mechanisms of Case-Based Reasoning 143

most-on-point cases may be useful to cite as counterexamples to an opponent's cited case.

Most-on-point near-miss cases are defined as those cases

- that are won by a side,
- to which there applies at least one Dimension that is a near miss for the cfs and favors that side,
- that are contained in an extended Claim Lattice in the root or in nodes that are closer to the root than (or as close as) any case-containing node on that branch from the root,
- that are not already a best case to cite.

Most-on-point near-miss cases are the cases in the CKB that would be most analogous to the fact situation if all of the Dimensions that were near misses to the fact situation suddenly applied. As such, these cases are potentially useful in making new points or responses.

Hypo's Best Case Selector selects the three types of most analogous cases for a cfs. The results of its selection are illustrated for the three fact situations of the *USM, Structural Dynamics,* and *Crown* cases in figures 8.3, 8.4, 8.6, and 8.10. Each figure shows an excerpt from the Case Analysis Records generated for the cases.

In selecting the most-on-point cases, the Best Case Selector avoids comparing apples and oranges; the on-pointness comparison of cases is confined to comparing cases on the same branch of the Claim Lattice. Cases selected as most analogous from different branches (whose subsets of the cfs's reference set, though maximal, are overlapping or disjoint) are not deemed by the Best Case Selector to be more or less on point than each other. That would be like comparing apples and oranges. In figure 8.5, for example, the *Analogic* and *Amoco* cases are deemed equally on point because each has a different, though maximal, subset of the *Structural Dynamics* case's reference set of Dimensions. Similarly, the cases below the *Analogic* case are not necessarily less on point than the cases below the *Amoco* case. In this instance, some are (*Space Aero* and *Yokana*) and some are not (*Telex, Eastern Marble,* and *Kewanee*), reflecting the fact that the Claim Lattice is a graph.

In selecting the most-on-point cases, the Best Case Selector does not compare numbers of Dimensions shared with the cfs but compares sets and subsets of such Dimensions. In figure 8.5, for example, the *Analogic* and *Amoco* cases are deemed equally on point despite the fact that the former has two Dimensions in common with the cfs as compared to the latter's three.

In selecting best cases to cite, the Best Case Selector weeds out cases that are most on point but would not make convincing legal points if cited in the first instance. As illustrated in figures 8.3 and 8.4, the Selector filters the most-on-point cases. The *Pressure Science* case, though a most-on-point case for the defendant, did not make the list of defendant's best cases to cite because the Dimension it shared with the cfs did not represent a strength of the defendant's case. In *Pressure Science* the defendant won despite the fact that it had gained a competitive head start over the plaintiff. In trade secrets law, the fact that a defendant who has access to plaintiff's trade secrets gains a competitive head start tends to support an argument that it misappropriated plaintiff's trade secret. That knowledge is captured in the *Competitive-Advantage* Dimension. Thus *Pressure Science* is not a convincing case to cite in an initial argument that a defendant should win. *Pressure Science* does, however, make an effective counterexample to cite in response to the argument by a plaintiff that a defendant should lose where it gained a competitive head start. Similarly, in figure 8.10, neither *Space Aero* nor *Data General* is a best case to cite for the plaintiff, but both make good counterexamples.

As the number of cases in the CKB increases, so will the average number of cases contained in a typical Claim Lattice node. A different kind of filter could be used to select the "least not on-point" cases within a particular node. In other words, a node's cases could be screened in terms of the number of Dimensions not shared with the cfs. The Best Case Selector could then select the case that has the least number of Dimensions that make the case distinguishable from the cfs. This secondary filter has not been implemented.

8.3 Identifying Configurations of Counterexamples

All case-based reasoning involves recognizing and using cases as counterexamples. When cases equally analogous lead to contradictory results, the cases can be thought of as counterexamples to one another. Each case is a counterexample to the proposition that the fact situation should be decided in accord with the other. The existence of the counterexample is important because it makes reliance on the other case much more dubious.

Although case-based reasoners should be able to recognize counterexamples and call attention to them, in most case-based reasoners, conflicts among most analogous cases are resolved by the matcher. There is a static hierarchy of features: the case match with the highest score wins, and the defeated cases are ignored. The static hierarchies are also flawed in another sense. Although one feature may be more important than another in some or most cases, that may not be true if there are other countervailing features in a problem situation or where feature magnitudes may differ. A matcher employing a static hierarchy of features for selecting among conflicting analogous cases is not appropriate where assessing the weights of features is highly context dependent and where explicating the comparisons and contrasts among a fact situation, the most analogous precedents, and their counterexamples conveys valuable information, as it does in legal argument.

Across case-based domains, the definitions and uses of counterexamples differ. In Hypo, the 3-Ply Arguer looks for four kinds of counterexamples that have legal significance in the light of the Argument Evaluation Criteria:

- More on point (trumping), cases that had a contrary outcome from and are more on point than a given case. These are good for citing as trumping counterexamples.

- Potentially more on point (potentially trumping), for each side, cases that are potentially most on point or more on point than opponents' cases. These are potential counterexamples and are the basis of hypothetical variations of the fact situation that turn up new points and stronger responses. They also illustrate how the arguments about a fact situation change as factors are added, subtracted, exaggerated, or combined with factors of conflicting cases.

- As-on-point or partial, cases that had a contrary outcome from a given case although they share all or some of the same Dimensions of that case in common with the cfs

- Boundary, cases that had a contrary outcome from and are more extreme along a shared Dimension than a given case

The first three kinds of counterexamples are represented by the configurations in a regular or extended Claim Lattice of cases having contradictory outcomes. For a given case, a counterexample is a case won by the opposing side and located as follows:

- More-on-point counterexamples, if they exist, are located in nodes of a regular Claim Lattice closer to the root on any of the branches connecting the case and the root.

- Potentially more-on-point counterexamples are located in nodes of the extended Claim Lattice closer to the root on any of the branches connecting the case and the root.

- As-on-point or partial counterexamples are located in the same node of the regular Claim Lattice as the given case or in any node whose list of Dimensions contains a proper subset of that node's Dimensions.

- Boundary counterexamples are located along a Dimension shared with the fact situation and have an extreme value along that shared Dimension.

For a particular cited case, the 3-Ply Arguer compares the case to the most-on-point or most-on-point near-miss cases listed in the Case Analysis Record; these cases were previously selected by traversing the Claim Lattices. The Arguer looks for opposing cases that are more on point relative to the cfs than the cited case. These are the trumping or potentially trumping counterexamples. The Arguer also looks along shared Dimensions for more extreme opposing cases to use as boundary counterexamples.

The absence of counterexamples is significant. The 3-Ply Arguer looks for the absence of more-on-point counterexamples when it seeks nontrumped cases to cite in points. These are the best cases to cite for each side for which there are no more-on-point pro-opponent cases. The Arguer compares the strengths of each side's argument in terms of whether the side can cite nontrumped cases; if only one side has such cases, that side has a stronger argument.

The various configurations of counterexample are illustrated in the Claim Lattices of the accompanying figures. In figure 8.1, *Space Aero* is a more-on-point counterexample to any of the pro-defendant cases below it, including the *Pressure Science* case. Although the defendant won *Pressure Science* even though it gained a competitive advantage, in *Space Aero*, just as in the cfs, defendant not only gained a competitive head start but plaintiff took security measures too. In fact, there are no more-on-point counterexamples to the *Space Aero* case, a fact that the Arguer takes into account in deciding that plaintiff has the stronger argument. As a look at figure 8.2 will show, there are no counterexamples potentially more on point than *Space Aero*. That means the Arguer will not be able to suggest a hypothetical to strengthen defendant's response to citing the *Space Aero* case. By contrast, in figure 8.8, the *Data General* case is potentially a more-on-point counterexample to the *Yokana* and *Midland Ross* cases. The Arguer can suggest a hypothetical: if the disclosures in the cfs were subject to restrictions, *Data General* would be a trumping counterexample strengthening plaintiff's response to those cases. In figure 8.5, the *Analogic* and *Amoco* cases are not trumping counterexamples. Each involved a nondisclosure agreement between plaintiff and defendant and came to contradictory results, but neither is more on point than the other.

By making it easy to find configurations of counterexamples, Claim Lattices allow the program to recognize among the welter of relevant cases those legally interesting patterns among contradictory cases that are the stuff of legal arguments.

8.4 Hypothetical Modifications to Explore Contingencies

All case-based reasoners should support posing hypothetical modifications of cases to explore the consequences of making a problem situation or retrieved analogous case more or less like other analogous cases, particularly counterexamples. By posing hypotheticals, the system can explore how small variations in the fact situation can drastically affect an outcome.

8.4.1 Suggesting Interesting Hypotheticals to Pose

Hypo generates hypotheticals to change the results of the comparisons among the most analogous cases and alter the resulting arguments in predictable and useful ways. Hypo has heuristics for generating hypothetical modifications of a seed case to make it more or less like one or more target cases. Two interesting hypotheticals are produced from particular seed-target case combinations:

- cfs spinoffs: hypotheticals posed using the cfs as a seed and a most-on-point near-miss case, especially a potential counterexample, as a target

- hybrids: hypotheticals posed using a pro-plaintiff most-on-point case as a seed and a pro-defendant most-on-point case from a different branch of the Claim Lattice as a target (or vice versa)

Posing cfs spinoffs by hypothetically varying the cfs to make it more like potential counterexamples is a good way to apprise an attorney of the kinds of facts that could improve a response. Having found a suitable potential counterexample, the Explainer poses a hypothetical based on the cfs as seed but supplies the missing triggering facts of the near-miss Dimensions associated with the potential counterexample. By recursively calling the basic processing loop on the hypothetical, the Arguer generates new arguments, which, when compared with the old, point out the improvement in the response. A similar approach can be used to show the attorney how to make a new point in favor of a side. The Explainer chooses as a target case a most-on-point near-miss case whose outcome favored that side.

Hybrids combine the pro-plaintiff factors that the seed case shares with the cfs with the shared pro-defendant factors of the target case. No case in the CKB has that particular combination of factors. If it did, it would have been more on point than either seed or target. Hybrids are interesting because they implicitly raise the issue of which of the competing factors are more important and how such a case would be decided. The hybrid hypo can be made even more interesting by pushing the conflicting factors to extremes. In oral arguments, courts often create hybrid hypotheticals to use in slippery slope arguments to put pressure on an attorney's position. Starting with a case cited by the attorney as

Basic Mechanisms of Case-Based Reasoning 149

the seed, the court poses hypotheticals, making it look more and more like a case cited by the opponent. In the process, the attorney is forced to propose a criterion for drawing the line between the seed and target cases. Courts also pose hybrids as a way of noting that no decided case has ever presented that particular combination of factors.

8.4.2 Heuristics for Generating Hypotheticals

In order to generate a hypothetical from a seed case, the Hypo Generator first creates a copy of the seed case by dumping the copies of the Legal Case Frames of the seed case into a file and reinstantiating them, with names modified to avoid obliterating the seed case, thus creating a new version of the seed case. The Hypo Generator then applies heuristic modification methods to modify the copied case.

The Hypo Generator has five heuristics for hypothetically modifying a case:

> (H1) Pick a near-miss Dimension and modify the facts to make it applicable.
>
> (H2) Pick an applicable Dimension and make the case weaker or stronger along that Dimension.
>
> (H3) Pick a Dimension related to one of the applicable Dimensions and apply one of the other heuristics, particularly 1 or 2.
>
> (H4) Pick an applicable Dimension and make the case extreme with respect to that Dimension.
>
> (H5) Pick a target case that is a win and, using 1 and 2, move the seed case toward it to create a near win.

Each of the heuristic methods is described below and illustrated with an example. The example starts with the *Crown* case as the cfs. In *Crown* the plaintiff disclosed its secrets to seven outsiders (Dimension *Secrets-Disclosed-Outsiders* applied). (Hypo's arguments for the *Crown* case are set out in chapter 5.) In the following descriptions, the case being modified hypothetically is a copy of the *Crown* seed case.

H1, enable a near-miss Dimension. To modify a case hypothetically according to this heuristic method, the Hypo Generator selects a near-miss Dimension and fills in the missing prerequisite. Since the Dimension is a near miss, the missing prerequisite is the triggering prerequisite, the one associated with the Dimension's focal slot. The Hypo Generator invokes a store method to make the case satisfy the missing Factual Predicate. The store method instantiates underlying Legal Case Frame objects, adds them to the case, and makes appropriate cross-references. For example, to make the near-miss Dimension *Outsider-Disclosures-Restricted* apply to a copy of the *Crown* case, the Hypo Generator instantiates the missing focal slot prerequisite, "Disclosures to outsiders were subject to restriction," by making 100 percent of the disclosures to outsiders be subject to confidentiality restrictions. This strengthens the plaintiff's position.

H2, make a case weaker or stronger along an applicable Dimension. The Hypo Generator strengthens or weakens a case by changing the value of the Dimension's focal slot in the case. The change can be made independent of, or relative to, the corresponding value in a target case. To accomplish the former strengthening or weakening, the Generator changes the values of a focal slot in the manner specified by the range information of the Dimension. That range information specifies possible values of the focal slot and which kind of change will favor the plaintiff. The amount of the change is somewhat arbitrary. To accomplish a modification relative to a target case (for instance, to strengthen), the Generator adjusts the values of the focal slots of the copy of the seed case in the stronger direction so that it is further out than the target case's value. For example, the Generator makes the version of the *Crown* case even weaker along the *Secrets-Disclosed* Dimension relative to a target case like *Midland-Ross* by *increasing* the number of disclosees in the version from 7 to 150. Since *Midland-Ross* was decided for the defendant because there were too many disclosees (100), the version of *Crown* has passed the 100-disclosee threshold, thus losing the ability to distinguish *Midland-Ross* as in Argument [1] of the *Crown* extended example in chapter 5.

Hypo could make the version of *Crown* weaker still by increasing the number of disclosees near or above 6,000, the highest value of any case in the CKB, or even greater (in a target-independent way), to the highest value allowed by Hypo. The case in the CKB with 6,000 disclosures is *Data General*, where the plaintiff nevertheless won. In Argument [1] of chapter 5, Hypo cites *Data General* as a boundary counterexample to show that even a large number of disclosures is not fatal to plaintiff. If Hypo increased the number of disclosees to 10,000, however, the plaintiff could no longer rely on *Data General* as a boundary counterexample.

H3, generate a hypo on a related Dimension. Two Dimensions in Hypo are related when they favor opposite sides and there is a real case in which both appear. The case may turn out to be a useful counterexample in the context of a cfs involving both Dimensions. For example, the Dimensions *Outsider-Disclosures-Restricted* and *Secrets-Disclosed* favor conflicting sides and appear together in the *Data-General* case, which is a potentially more-on-point counterexample in the context of the *Crown* case. A case can be modified on a related Dimension by adding facts sufficient to make the related Dimension apply to it in a manner similar to that of heuristic H1. In the light of *Data General*'s strategic use as a counterexample, the example of modifying the version of the *Crown* case so that the *Outsider-Disclosures-Restricted* Dimension applies is also an example of H3. In this example, the related Dimension happens to be a near miss, but that need not always be true. A hypothetical generated on a conflicting Dimension is interesting because it is an example of a case where, at least arguably, facts associated with one Dimension can override the effects of the other Dimension's facts. Hypo poses such hypotheticals to probe for ways to strengthen the response to a point.

H4, examine an extreme case. To generate an extreme case, Hypo changes the value in the case of a Dimension's focal slot to be an extreme of the range of possible values. This can also be done in either a target-based or target-independent manner. The former method pushes the slot value to the extreme actually existing in a case in the CKB; the latter simply pushes the slot value to its permissible extreme. For instance, the extreme case on the strongest end of the *Secrets-Disclosed* Dimension for plaintiff would be 0 disclosees. The other extreme is the maximum value for number of disclosees in a case won by the plaintiff (6,000 in *Data General*) and in Hypo (10 million).

H5, manipulate a near win. A near win is one in which a version of a seed case that is strong for and was won by, let us say, the plaintiff is moved in the direction of a target case from the CKB decided in favor of the defendant. Using methods H1 through H3, Hypo endows the version situation with the factors that made the target case a strong case for the defendant. The resulting hypothetical is not as strong for the plaintiff as the seed; it is a near win. An argument can be made, based on the pro-defendant target case, that the near win should be decided in favor of the defendant. Manipulating a near win is especially useful in generating hybrids of most-on-point cases. For example, in figure 8.8, a hybrid can be created from the *Data General* and *Automated Systems* cases by creating a near win using the former as seed and the latter as target. In *Automated Systems* the court held in favor of the defendant where the confidential information that the plaintiff wanted to protect was about a customer's business operations; that is, the knowledge was about a "vertical market" and the plaintiff had disclosed the information to defendant in negotiations. The Hypo Generator creates a near win out of *Data General* as the seed by making the confidential information be vertical knowledge (about customer business operations) and by introducing disclosures to defendant in negotiations. As a result, an argument could be based on *Automated Systems* that, in the near-win version of *Data General*, the defendant should win.

The 3-Ply Arguer directs the Hypo Generator as to which applicable, near-miss, or related Dimensions to use in modifying the version of the seed case with the five heuristic methods and what target values to use, if any. Given a seed and target case, the Arguer computes the relevant differences between them and generates a specification for a hypothetical. For a cfs spinoff, the relevant differences are some of the same differences that the Arguer would use to distinguish the target case from the seed: unshared Dimensions (applicable to the target but near misses as to the seed that favor the side of the target's winner) and differences along shared Dimensions that favor the side of the target's winner.

The specification for a hypothetical, including the seed case, target case (if any), and relevant differences, is passed along to the Hypo Generator module.

Some of the hypothetical modifications suggested by the Explainer to explore the possible legal ramifications implicit in the *Crown* Extended Example of chapter 5 are shown below. The first two hypotheticals suggest how to bolster responses to points in Arguments [1] and [4]. The last three suggest the bases for three new points.

Hypothetical Variations of the *Crown* Case Suggested by Hypo

1. Plaintiff's response would be strengthened if: Plaintiff's disclosures to outsiders were restricted.
Cf. Data General Corp. v. Digital Computer Controls Inc. 357 A.2d 105 (Del. Ch. 1975) (e.g., see argument [1])

2. Plaintiff's response would be strengthened if: Defendant's access to plaintiff's product information saved it time or expense. Plaintiff adopted security measures.
Cf. Space Aero Products Co. v. R.E. Darling Co. 208 A.2d 74 (Ct. App., Md., 1965) (see argument [4])

3. Plaintiff's position would be strengthened in following situations: Suppose:
(a) Plaintiff and defendant entered into a nondisclosure agreement. Plaintiff adopted security measures.
Cf. Eastern Marble Products Corp. v. Roman Marble, Inc. 364 N.E.2d 799 (Mass., 1977)
(b) Defendant's access to plaintiff's product information saved it time or expense. Plaintiff and defendant entered into a nondisclosure agreement.
Cf. Telex Corp. v. IBM Corp. (1) 510 F.2d 894 (10 Cir., 1975)

4. Defendant's position would be strengthened in following situations: Suppose:
(a) Plaintiff's product information was about customer business relations.
Cf. Automated-Systems v. Service-Bureau 401 F.2d 619 (10 Cir., 1968)
(b) Plaintiff disclosed to 6,000 outsiders, as many as in *Data General*. Suppose it disclosed to 10,000? 10,000,000?

Hypo generates versions of the *Crown* case that strengthen or weaken the plaintiff's position in a variety of ways. The first two suggested modifications are implemented using H3 and H1 moves to related, conflicting near-miss Dimensions (*Outsider-Disclosures-Restricted* in variation 1; *Competitive-Advantage-Gained* and *Security-Measures* in variation 2). The conflict relations among the Dimensions were noted by the 3-Ply Arguer in identifying *Data General* and *Space Aero* as potentially more-on-point counterexamples. Suggested modifications in 3 and 4(a) are implemented with H1 moves to near-miss Dimensions. The 3-Ply Arguer focused on particular near-miss Dimensions because it discovered most-on-point near-miss cases with those Dimensions that could be cited on behalf of plaintiff or defendant. In suggested modification 4(b), the version is moved using H2 and H4 past the values in *Midland-Ross* to the extreme value in *Data General* and beyond. The program does not know to speculate that a secret told to 10,000 people is not a secret, even if they promise not to tell anyone else, but the program does know that two Dimensions in *Data General* conflict and that moving to an extreme on one Dimension may cause the conflict to be moot.

The results of generating the first suggested hypothetical are shown in the *Crown* Extended Example in chapter 5, where a cfs spinoff, Version 4 of the *Crown* case, was generated using H3 and H1. Version 4 has the same facts as the *Crown* case, except for one modification: all seven disclosures to outsiders are now subject to restrictions.

8.5 Comparing Case-Based Analyses of Different Problem Situations

All case-based reasoners should support comparing case-based analyses of different problem situations as a tool for explanation. One excellent way of explaining a case-based analysis is to contrast it to the analysis of a fact situation that is similar but has some crucial differences. In addition, the results of the comparison can be used to draw conclusions about the original analysis. Good fact situations to compare are the problem situation and a hypothetical variant of it or a retrieved case and a counterexample.

The 3-Ply Arguer compares the strength of arguments that can be made in favor of a claim in different fact situations by comparing Claim Lattices. For example, to demonstrate the effects on an argument of a hypothetical change in the facts, the program compares the Claim Lattices before and after the change. Changes in the number of and relationships among the most analogous cases indicate shifts in the balance of the argument (for example, introducing a new best case for a particular side to cite or supplanting an old one with a new most-on-point counterexample).

One comparison is shown in the *Crown* Extended Example of chapter 5. The arguments that can be made in the context of two related fact situations, the *Crown* case and hypothetical Version 4 of the *Crown* case, are compared. The overall difference in the arguments is shown in the Citation Summary for Version 4. Where previously only the defendant could make untrumped points, now both plaintiff and defendant can make such points. Furthermore, as the comparison of Arguments [1] and [5] shows, the response to the point citing the *Midland Ross* case is improved; *Data General* can be cited in the response as a trumping counterexample. The attorney must now find out whether the disclosures are restricted in the *Crown* case.

The positions of cases in Claim Lattices reflect the comparative weaknesses and strengths of arguments citing the cases. The underlying comparison among Claim Lattices that gives rise to the differences in argument is clear in figures 8.8 and 8.9. The former shows an excerpt of the extended Claim Lattice for the *Crown* case; the latter shows the extended Claim Lattice for a variant of the *Crown* case in which the disclosures to outsiders have been made subject to restrictions. In figure 8.9, the *Secrets-Disclosed-Outsiders* has changed from a near miss to an applicable Dimension. The *Data General* case has changed from being a counterexample potentially more on point than *Midland-Ross* to being a real trumping counterexample.

9 A Theory of Case-Based Argument in Hypo

This chapter presents a partial theory of arguing with precedents. It provides a theoretical description of the aspects of legal argument that underlie the program—in other words, the theory that Hypo, in effect, implements. The theory defines the circumstances in which past cases can be cited as reasonable justifications in arguments and how those arguments, to some extent, can be evaluated. Definitions are provided in the terminology of sets for the four roles of precedents in arguments: cited cases, distinguished cases, counterexamples, and targets for hypotheticals.

Depending on its role in an argument, different aspects of a precedent are salient. *Salience* means strikingness or emphasis. An arguer emphasizes different aspects of a precedent depending on his or her viewpoint (for the plaintiff or for the defendant) and on whether he or she cites the case to justify a similar outcome, distinguishes it, or cites it as a counterexample to another case or as the target of a hypothetical.

Similarly, given a problem situation, different precedents in the CKB are significant in the light of the argument roles they may play. *Significance* means weight or import. An arguer wants to cite the most significant precedents in each of the argument roles.

For each of the argument roles, the theory provides a succinct expression of (1) the features of a precedent that are salient when used in that role and (2) the most significant cases in the CKB to fill the role. The theory also defines how a precedential argument, to a limited extent, can be evaluated.

The theory is an abstraction and oversimplification of legal argument with precedents. Nevertheless, succinct definitions of these aspects of precedential argument facilitate evaluating the theory's advantages and shortcomings as a model of analogical reasoning with precedents in law and point to ways of improving the theory.

9.1 Computationally Defining Salience and Significance

In this partial theory of precedential argument, as elsewhere in this book, a legal case is treated as a historical collection of factors, each with a particular magnitude, to which some authoritative decision maker, the judge, has assigned an outcome for plaintiff or defendant.

The following notations are useful in defining the argument roles for precedents. They enable one to speak more succinctly about cases and factors.

9.1.1 Set Theory and Logic Symbols

This chapter employs some symbols from set theory and logic. The following simple examples illustrate the symbols' meanings.

Let's assume that A is the set consisting of the letters a, b, and c, that is, $A = \{abc\}$. Let $B = \{cefg\}$. The intersection of sets A and B is $A \cap B = \{c\}$. The union of sets A and B is $A \cup B = \{abcefg\}$. The set difference between sets A and B is $A \setminus B = \{ab\}$. $B \setminus A = \{efg\}$.

Let $E = \{bc\}$. Set E is a subset or equal to A (i.e., $E \subseteq A$) because either $E = A$ or every member of E is a member of A. A is not a subset or equal to E (i.e., $A \nsubseteq E$) because there is at least one member of A, $\{a\}$, that is not a member of E. Since E is a subset or equal to A, A is a more inclusive set than or equal to E (i.e., $A \supseteq E$).

Let $G = \{xyz\}$. Sets A and G are disjoint because the intersection of A and G is the empty set. In symbols, $A \cap G = \emptyset$.

Assume that l is a variable that stands for some letter. The expression, $\forall l \in A$, means "for all letters l such that l is a member of set A." The expression, $\exists l \in A$, means "there exists some letter l such that l is a member of A."

Among logical symbols, $\vee$ means or, $\wedge$ means and, and $\neg$ means not.

9.1.2 Shorthand Notation for Factors

The symbol s means side in a lawsuit, either plaintiff (π) or defendant (δ). "$O(c_i) = \pi$" means the outcome of case c_i was for the plaintiff. F_s means the set of all factors, f, such that f generally favors side s, either plaintiff or defendant, for example,

$F_\pi \equiv$ the set of all factors, f, that generally favor plaintiff,

$F_\delta \equiv \{f \mid f \text{ generally favors defendant}\}$.

$F_{c_i} \equiv \{f \mid f \text{ applies to } c_i\}$, (i.e., the set of all factors, f, such that f applies to case c_i.) $Opp(s) \equiv$ opponent of side s, for example, $opp(\pi) = \delta$, that is, the opponent of plaintiff is defendant. For a given factor f^k, $M(f_{c_i}^k) \equiv$ the magnitude of factor f^k in case c_i. "$M(f_{c_i}^k) > M(f_{c_j}^k)$" means that the magnitude of factor f^k is greater for the plaintiff in case c_i than in case c_j. "$\setminus$" $\equiv$ set difference. CKB means the set of all past cases. Using this notation one can provide new explicit definitions for some now familiar concepts.

9.1.3 Relevant Similarities and Differences

Relevant similarities between two cases are shared factors. The set of relevant similarities between case c_1 and case c_2, S_{c_1,c_2}, is the set of factors the two cases share, specifically,

$$S_{c_1,c_2} \equiv F_{c_1} \cap F_{c_2}. \tag{9.1.1}$$

In English, the set of relevant similarities between cases c_1 and c_2 is the intersection of the sets of factors that apply to each case. One case was decided because, or in spite, of the factors that applied to it. Some of those factors also apply to the other case and justify the same outcome.

The set of relevant differences between c_1 and c_2, D_{c_1,c_2}, is defined as follows (assume that the outcome of c_2 was in favor of plaintiff):

$$\begin{aligned}D_{c_1,c_2} &\equiv [(F_{c_1} \setminus F_{c_2}) \cap F_\delta] \cup [(F_{c_2} \setminus F_{c_1}) \cap F_\pi] \\ &\cup \{f \mid (f \in S_{c_1,c_2}) \wedge (M(f_{c_2}) > M(f_{c_1}))\}\end{aligned} \tag{9.1.2}$$

In English, the set of relevant differences is the union of three sets: the pro-defendant factors that apply only to c_1, the pro-plaintiff factors that apply only to c_2, and the shared factors that favor plaintiff more strongly in c_2 than in c_1.

The relevant differences are reasons that the two cases should be decided differently. The relevant differences are the pro-defendant factors that apply only to c_1, the pro-plaintiff factors that apply only to c_2, and the shared factors that favor plaintiff more strongly in c_2 than in c_1. All of these relevant differences make c_1 a weaker case for plaintiff than c_2. As a result, c_2 is a weaker justification in a legal argument that plaintiff should win in c_1.

9.1.4 Most Analogous Precedents

The theory defines the sense in which a precedent is analogous or on point to a problem.

Cases that are on point are relevantly similar to a problem situation. The set of cases that are on point to a problem, OP, is defined as follows:

$$OP \equiv \{c_i \mid (c_i \in CKB) \land (S_{p,c_i} \neq \emptyset)\} \tag{9.1.3}$$

Saying that one case, c_i, is more on point than another case, c_k, relative to a problem, p, means that

$$S_{p,c_i} \supset S_{p,c_k}. \tag{9.1.4}$$

In English, the set of relevant similarities between the problem situation and c_i includes the set of relevant similarities between the problem and c_k.

Cases that are most on point to the problem are the most relevantly similar of all the on-point cases. The set of most-on-point cases for a side s, MOP_s, is defined as the set of all cases, c_i, such that for each c_i, s won c_i and there is no on-point case won by s that is more on point than c_i. Specifically, MOP_s is defined as follows:

$$\begin{aligned} MOP_s \equiv\ & \{c_i \mid (c_i \in OP) \land (O(c_i) = s) \land \\ & (\forall c_k (c_k \in OP) \land (O(c_k) = s) \land \\ & ((S_{p,c_i} \cap S_{p,c_k} = \emptyset) \lor (S_{p,c_i} \supseteq S_{p,c_k}) \lor \\ & ((S_{p,c_i} \not\subseteq S_{p,c_k}) \land (S_{p,c_k} \not\subseteq S_{p,c_i}))))\} \end{aligned} \tag{9.1.5}$$

In English, MOP_s is the set of all cases, c_i, such that c_i is on point, s won c_i, and for all other on-point cases c_k won by s, either c_i and c_k have no similarities in common with the problem situation or c_i is as or more on point than c_k, or neither is more on point than the other.

Intuitively, MOP contains the cases that are candidates for the best cases to cite for a side in an argument on how to decide the problem. Of all the cases in the CKB, they are closest in that they share with the problem the greatest overlap of factual strengths and weaknesses as represented by factors.

As the definitions of "more on point" and MOP indicate, in this theory the relative closeness of two cases to the problem is not defined in terms of the comparative numbers of factors they share with the problem but in terms of the relative overlaps of the sets of factors they share with the problem. A case that has two similarities to the problem may be in MOP along with a case that has four similarities as long as the relevant similarities comprise different sets and the smaller set is not a proper subset of the larger.

9.2 Argument Roles for Precedents

According to the theory, a precedent can be employed in four roles in a legal argument, the same roles in which they are used in Hypo's 3-Ply Arguments:

1. As a cited case to justify a legal conclusion that the problem should have the same outcome as the cited case

2. As a distinguished case to respond to an assertion that the problem should have the same outcome as the cited case

3. As a counterexample to respond in another way to an assertion that the problem should have the same outcome as the cited case

4. As a target case to motivate a hypothetical modification of the problem that will strengthen or weaken an argument

For each of the argument roles, the theory allows a succinct expression of the best cases in the CKB to fill the role, as well as the features of a precedent that are salient when used in that role. In the expressions, the following abbreviations are employed: p stands for the problem situation, cc is the cited case, dc is the distinguished case, cex is the counterexample, and t is the target.

In defining the best cases to cite and the features of a precedent that are salient, the expressions take context into account. They contain terms that reflect the facts of the problem situation, the side on whose behalf one argues, the role that a precedent plays in the argument, and the facts of other cases in the CKB. This is the key to the theory's ability to assess relevance dynamically and to support multiple interpretations of a given precedent.

9.2.1 Cited Case

The basic role for precedents in legal arguments is as cited cases. Although any on-point case could reasonably be cited in support of a side, some precedents are better to cite than others.

The best cases in the CKB for a side to cite in support of its position are certain most-on-point cases whose outcomes favored that side and with respect to which there are no better cases for the opponent to cite as counterexamples. The opponent's better cases, if any, are referred to as trumping counterexamples. More concisely, the set of best untrumped cases for a side s to cite, BUC_s, is defined as follows:

$$\begin{aligned} BUC_s \equiv \ & \{c_i \mid (c_i \in MOP_s) \land \\ & (\exists f^i((f^i \in F_s) \land (f^i \in S_{p,c_i}))) \land \\ & (TCX_{opp(s),c_i} = \emptyset)\} \end{aligned} \qquad (9.2.6)$$

In the definition of BUC_s, $TCX_{opp(s),c_i}$ is the set of trumping counterexamples to c_i that the opponent of s can cite. In English, the set of best untrumped cases to cite for a side s is the set of cases, c_i, such that c_i is a most-on-point case and c_i shares some factor with the problem that favors side s and there is no trumping counterexample to c_i for s's opponent to cite.

A trumping counterexample is a case with the opposite outcome that has all the cited case's similarities and some additional ones. This kind of counterexample trumps the cited case. It is more on point than the cited case because it has a more inclusive set of relevant similarities to the problem. As such, it is a better, more persuasive case than the cited case, and it favors the opponent. More specifically, the set of trumping counterexamples that can be cited by a side, s, in response to a cited case, cc, $TCX_{s,cc}$ is defined as follows:

$$TCX_{s,cc} \equiv \{c_i \mid (c_i \in MOP_s) \land (S_{p,c_i} \supset S_{p,cc})\} \qquad (9.2.7)$$

In English, the set of all cases that a side s can cite as trumping counterexamples to a cited case cc is the set of all most-on-point cases, c_i, such that the outcome of c_i favors s and c_i is more on point than cc.

The salient features of a precedent playing the role of a cited case are its relevant similarities to the problem situation:

A Theory of Case-Based Argument in Hypo

$$S_{p,cc} = F_p \cap F_{cc} \tag{9.2.8}$$

In citing a case, an arguer should emphasize these similarities because they justify the same outcome in the problem as in the cited case.

A major difference between arguing with factors and cases and arguing with factors alone can be demonstrated by the fact that a cited case's salient features include not only the shared factors that favor a conclusion that the plaintiff should win but also those that favor a conclusion that the plaintiff should lose. An arguer who knew only factors and no specific cases might argue for the plaintiff by emphasizing only the pro-plaintiff factors and ignoring the pro-defendant factors. With a specific case that combined the competing factors and whose outcome favored the plaintiff, the arguer has some persuasive evidence that the current dispute should be decided for the plaintiff despite the pro-defendant factors. The past case shows that pro-plaintiff factors outweigh the competing factors.

9.2.2 Distinguished Case

The basic way of responding to a cited case is by distinguishing it. Distinguishing points out the relevant differences between it and the cited case as a way of arguing that the problem should be decided differently.

The best cases for a side to distinguish are the best untrumped cases that the opponent can cite: $BUC_{opp(s)}$ (see definition 9.2.6).

The salient features of a precedent, dc, that s should emphasize in distinguishing it are the relevant differences from s's viewpoint between the problem and the distinguished case, $D_{p,dc}$, as defined in expression 9.1.2.

9.2.3 Counterexample

Another way of responding to a cited case is by citing another precedent as a counterexample to it. There are four kinds of counterexamples in this theory, each involving a case that is "contrary" to the cited case in the sense that it had the opposite outcome, focuses on a different set of salient features, and can be used to disparage the impact of the cited case.

Trumping counterexample: This is a contrary case that has a more inclusive set of relevant similarities to the problem than the cited case. Trumping counterexamples were defined in expression 9.2.7. The salient features of a trumping counterexample (the ones that a side will emphasize in describing the counterexample) are the extra similarities that it shares with the problem that the cited case does not, specifically,

$$S_{p,cex} \setminus S_{p,cc} \qquad (9.2.9)$$

An argument citing a trumping counterexample says, in effect, that when the extra similarities are taken into account, the cited case should not be followed.

As-on-point or partial counterexample: Here a contrary case has the same set or some nonempty subset of similarities to the problem as the cited case. This kind of counterexample shows, somewhat more weakly than a trumping counterexample, that the shared similarities do not always lead to the same outcome as the cited case. The set of as-on-point or partial counterexamples that can be cited by a side, s, in response to a cited case, cc, $ACX_{s,cc}$ is defined as follows:

$$ACX_{s,cc} \equiv \{c_i \mid (c_i \in OP) \wedge (O(c_i) = s) \wedge \\ (S_{p,c_i} \cap S_{p,cc} \neq \emptyset) \wedge (S_{p,c_i} \subseteq S_{p,cc})\} \qquad (9.2.10)$$

In English, the set of all cases that a side s can cite as as-on-point or partial counterexamples to a cited case cc is the set of all cases, c_i, such that the outcome of c_i favors s and c_i shares all or some of the same factors with the problem as cc.

The salient features of an as-on-point or partial counterexample are the similarities that both counterexample and cited case have to the problem:

$$S_{p,cex} \cap S_{p,cc} \qquad (S_{p,cex} \subseteq S_{p,cc}) \qquad (9.2.11)$$

Boundary counterexample: This is a contrary case that is an extreme example of some factor, f^i, that is a relevant similarity between the problem and the cited case and favored the winner of the cited case. The set of boundary counterexamples that can be cited by a side, s, in response to a cited case, cc, $BCX_{s,cc}$, is defined as follows (assume that s is the plaintiff and that defendant won the cited case):

A Theory of Case-Based Argument in Hypo

$$BCX_{s,cc} \equiv \{c_j \mid (O(c_j) = s) \land (c_j \in OP) \land$$
$$(\exists f^i (f^i \in F_{opp(s)}) \land (f^i \in S_{p,cc}) \land$$
$$(f^i \in S_{p,c_j}) \land (M(f^i_{cc}) > M(f^i_{c_j})))\} \quad (9.2.12)$$

In English, the set of all cases that a side s can cite as boundary counterexamples to a cited case cc is the set of all on-point cases, c_j, such that the outcome of c_j favors s and there is some factor, f^i, such that c_j and cc share f^i with the problem, and the magnitude of f^i in cc is greater in favor of s, the plaintiff, than in c_j.

For a given boundary counterexample, cex, the salient features include each factor, f^i, of which the counterexample is a more extreme example than the cited case and the relative magnitudes of f^i in the counterexample and the cited case. By emphasizing that the plaintiff won despite the fact that the counterexample was worse for the plaintiff along factor f^i than the cited case, a boundary counterexample tends to show that f^i is not a very significant factor.

Potentially trumping counterexample: This last counterexample is a contrary case that would be a good counterexample with which to trump the cited case if the problem had certain additional factors. Potentially trumping counterexamples identify ways to strengthen or weaken a side's argument. They make good targets for hypothetical modifications of the problem in which the the potential counterexample would be a real trumping counterexample to a given cited case. The set of potentially trumping counterexamples that can be cited by a side, s, in response to a cited case, cc, $PTCX_{s,cc}$ is defined as follows (let $pvar$ denote a hypothetical variant of the problem):

$$PTCX_{s,cc} \equiv$$
$$\{c_j \mid (O(c_j) = s) \land (\exists pvar(S_{pvar,c_j} \supset S_{p,cc})\} \quad (9.2.13)$$

In English, the set of all cases that a side s can cite as potentially trumping counterexamples to a cited case cc is the set of all cases, c_j, such that the outcome of c_j favors s and there is some hypothetical variant of the problem, $pvar$, such that c_j is more on point with respect to *pvar* than *cc*. Hypo uses a number of heuristics for hypothetically modifying a problem situation to generate *pvar*.

The salient features of a potential counterexample are the extra similarities between it and the hypothetical variant of the problem (*pvar*):

$$S_{pvar,cex} \setminus S_{p,cc} \qquad (9.2.14)$$

These salient features are the difference between the problem situation and a hypothetically modified problem in which a side's arsenal of cases to cite is strengthened by the addition of a new trumping counterexample.

9.2.4 Target for Hypotheticals

A final role of a precedent in this theory is as the target of a hypothetical modification of the problem that would strengthen or weaken the plaintiff's position. The salient features of a case, t, that is a target for a hypothetical variation of another case to be modified (*cmod*) are those factors in $F_t \setminus F_{cmod}$ that are added, or those factors in $S_{cmod,t}$ whose magnitudes are changed, to make the hypothetical more like or more extreme than the target. The set of targets for hypothetical modifications of the problem depends on what the hypothetical is designed to accomplish. For example, the set of potentially trumping counterexamples, $PTCX_{s,cc}$ is the set of targets for hypotheticals in which side s has a stronger response against *cc*.

9.3 Evaluating Precedential Arguments

Here is how Hypo's principal argument evaluation criterion is expressed in terms of the theory. With respect to the ability to cite precedents, a side, s, has a stronger argument if

$$(BUC_s \neq \emptyset) \wedge (BUC_{opp(s)} = \emptyset). \qquad (9.3.15)$$

In English, side s has the stronger argument if only it has best cases to cite for which there are no trumping counterexamples. If neither BUC_s nor $BUC_{opp(s)}$ is empty, then both sides can make strong arguments.

Although the theory permits evaluating competing precedential arguments only to a limited extent, the theory's evaluation criterion assesses the relative qualitative strengths of an argument. The theory does not resort to "nonlegal" criteria for assessing argument strength, such as counting precedents on both sides. On the other hand, the theory does not take into account criteria like the recentness of precedents or the pedigrees of the deciding courts. Such commonly used legal criteria could be incorporated into the theory, for example, to break ties between equally balanced arguments.

9.4 An Example of Computing Salience

The theory's expressions determine the features of a past case that are salient when the case is cited in the four argument roles. Hypo, which implements the theory, tailors its descriptions of a precedent to emphasize the features, specifically factors, that are salient depending on the precedent's argument role and the viewpoint the program takes (for plaintiff or defendant).

A representative sample of the variety of descriptions that Hypo generates for a single case in its knowledge base depending on the argument role and context follows. These alternative descriptions of the *Data General* case are excerpted from the complete 3-Ply Arguments for the *Crown* Extended Example of chapter 5, which are reproduced in figures 9.1 through 9.4.

Descriptions of *Data General* Case in Four Contexts

1. As cited case: Even though plaintiff disclosed its product information to outsiders, plaintiff should win a claim for trade secrets misappropriation. Cite: *Data General*

2. As distinguished case: *Data General* is distinguishable because in *Crown Industries*, plaintiff disclosed its product information in negotiations with defendant. Not so in *Data General*. In *Data General*, plaintiff's disclosures to outsiders were restricted. Not so in *Crown Industries*.

3. As counterexample: *Data General* is more on point [than *Midland Ross*] and held for plaintiff, and plaintiff's disclosures to outsiders were restricted. *Data General* held for plaintiff even though in *Data General* plaintiff disclosed its product information to more outsiders than in *Midland Ross*.

⟹ Point for Plaintiff as Side 1:

Where:

Even Though: Plaintiff disclosed its product information to outsiders.

Plaintiff should win a claim for Trade Secrets Misappropriation.

Cite: Data General Corp. v. Digital Computer Controls Inc. 357 A.2d 105 (Del. Ch. 1975).

⟸ Response for Defendant as Side 2:

Data General Corp. v. Digital Computer Controls Inc. is distinguishable because:
In Crown Industries, plaintiff disclosed its product information in negotiations with defendant. Not so in Data General.
In Data General, plaintiff's disclosures to outsiders were restricted. Not so in Crown Industries.

⟹ Rebuttal for Plaintiff as Side 1: None.

Figure 9.1
Citing and Distinguishing *Data General* Where CFS Is the *Crown* Case

4. As target case: Plaintiff's response would be strengthened if plaintiff's disclosures to outsiders were restricted. Cf. *Data General*.

As the descriptions of the *Data General* case illustrate, Hypo emphasizes various aspects of the case, sometimes focusing on similarities, sometimes differences, sometimes factor magnitudes, sometimes factors significant because they do not apply. The example illustrates how the theory's expressions for salience apply to a particular case cited in a variety of roles. For each of the argument roles, the following discussion demonstrates how the expressions compute the salient features of the *Data General* case. The example involves three factors and four cases. For convenience, the cases are summarized abstractly in terms of an outcome, a set of applicable factors, and the magnitudes of those factors.

The three factors are those associated with three familiar Dimensions:

[1]

$\Longrightarrow$ Point for Defendant as Side 1:

Where: Plaintiff disclosed its product information to outsiders.

Defendant should win a claim for Trade Secrets Misappropriation.

Cite: Midland-Ross Corp. v. Sunbeam Equipment Corp. 316 F. Supp. 171 (W.D. Pa., 1970).

$\Longleftarrow$ Response for Plaintiff as Side 2:

Midland-Ross Corp. v. Sunbeam Equipment Corp. is distinguishable because: In Midland-Ross, plaintiff disclosed its product information to more outsiders than in Crown Industries

Counterexamples:

Data General Corp. v. Digital Computer Controls Inc. 357 A.2d 105 (Del. Ch. 1975), held for plaintiff even though in Data General plaintiff disclosed its product information to more outsiders than in Midland-Ross Corp. v. Sunbeam Equipment Corp.

$\Longrightarrow$ Rebuttal for Defendant as Side 1:

Data General Corp. v. Digital Computer Controls Inc. is distinguishable because:
In Crown Industries, Plaintiff disclosed its product information in negotiations with defendant. Not so in Data General.
In Data General, plaintiff's disclosures to outsiders were restricted. Not so in Crown Industries.

Note:
Plaintiff's response would be strengthened if: Plaintiff's disclosures to outsiders were restricted.
Cf. Data General Corp. v. Digital Computer Controls Inc. 357 A.2d 105 (Del. Ch. 1975)

Figure 9.2
Data General Cited as Boundary and Potentially More-On-Point Counterexamples in Argument [1], *Crown* Extended Example

[5]

$\Longrightarrow$ Point for Defendant as Side 1:

Where: Plaintiff disclosed its product information to outsiders.

Defendant should win a claim for Trade Secrets Misappropriation.

Cite: Midland-Ross Corp. v. Sunbeam Equipment Corp. 316 F. Supp. 171 (W.D. Pa., 1970).

$\Longleftarrow$ Response for Plaintiff as Side 2:

Midland-Ross Corp. v. Sunbeam Equipment Corp. is distinguishable because:

In Midland-Ross, plaintiff disclosed its product information to more outsiders than in Crown Industries—4

Counterexamples:

Data General Corp. v. Digital Computer Controls Inc. 357 A.2d 105 (Del. Ch. 1975), is more on point and held for plaintiff where it was also the case that: Plaintiff's disclosures to outsiders were restricted.

Data General Corp. v. Digital Computer Controls Inc. 357 A.2d 105 (Del. Ch. 1975), held for plaintiff even though in Data General plaintiff disclosed its product information to more outsiders than in Midland-Ross Corp. v. Sunbeam Equipment Corp.

$\Longrightarrow$ Rebuttal for Defendant as Side 1:

Data General Corp. v. Digital Computer Controls Inc. is distinguishable because: In Crown Industries, Plaintiff disclosed its product information in negotiations with defendant. Not so in Data General.

Figure 9.3
Data General Cited as Trumping and Boundary Counterexamples in Argument [5], *Crown* Extended Example

Hypotheticals to Consider on Claim of Trade Secrets Misappropriation in Fact Situation of Crown Industries:

Plaintiff's position would be strengthened in following situations:

Suppose:

Plaintiff's disclosures to outsiders were restricted. Cf. Data General Corp. v. Digital Computer Controls Inc.
357 A.2d 105 (Del. Ch. 1975)

Figure 9.4
Data General Cited as Target for Hypothetical Where a New Point Could Be Made (From *Crown* Extended Example)

1. $f^1 \equiv$ Secrets-Disclosed-Outsiders (Helps defendant (δ) to extent that plaintiff has disclosed secrets to outsiders)

2. $f^2 \equiv$ Outsider-Disclosures-Restricted (Helps plaintiff (π) if all disclosures to outsiders are confidential)

3. $f^3 \equiv$ Disclosure-in-Negotiations (Helps defendant (δ) if plaintiff disclosed secrets to defendant in negotiations)

The four cases are also familiar:

1. *Crown Industries*
   Outcome: Defendant won
   Factors: $\{ f^1 f^3 \}$
   Magnitudes:
   $M(f^1_{Crown}) =$ disclosures to 7 outsiders

2. *Midland Ross*
   Outcome: Defendant won
   Factors: $\{ f^1 \}$
   Magnitudes:
   $M(f^1_{MidlandRoss}) =$ disclosures to 100 outsiders

3. *Data General*
   Outcome: Plaintiff won
   Factors: $\{ f^1 f^2 \}$
   Magnitudes:
   $M(f^1_{DataGeneral}) =$ disclosures to 6,000 outsiders
   $M(f^2_{DataGeneral}) =$ all disclosures restricted

4. *Crown Industries*—Variant
   Outcome: Defendant won
   Factors: $\{\, f^1 f^2 f^3 \,\}$
   Magnitudes:
   $M(f^1_{Crown-var})$ = disclosures to 7 outsiders
   $M(f^2_{Crown-var})$ = all disclosures restricted

9.4.1 Cited Case

Description 1 shows how Hypo describes the *Data General* case as cited case (*cc*), where the problem situation (*p*) is that of the *Crown Industries* case. Using equation 9.1.1, the set of salient features is

$$S_{Crown, DataGeneral} = \{f^1 f^3\} \cap \{f^1 f^2\} = \{f^1\}.$$

Consequently, Hypo's description of the *Data General* case in Description 1 emphasizes f^1 and ignores f^2. Intuitively, this makes sense. To call attention to f^2 at this point would not be tactically sound since f^2 is not a relevant similarity but a relevant difference (it is a pro-plaintiff factor that *Data General* does not share with the problem). It is up to the defendant to point out the differences (which Hypo does in distinguishing).

Note that Hypo prefaces the description with "Even though" in recognition of the fact that although f^1 is a relevant similarity, plaintiff's disclosures to outsiders are not normally reasons for deciding in plaintiff's favor. Had there been some relevant similarities that favored the plaintiff, for example, that the plaintiff had taken substantial precautions to secure its secrets, Hypo would have stated them first. That is, Hypo would say, "Where: plaintiff took substantial security precautions, Even though: plaintiff disclosed its product information to outsiders, plaintiff should win...."

9.4.2 Distinguished Case

The salient features in distinguishing a case are the relevant differences between the problem and the distinguished case, $D_{p,dc}$. Description 2 shows how Hypo describes the *Data General* case as a distinguished case (*dc*), where the problem situation (*p*) again is the *Crown* case. Making the substitutions for the three terms in definition 9.1.2 of relevant differences:

A Theory of Case-Based Argument in Hypo

$$(F_{Crown} \setminus F_{DataGeneral}) \cap F_\delta = \{f^1 f^3\} \setminus \{f^1 f^2\} \cap F_\delta = \{f^3\}$$
$$(F_{DataGeneral} \setminus F_{Crown}) \cap F_\pi = \{f^1 f^2\} \setminus \{f^1 f^3\} \cap F_\pi = \{f^2\}$$
$$\emptyset \quad (M(f^1_{DataGeneral}) \not> M(f^1_{Crown}))$$

The last term is empty because a total of 6,000 disclosures is worse, not better, for plaintiff than 7 disclosures. Taking the union of the terms yields the set of salient differences between the *Crown* case and *Data General*: $D_{Crown, DataGeneral} = \{f^3\} \cup \{f^2\} \cup \emptyset = \{f^3 f^2\}$.

Hypo recites these differences in Description 2. The differences tend to explain away the outcome in *Data General* and show that the *Crown* case need not have the same result.

The analysis allows Hypo to select those differences in factor magnitudes that are salient in a given context. Although the magnitudes of *Data General* and *Crown* along f^1 are different, Hypo sensibly does not call attention to this difference. The difference does not help, indeed it hurts, the defendant's argument. *Crown* is much stronger for plaintiff than *Data General* in terms of the numbers of disclosures to outsiders.

The analysis also allows Hypo to point out those factors that are salient in a context because they do not apply to a case. For example, in the context of distinguishing *Data General*, f^3 is significant because it does not apply to *Data General*. The importance of this "nonfeature" becomes apparent only in the light of the process of distinguishing *Data General* from *Crown*.

9.4.3 Counterexample

Description 3 shows how Hypo describes the *Data General* case as a trumping and boundary counterexample (*cex*). Here, the problem situation (*p*) is a variant of the *Crown* case in which all seven disclosures to outsiders were subject to confidentiality restrictions ($F_{Crown-var} = \{f^1 f^2 f^3\}$ and $M(f^1_{Crown-var}) = 7$) and the case cited for the defendant (*cc*) is the *Midland Ross* case. The salient features when used as a trumping counterexample are (from expression 9.2.9):

$$\{f^1 f^2\} \setminus \{f^1\} = \{f^2\}$$

In the first sentence of Description 3, Hypo cites *Data General* as a counterexample to trump *Midland Ross* and emphasizes the extra similarities that led to the opposite result in *Data General*: f^2.

When used as a boundary counterexample, the salient feature of *Data General* is f^1 because f^1 satisfies the requirement of definition 9.2.12:

$$[f^1 \in F_\delta] \wedge [f^1 \in S_{Crown-var, Midland}] \wedge$$
$$[M(f^1_{Midland}) > M(f^1_{DataGeneral})]$$

In the second sentence of Description 3, Hypo cites *Data General* as a boundary counterexample, emphasizing the fact that the plaintiff won in *Data General* though it was a much worse case than *Crown* in terms of disclosures to outsiders (6,000 outsiders versus 7).

9.4.4 Target for Hypothetical

Description 4 shows how Hypo describes the *Data General* case used as a target for a hypothetical modification of the *Crown* case with the result that *Data General* would become a counterexample with which to trump *Midland Ross*. The salient feature of *Data General* in this context is the extra factor, f_2. ($F_t \setminus F_{cmod} \cap F_\pi = (F_{DataGeneral} \setminus F_{Crown}) \cap F_\pi = \{f^1 f^2\} \setminus \{f^1 f^3\} \cap F_\pi = \{f^2\}$.)

The example has illustrated how Hypo tailors a description of a precedent to suit alternative viewpoints and argument roles. The interpretation of a particular precedent is flexible. For each context, the theory specifies the features of the precedent that are salient.

The theory also accounts for the significance of precedents in an argument. For each argument role, the theory determines the best cases to cite in that role. For example, definition 9.2.6 specifies the best untrumped cases to cite for a side, BUC, and definition 9.2.7 specifies the best precedents to cite as trumping counterexamples, TCX.

Descriptions and examples of how Hypo selects significant cases for making argument points and responses may be found in chapters 5 and 8. Hypo's mechanisms for selecting best cases to cite and counterexamples, in effect, implement the definitions of BUC, TCX, and $PTCX$.

9.5 Factor Weights

The theory of case-based argument assumes that cases can be represented as collections factors to which a decision maker assigns an outcome. The theory describes the precedential arguments and some relatively weak criteria for evaluating those arguments. It does not provide a formula or algorithm that the decision maker can apply to decide a case.

Given the theory's reliance on factors, it is tempting to ask if there is some mathematical method for combining factors to come to a decision. In any given case, the factors may compete, some favoring an outcome and others militating against it. If it were possible to assign numerical weights to the factors or organize them into a hierarchy, a computer program could sum the competing factors and assign an outcome.

That is not the approach taken in Hypo. I have avoided assigning weights to factors because the concept of a factor's weight, though intuitively attractive, is, on closer view, highly problematic. A factor's weight in an argument is some kind of measure of the degree of support it lends to a conclusion. The weight should be distinguished from its magnitude. I have defined a factor's magnitude as a value along a predefined range of possible values that indicates how extreme a case is as an example of that factor.

For a number of reasons, representing a factor's weight as a number or position in a hierarchy is problematic.

- A factor's weight is highly contextual and depends on individual problem situations. Although an attorney may consider one factor generally to be more important than another, she or he is always mindful of peculiar cases where the opposite is true because of the relative magnitudes of the factors, the fact that other factors apply to complicate matters, or because some judge or jurisdiction simply treats them that way.

- Domain experts may not reason in terms of weighting schemes, especially numerical ones. Attorneys generally concede that factors are useful in analyzing legal problems, but they rarely are willing to apply weights or probabilities to those factors.

- Weighting factors is not justified by any authoritative means. Even if attorneys did assign weights to factors, they would disagree on what those weights should be. In addition, attorneys would not actually be able to cite factor weights in their arguments to a court because weighting is not an accepted kind of argument.

- Premature commitment to a weighting scheme may cut off fruitful lines of inquiry. A rigid scheme may cause an attorney to overlook a factor that, although not generally important, is crucial in a particular situation.

- Reduction to numerical weights obliterates information needed for symbolic comparison of cases. The business of attorneys is arguing about the competing factors in the light of the precedents. If the factors are collapsed into a number, there is nothing left to argue about.

Given these problems, the theory does not assign weights to factors. Instead, the precedent-citing arguments symbolically represent the weights of competing factors. The theory's expressions for the most significant cases to cite in the argument roles and their salient features in those roles in effect determine the factors that are most weighty in the context of a particular fact situation and CKB. Those are the factors that are at the crux of the argument.

To put the point another way, what does it mean in the law to say that of two competing factors, A and B, factor A has more weight? As a practical matter of legal argument, one has to be able to produce some demonstration that factor A is more important. For example, one could find two cases, each the same except for the presence of factor A but where the outcomes differ by virtue of the extra factor. Or one could find a case involving A and B in which factor B is exaggerated to an extreme value with no difference in outcome. If no such cases are to be found, then one could pose hypothetical cases to demonstrate the point. The demonstration, of course, is not unassailable. The opponent may be able to distinguish the case or cite a counterexample. A good counterexample would be another case involving factors A and B where A did not affect the outcome. That is the kind of symbolic reasoning about factors and cases that Hypo performs. Its precedent-citing arguments, including distinguishing, counterexamples, and hypotheticals, are demonstrations for and against an assertion that competing factors should be resolved in a particular way.

In procedural terms, Hypo deals symbolically with factor weights in three phases. Having determined the factors that apply to the problem and selected the most-on-point cases, Hypo clusters the applicable factors according to how they appear in the most-on-point cases, interprets the effect of the clustered factors in the light of the outcomes of the most-on-point cases, and criticizes and tests the interpretations in the light of the salient differences among the most-on-point cases by distinguishing precedents, citing counterexamples, and posing hypotheticals that change magnitudes and combinations of factors in the problem.

The three phases, described in more detail in [Ashley and Rissland 1988b], enable Hypo to reason about the relative significance of the competing factors in the problem situation in the light of how the most analogous precedents have dealt with those factors.

In the Cluster Phase, Hypo divides the most-on-point cases into groups, each group containing all of the most-on-point cases that share the same cluster of factors with the problem situation. These groups or equivalence classes correspond to the nodes of the Claim Lattice that contain most-on-point cases. In grouping these cases, Hypo temporarily ignores certain differences between the precedents in a group, such as differences in factor magnitudes or extra factors that apply to one case in the group but not to others.

In the Interpretation Phase, Hypo assigns a combined effect to each cluster of factors according to the outcomes of the associated most-on-point cases. This is easy if all of the cases in the group have the same outcome; if all of the cases in the group held for the plaintiff, then Hypo treats the associated cluster of factors as favoring the plaintiff. Often, however, the cases in a group do not have the same outcome; some favor the plaintiff, and others favor the defendant. When that happens, Hypo applies heuristics in trying to settle the tie. The program attacks one of the conflicting interpretations by attacking the associated precedents. It does so by distinguishing the precedents from the problem situation, now taking into account the differences previously ignored in the Cluster Phase. It attempts to explain away the result in a particular most-on-point case by pointing out relevant differences (unshared factors or a difference in magnitudes of a shared factor).

In the Criticize and Test Phase, Hypo attacks an interpretation of a cluster of factors by pointing out various kinds of counterexamples. It cites a counterexample to show that even an extreme example of a particular factor in the cluster does not warrant a given outcome (a boundary counterexample), or it suggests hypothetical changes in the problem situation, adding factors that would lead to the opposite result by promoting one case in the group into a trumping counterexample.

The outputs of the Interpretation and Criticize and Test Phases are Hypo's 3-Ply Arguments citing the most-on-point precedents, distinguishing them, citing counterexamples, and posing hypotheticals. In the context of the example of the previous section, when Hypo poses *Data General* as a boundary counterexample, in effect, it criticizes the interpretation of factor f^1 as favoring the defendant. Similarly when Hypo poses *Data General* as a potentially trumping counterexample, it suggests that a new cluster consisting of f^1 and f^2 would also lead to a different interpretation of f^1. When it distinguishes *Data General* from the defendant's viewpoint, Hypo supports the interpretation that factor f^1 favors defendant by attempting to explain away the *Data General* case.

Although by the end of the Criticize and Test Phase, Hypo has not assigned actual weights to the competing factors, it has dealt symbolically with the problem of weighting. It has generated precedent-citing arguments in favor of alternative interpretations of the weights of the factors within the context of the problem.

9.6 Computing Citation Labels

Hypo's computational expressions for the best cases to cite provide a computational interpretation of a standard legal method for characterizing the significance of precedents, *Blue Book* citations.

Hypo summarizes the significance of precedents with citation displays. Citation displays summarize the 3-Ply Arguments and characterize the degree of support that precedents lend to the proposition that a side should win a claim. The precedents are labeled with "citation signals" that show the strength of the precedential support.

In the legal profession, standards have been adopted for the use and interpretation of citations. The most influential standard setter is the so-called *Blue Book, A Uniform System of Citation*, published by the Harvard Law Review Association. A sampling of standard citation signals and their legal meanings is set forth below (see [BlueBook 1986, pp. 6–7]):

1. *Accord* or [no signal]: directly supports

2. *See*: supports

3. *Cf.*: analogously supports

4. *Contra*: directly supports contrary

5. *But See*: supports contrary

6. *But Cf.*: supports analogous contrary

For example, an "Accord" label means that a precedent strongly supports a proposition. "Contra" means that it directly supports the contrary. Note that the default, no signal at all, is equivalent to "Accord" (no signal indicates that the cited case directly supports the proposition).

Hypo has computational equivalents of the *Blue Book* citation signals, defined in terms of Hypo's various categories of most analogous cases and counterexamples. For each signal, one could write an expression in terms of the sets defined above, MOP, BUC, TCX, BCX, $PTCX$, which would define a computational meaning for the signal. Hypo's computational equivalents are

1. *Accord* or [no signal]: best pro case to cite, no trumping counterexamples

2. *See*: relevant pro case, not best untrumped case to cite

3. *Cf.*: most-on-point, near-miss pro case

4. *Contra*: Trumping or as-on-point counterexample

5. *But See*: Boundary or partial counterexample

6. *But Cf.*: Potentially more-on-point counterexample

With computational definitions of the signals, Hypo can summarize the significance of precedents in a manner familiar to attorneys. An "Accord" label (and the default of no signal) shows that a precedent strongly supports the proposition that a side should win a claim. A "See" cite conveys less support. "Contra," "But See," and "But Cf." labels are warning signals; they label cases that may seriously affect the reliability of the precedent in supporting the proposition. A "Contra" case is a counterexample that yields just as strong or stronger support for the opposite side on the proposition. "But See" cases yield some support for the opposite side. "But Cf." indicates that the listed cases may potentially support the opposite side and should be checked.

The information that Hypo's citation displays summarize about a precedent's contextual significance can be played out in a 3-Ply Argument. The citation summaries that introduce the 3-Ply Arguments of the Extended Examples in chapter 5 and appendix H illustrate some simple citation displays where the "[no signal]" default option indicates that the listed cases directly support the proposition that a party should win the claim (the cases are the best ones to cite and have no trumping counterexamples). In addition, Hypo's lists of suggested hypotheticals following the 3-Ply Arguments use "cf." cites to indicate that they potentially support the proposition. (See figures 9.2 and 9.4.)

As summaries of precedential support, citation displays have much of the utility of published compilations of citations like those of legal treatises described in chapter 2, but the displays are compiled dynamically in the light of the cases in the CKB and tailored to the specific fact situation presented by the attorney. Citation displays also flag the changes in an argument caused by hypothetical changes to the facts. For example, the stronger argument that plaintiff can make in the hypothetical variant of the *Crown* case in chapter 5 is flagged by the changes in the cases citable in the citation summary where *Data General* gets promoted from a "cf." cite in the former display to a full "Accord" in the latter.

The theory's computational interpretations of *Blue Book* signals will not correspond to every attorney's sense of their meanings. Indeed, the accepted meanings of the signals are not very well specified and often controversial. The methodological point is that the partial theory's definitions supply the signals with a meaning that is sufficiently concrete for a computerized case retrieval system to compute them but also flexible enough for the system to apply them intelligently in context.

9.7 Conclusion

In Hypo's theory, as in law, determining the features of a precedent that are salient and the precedents that are significant in an argument depends on context: the facts of the problem, the facts and outcomes of other cases in the CKB, the viewpoint of the arguer, and the contextual role of the case in the argument.

The theory's formulas for defining the salience and significance of precedents in arguments take all of these contextual components into account. Although the theory does not assign numerical weights to factors, Hypo's arguments symbolically represent alternative interpretations of the weights of competing factors in the context of a particular problem.

10 Evaluating Hypo's Performance

The Hypo program performs significant tasks of legal reasoning. Hypo manipulates precedents to the same ends as attorneys, and with substantially similar results: to make and respond to legal points about a fact situation, to select and highlight the best precedents for each side, to evaluate the strengths of each side's argument, to pose hypotheticals to focus on factual issues important in the light of the arguments.

10.1 Comparing Hypo's Points and Responses to Court Opinions

Hypo's facility for reasoning with precedents is demonstrated by comparing Hypo's output to that of actual judges and attorneys. Current fact situations based on legal cases were submitted to Hypo. The 3-Ply Arguments and hypotheticals Hypo posed were compared to the points and responses made in the attorneys' briefs or the judges' opinions. The comparisons focused on the following questions: Did Hypo's evaluation of the relative overall strength of the parties' arguments tally with who won the case? Did Hypo make points and responses for each side citing the same precedents and in the same way as the precedents were cited in the briefs and opinions? Did Hypo's citation of precedents and posing of hypotheticals raise the same issues as were raised in the briefs and opinions?

Detailed comparisons were undertaken for the following cases:

- *USM Corp. v. Marson Fastener Corp.* 379 Mass. 90 (1979). Hypo's outputs are shown in appendix H.

- *Crown Industries, Inc. v. Kawneer Co.* 335 F. Supp. 749 (N.D. Ill., 1971). Hypo's outputs are shown in the *Crown* Extended Example in chapter 5.

- *Amoco Production Co. v. Lindley* 600 P.2d 733. Hypo's outputs are shown in the outputs for the *Amexxco* example in appendix H.

- *Structural Dynamics Research Corp. v. Engineering Mechanics Research Corp.* 401 F. Supp. 1102 (E.D. Mich., 1975). Hypo's outputs are shown in appendix H.

10.1.1 USM Corp. v. Marson

Opinion and Briefs The case of *USM Corp. v. Marson Fastener Corp.* involved a claim by plaintiff USM Corp. that defendant Marson Fastener misappropriated its trade secrets concerning a rivet-making machine. The main issue the court addressed in its opinion was whether the plaintiff had taken adequate steps to protect its supposed trade secrets. The court decided the case in favor of the plaintiff, holding that USM Corp. had taken adequate steps.

Some excerpts of the Court's opinion in the *USM Corp.* case are set forth in appendix I. The court justified holding for the plaintiff by analogizing the fact situation to cases that held for the plaintiff like *Space Aero* and *Eastern Marble*. It distinguished cases that held for the defendant like *Motorola, Inc.* and the *Healy* case. The argument in the court's opinion was the culmination of a series of previous arguments in the case. Both plaintiff and defendant had submitted to the judge formal written arguments, known as briefs, that set out a summary description of the facts of the case and the law from each side's viewpoint. In the briefs, the parties justify their positions by citing analogous precedent cases and by distinguishing the opponent's cases. Excerpts from the parties' briefs are presented in appendix I.

The main points and responses drawn from the court's opinion and the briefs of plaintiff and defendant may be summarized as follows.

The court (and plaintiff) favorably cited the *Space Aero* and *Eastern Marble* cases where plaintiff took adequate measures to protect its trade secrets. In *Eastern Marble* as in *USM*, the plaintiff had undertaken security measures to protect its trade secrets. 379 Mass. at 102, 103.

The court (and plaintiff) distinguished the pro-defendant *Healy* case by contrasting the precautions taken by USM Corp. with the lack of precautions taken by the plaintiff in that case. 379 Mass. at 102.

Defendant distinguished *Eastern Marble* by pointing out that it involved specific nondisclosure agreements between the plaintiff and its employee and cited the *Motorola* case where the court declared that absent specific nondisclosure agreements, the defendant should win.

The court responded by distinguishing *Motorola, Inc.* as involving inadequate security measures, contrasted that case with *Plant Industries* where the security measures were adequate, and cited a counterexample, the *A. H. Emery Co.* case, where detailed drawings and blueprints were protected despite the absence of express warnings about what information was confidential, to show that the absence of warnings did not matter. The court also cited the *Schulenburg* case for the proposition that blueprints and drawings may be trade secrets. 379 Mass. 100.

Hypo's Citation Summary, 3-Ply Arguments, and Hypotheticals As shown in the Citation Summary for *USM* in appendix H, Hypo also determined that plaintiff had the stronger argument on a claim for breach of trade secrets misappropriation and cited as plaintiff's most supportive cases (the best cases to cite with no trumping counterexamples) two cases that the court had relied on: *Space Aero* and *Plant Industries*. The other case Hypo cited, *Peggy Lawton Kitchens*, was decided in 1984 and was not in existence when the *USM* case opinion was written.

A comparison of Hypo's selections of analogous precedents for the *USM* case, shown in figures 8.3 and 8.4, and the cases cited in the court's opinion shows the following results:

Of the nine cases Hypo, after its own analysis of the fact situation, selected as plaintiff's best cases to cite, seven of the cases had actually been cited by the court as supporting the plaintiff's side. Of the other two cases, one was the more recent *Kitchens* case, and the other was a hypothetical fact situation in Hypo's CKB.

Of the three cases Hypo chose as defendant's most-on-point cases, one was the *Healy* case, which the court distinguished, one was decided subsequent to the date of the *USM* decision, and the last was not mentioned by the court.

With respect to the merits of the trade secrets misappropriation claim, the court cited or distinguished thirty-one cases that Hypo did not cite because none of the cases is in the CKB. Of the ten cases in Hypo's CKB that were either cited or distinguished by the court, Hypo selected nine of them as most-on-point or best cases. Hypo treated only one, the *Structural Dynamics* case, as irrelevant to the fact situation. Of five cases (*Telex, Kewanee, Analogic, Amoco*, and *Pressure Science*) not cited by the court but that Hypo treated as important (most-on-point or best case to cite), the *Amoco* case postdated the *USM* decision.

Comparison with the Hypo-generated 3-Ply Arguments for *USM* in appendix H shows that Hypo identified the major points and responses. In the 3-Ply Arguments, Hypo cited or distinguished the following cases in ways very similar to the court:

In Arguments [6] and [7], Hypo cited the *Space Aero* and *Eastern Marble* cases for the plaintiff, drawing the analogy to the fact that plaintiffs adopted security measures in each. In responding to *Eastern Marble*, by posing *Healy* as an as-on-point counterexample, Hypo evidenced the same juxtaposition of conflicting precedents that the actual arguers and the court focused on. Hypo also distinguished the *Eastern Marble* case in the same way as the defendant did, by focusing on the nondisclosure agreement between plaintiff and defendant in that case.

In Arguments [6] and [8], Hypo distinguished the *Healy* case in the same way that the court did by pointing out that the plaintiff in *USM* took more security measures than in *Healy*. In addition, Hypo suggests a way of distinguishing *Healy* that the court did not think of by focusing on the competitive advantage gained by the defendant in *USM*.

As shown in Argument [9], Hypo distinguished the *Motorola* case from the *Eastern Marble* case in the same way that the court did–by focusing on the greater security measures taken in the latter. Argument [9] was generated with *Eastern Marble* as the cfs.

10.1.2 *Crown v. Kawneer*

Hypo's behavior also comports well with the way courts analyzed and decided *Crown Industries, Inc. v. Kawneer Co.* and similar cases. The fact situation of *Crown* is described in chapter 5. The court held in favor of the defendant, Kawneer, where the plaintiff had made disclosures of its supposed trade secrets to various outsiders.

Court Opinions The following quotations indicate how the court in *Crown* and in two other cases raising similar issues made arguments citing or distinguishing the nearly identical *Midland-Ross* and *Yokana* cases. This is how the court analyzed the *Crown* case in its opinion:

> Even though the Plaintiff's power packs, exemplified by PX-121, might have had to be rendered inoperative and examined by an engineer in order to discover the alleged trade secrets contained therein, the sale of the power packs nevertheless constituted a public disclosure which defeats a claim founded upon alleged misappropriation of the trade secrets allegedly contained in the power packs. *Midland-Ross Corp. v. Sunbeam Equipment Co.*, 316 F. Supp. 171, 177 (W.D. Pa. 1970), affirmed, 435 F.2d 159 (3d Cir. 1970). 335 F. Supp. at 761.

No confidential relationship existed between the Plaintiff, Crown, and the Defendant, Kawneer, because Plaintiff never requested Defendant to keep the nature or details of Plaintiff's power pack in confidence; nor was the relationship between Plaintiff and Defendant of the type from which such a confidential relationship could be implied. 335 F. Supp. at 762.

In another case with similar issues, *National Rejectors, Inc. v. Trieman* 409 S.W.2d 1, 40–42 (Sup. Ct. Mo., 1966), the court said,

[W]e do find some significant parallels between the facts of this case and those of *Midland-Ross Corporation v. Yokana* (D.C.N.J.), 185 F. Supp. 594 [The *Yokana* case involved the same plaintiff as *Midland-Ross Corp. v. Sunbeam Equipment Co.* and the same defense that plaintiff had disclosed its secrets to outsiders].... Thus the claim of trade secrets by National and by plaintiff in Midland-Ross have essentially the same basis.... What was lacking in *Yokana* as in this case, was any evidence that, prior to defendant's competition, plaintiff considered the information which Yokana sought to use trade secrets. The court pointed out that plaintiff's blueprints in *Midland-Ross* were furnished plaintiff's suppliers and customers and potential customers. The court found an absence of precautions on the part of plaintiff to keep secret information regarding its machines.

Although the following cases do not parallel the present case as closely as *Yokana* our conclusion here is consistent with that reached in [citing and describing other cases].

Not only are the facts of *Midland-Ross Corporation v. Yokana* comparable to those in this situation, but we find the relief afforded in that case also appropriate in this.

In *Mixing Equipment Co. v. Philadelphia Gear, Inc.*, 436 F.2d 1308, 1315 (3d Cir., 1971), also a case with issues similar to *Crown*, the court distinguished the *Yokana* case as follows: "[Another case] and *Midland-Ross Corp. v. Yokana*, 293 F.2d 411 (3 Cir. 1961) cited by appellants are inapposite. They involve situations in which restrictive covenants had not been utilized by the former employer."

Hypo's Citation Summary, 3-Ply Arguments, and Hypotheticals Like the court, Hypo determined that the defendant had the stronger argument. (Hypo's outputs for the *Crown* case are shown in chapter 5.) In its selection of the *Midland-Ross* and *Yokana* cases as among defendant's best cases to cite, Hypo agreed with the courts in *Crown* and the other cases. Hypo's analysis of the cfs by comparing and contrasting it with the most analogous cases is similar to that actually performed by the courts, and, in particular, the points in Arguments [1] and [2] show that Hypo draws the same analogy as the courts did. In both arguments, Hypo's distinction between the *Data General* case and the cfs is the obverse of the court's distinction between the *Yokana* case and the fact situation in *Mixing Equipment*.

Arguments [3] and [4] show that, like the courts, Hypo also addresses the issue of Crown's having disclosed its information to the defendant without having secured a confidentiality agreement. The suggested hypotheticals focus on how Crown's argument would be improved if the plaintiff and defendant had entered into a nondisclosure agreement.

10.1.3 *Amoco Production Co. v. Lindley*

In several important respects, Hypo's analysis of the *Amexxco* fact situation of chapter 2 compares favorably with that of the court in *Amoco Production Co. v. Lindley*, 609 P.2d 733 (Okla., 1980) upon which the case was based. In all material respects, the *Amexxco* fact situation closely tracks that of the *Amoco Production* case. New names for the parties and products were substituted.

The Court's Opinion A description of the *Amoco Production* case is set forth in appendix E. The court held for the defendant Lindley where Lindley was the sole developer of the Lindley system, a program to analyze oil well probe information, and although Lindley had entered into a nondisclosure agreement, the agreement did not specifically refer to the Lindley system. The court said,

> [Other] user manuals [of the plaintiff] were stamped confidential, numbered, and controlled centrally by management. This was not true of the Lindley System. Trade secret status is difficult to establish and often entails establishing that affirmative and elaborate steps were taken to insure that the secret claimed would remain so. *Telex Corp. v. International Business Machines Corp.*, 367 F. Supp. 258 (N.D. Okl. 1973), rev'd on other grounds, 510 F.2d 894 (10th Cir. 1975).... 609 P.2d at 743.
>
> In *Structural Dynamics Res. Corp. v. Engineering Mechanics Res. Corp.*, 401 F. Supp. 1102 (E.D. Mich. 1975), the Court dealt with charges against three former employees of Structural Dynamics Research Corp. [S.-D.R.C.] for unfair competition, misappropriation, and misuse of confidential trade secret material and breach of contractual duty not to disclose confidential information.... This language [of the S.D.R.C. contract with its employees] was embracive enough to cover the subsequent actions of defendants in setting up a business using a computer system very similar to the one they had created for their former employer. The language of the Amoco employment

contract is not so comprehensive. 609 P.2d at 744, 745.

Hypo's Citation Summary, 3-Ply Arguments, and Hypotheticals Hypo's Citation Summary for the *Amoco* case is shown below:

Hypo's Citation Summary for *Amoco*

3-Ply Arguments for Best Cases to Cite on Claim of Trade Secrets Misappropriation in Fact Situation of Amoco:

On a claim for Trade Secrets Misappropriation, plaintiff can make a stronger argument. Plaintiff can cite the following cases for which there are no more-on-point counterexamples:

Structural Dynamics Research Corp. v. Engineering Mechanics Research Corp. 401 F. Supp. 1102 (E.D. Mich., 1975)

Eastern Marble Products Corp. v. Roman Marble, Inc. 364 N.E.2d 799 (Mass. 1977)

Although Hypo determined that the plaintiff had a stronger argument (the court held for defendant) like the court, Hypo treated the *Structural Dynamics* case as one of plaintiff's strongest cases to cite. Hypo's outputs for the *Amexxco* fact situation are shown in appendix H. There Hypo determined that both sides had a strong argument of a claim for trade secrets misappropriation. Hypo did so because it cited the *Amoco* case for the plaintiff. That, of course, was not an option for the court that decided the *Amoco* case.

The 3-Ply Arguments and hypotheticals that Hypo made for the *Amoco* case are similar to those shown for the *Amexxco* fact situation in appendix H. Comparison of Argument [2] with above-quoted language shows that Hypo distinguished *Structural Dynamics* for the defendant in the same way that the court did; by pointing out the difference in the specificity of the agreements. In the absence of a trumping counterexample, the court gave greater weight to that distinction than Hypo did. Argument [5] shows, however, that Hypo analyzed the issue of the employee's having been sole developer of the trade secrets in the same way that the court did. Note how Hypo responded to citation of the *Wexler* case by focusing on the fact that there was a nondisclosure agreement in *Amexxco*, a distinction that made *Structural Dynamics* into a pro-plaintiff counterexample.

Argument [1] shows that Hypo focused, as the court did, on the issue of how many security measures the plaintiff took. Hypo distinguished the *Eastern Marble* case by pointing out that plaintiff there took more precautions than in *Amexxco*.

Hypo's citations of cases, particularly the suggested targets for hypotheticals, including the *Telex* case, are used in much the same way that the court used them to guide the inquiry as to what facts to look for and how to evaluate them legally. The court in the *Amoco* case did not decide the merits of the trade secrets claim but instead sent the case back to the trial court for further action. In effect, the court's citing cases like *Telex* and *Structural Dynamics* was to instruct the lower court as to the factual findings that would be significant.

10.1.4 *Structural Dynamics v. Engineering Mechanics*

The Court's Opinion The *Structural Dynamics* case is summarized in chapter 8. The court addressed claims for breach of a nondisclosure agreement and for trade secrets misappropriation. It held in favor of the plaintiff's claim for breach of the nondisclosure agreement. The court indicated, however, that since the defendant employees were the sole developers of the trade secret information, it would have held against plaintiff's trade secrets claim except for the fact that the employees had also entered into an agreement not to disclose confidential information to outsiders. The court said,

In this case Surana and Kothawala [the defendant employees] did not obtain the claimed trade secrets through improper means. In substantial measure they were the developers and innovators.... In such a case, absent an express contractual obligation by the employee not to use or disclose such confidential information acquired during his employment adverse to his employer's interest, he is free to use or disclose it in subsequent employment activity.

In *Wexler v. Greenberg*, 399 Pa. 569, 160 A.2d 430 (1960), the Pennsylvania Supreme Court held that in the absence of a contractual obligation not to use or disclose, no duty arose from the employment relationship itself that would prevent a chemist from using and disclosing secret chemical formulae developed by him in the course of his former employment. The court distinguished the cases in which an employer discloses to his employee a preexisting trade secret from those in which the employee himself develops the trade secret sought to be protected. 101 F. Supp. at 1111, 2.

A quantity of documents belonging to SDRC were also found in possession of defendants when this action was commenced. 101 F. Supp. at 1116.

Although SDRC did not use the ultimate in policing measures, the professional calibre of its employees, and the nature of its development work made heavy-handed measures unnecessary. Moreover, the confidential nature of development work was specifically called to each employee's attention in his individual confidential disclosure agreement. 101 F. Supp. at 1117.

Hypo's Citation Summary, 3-Ply Arguments, and Hypotheticals Like the court, Hypo treated the fact situation as raising claims for both breach of a nondisclosure agreement and trade secrets misappropriation. On the claim for trade secrets misappropriation, Hypo determined that both sides could make strong arguments. On the claim of breach of a nondisclosure agreement, Hypo came to the same conclusion as the court that the plaintiff had the stronger argument.

Although the cases that Hypo relied on postdated the *Structural Dynamics* case, examination of Hypo's points in Arguments [1] and [2] shows that Hypo focused on the same issues important to the court: that plaintiff and defendant entered into nondisclosure agreements, that the defendants were the sole developers of the trade secrets, and that the employees brought various product development tools with them from the plaintiff.

Argument [3] shows that Hypo distinguishes the *Wexler* case just as the court did: by focusing on the fact that the employee had not entered into a nondisclosure agreement.

10.2 Comparing Hypo's Citation Displays to Treatise Notes

Hypo's Citation Summaries, 3-Ply Arguments, and Suggested Hypotheticals compare favorably with the compilations of footnotes in legal treatises. Figure 10.1 shows cases cited in various footnotes having to do with the effect of disclosures to outsiders. Hypo's outputs for the *Crown* case have much of the utility for helping an attorney to plan an argument that the compilations of citations in the treatise footnotes have. The difference is that whereas an attorney needs to find the right treatise footnotes manually, Hypo generates the compilation dynamically and automatically from its analysis of the cfs.

Legal Proposition: When a product is marketed, put on display or advertised in such a manner as to allow its secret to be known, the "secret" is lost.

Authorities

Crown Industries, Inc. v. Kawneer Co., 335 F. Supp. 749, 761 (N.D. Ill. 1971) (sale terminates trade secret status even if product would have to be rendered inoperative and disassembled by an engineer, i.e., if product that can be readily reverse engineered is sold, secrecy is lost),

Midland-Ross Corp. v. Sunbeam Equipment Corp., 316 F. Supp. 171 (W.D. Pa.) *aff'd*, 435 F.2d 159 (3d Cir. 1970) (disclosure of trade secret by reason of operating instructions provided to customers),

Speedry Chems. & Prods., Inc. v. Carter's Ink Co., 306 F.2d 328, 334 (2d Cir. 1962),

Cf. *Telex Corp. v. IBM*, 367 F. Supp. 258, 358 (N.D. Okla. 1973), *antitrust aspects rev'd, trade secret aspects aff'd although computation of damages modified*, 510 F.2d 894, (10th Cir. 1975) (although some of IBM's trade secrets lost through IBM's marketing products, Telex's pervasive, willful trade secret misappropriation grounds for injunctive relief designed to limit further misappropriation),

But cf. *Data Gen. Corp. v. Digital Computer Controls, Inc.*, 357 A.2d 105 (Del. Ch. 1975) (despite arguably broad distribution of maintenance manual—restrictively legended—from which defendant copied plaintiff's minicomputer circuitry, court found (a) trade secret continued and (b) an absence of independent development by defendant),

Figure 10.1
Sample Compilation of Citations Excerpts from three footnotes, citing more than 100 cases, in the legal treatise *Milgrim on Trade Secrets*, vol. 12, sec. 2.05[2], nn. 8–10.

10.3 Discussion

Hypo is a promising prototype of an automated "brief writers' assistant." Attorneys need to find precedents and to organize them into arguments about a fact situation. That is what Hypo does. Although Hypo's judgments about the overall strength of an argument do not always coincide with the courts' ultimate decisions, nevertheless, Hypo treats as significant many of the same precedents that the courts do, demonstrates both sides of an argument based on the precedents, and distinguishes and cites counterexamples to the precedents in the same way as the courts.

Empirical experiments are planned to provide a more detailed benchmark of Hypo's performance and in particular to confirm what we know in an informal way: Hypo's arguments and hypotheticals impress attorneys as reasonable from a legal viewpoint and as helpful pointers to useful precedents organized according to their utility in arguments. In one experiment, modeled on the Mycin evaluation [Yu et al. 1984], subjects (lawyers and law students) will be provided with a hypothetical fact situation and the same cases that Hypo has in its CKB. They will be asked to select the cases that they would cite in favor of each side in the fact situation. For the cases they select, they will also be asked to outline a point citing the case for a side, a response to the point on behalf of the opponent, and a rebuttal. In a blind test, legal experts will be provided the subjects' outputs, as well as Hypo's selections of cases and 3-Ply Arguments, and asked to rank them according to acceptability. The experiment will show whether Hypo performs the tasks of selecting and organizing precedents for arguments on a par with the subjects.

As the size and scope of Hypo's CKB expands, it will be possible to compare its performance with those of existing full text retrieval systems like Lexis and Westlaw insofar as the quality of the assistance they give to attorneys who need to make arguments about specific fact situations.

11 Adversarial Case-Based Reasoning beyond the Law

Lawyers are not the only ones who argue with cases. Although up to this point, we have focused on legal cases, adversarial case-based reasoning is a general phenomenon.

11.1 Examples

11.1.1 An Everyday Example

All of us reason adversarially with cases every day. Consider this example:

> George, a twelve year old whose birthday is next month, argues with his overprotective parents because they will not allow him to go to the midnight showing of *Rocky Horror Picture Show*.
>
> George: "That's not fair. You let Sarah go to see that movie!" (Sarah is George's fifteen-year-old sister.)
>
> Parents: "Your sister can go because she is three years older than you are."
>
> George: "Why does *that* make any difference?"
>
> Parents:
> - i. "Your sister is more mature than you are."
> - ii. "The movie gets out too late; it's past your bedtime."
> - iii. "The movie is rated PG-13; it's for teenagers."
>
> George:
> - a. "But I *am* a teenager! I'm going to be 13 next month."
> - b. "Noah is 12, and his parents let *him* go see it."
> - c. "Great! On a VCR I could see it but not at the movies!"

Hallmarks of Adversarial Reasoning with Cases George's arguments show some of the hallmarks of arguing with cases. Indeed, like most other children, George shows a certain aptitude for arguing like a Philadelphia lawyer. Below are some similarities.

Arguing with cases is a basic kind of argument. In order to persuade, an arguer often cites a similar prior case as a justification for doing the same thing in a new case, a justification that needs to be honored, if only in the breach, by giving a reason for not following it. (Little brothers making the fairness argument often cite their big sisters as similar cases, at least for that purpose.)

The arguers share expectations about how to interpret the case-based arguments. In particular, they expect that (a) the poser would like his own case, α, to be treated in the same way as the posed analogous case, β, was treated (little brother wants to go to the movies too); (b) there are some particular similarities between α and β; and (c) those similarities justify, or at least purport to justify, treating the two cases in the same way. The common interpretation guides common ways of responding to the argument.

The arguers usually dispute the existence or significance of the purported similarities. Implicitly, the parents' response denies the implied assertion that common origin of sister and brother justifies allowing the latter to go to this movie.

Being able to spell out why two cases are relevantly different is just as important as being able to tell why they are similar. In distinguishing the allegedly similar case, the arguers point out what is different about the two cases and why that difference justifies not treating the cases the same way. For example, the parents try to distinguish the brother's case from the sister's. They point out factual differences (the children's ages, maturity, and bedtimes), as well as theoretical justifications (why the differences matter, ranging from the invocation of a simple rule that a movie should only be seen by the age group for which it is rated to an implied, complex theory about certain movies requiring maturity and the relation of children's ages to maturity).

The dialectical need to distinguish drives the distinguisher both to investigate for new differences and to find or create theories that assign the desired significance to the differences. The factual difference and the theoretical justification are, of course, intimately related. Consider some other (even more dubious) parental distinctions:

  iv. "Sarah is a girl, and you're a boy."
  v. "Sarah has more money than you do."
  vi. "Sarah has more homework than you do."

The fact that George and his sister are of different gender, for example, may not appear relevant except, arguably, in the light of the theory that girls mature faster than boys and are thus better equipped to deal with mature themes sooner. The fact that George's sister has more money may be a relevant difference, but the theory on which this difference is relevant only confirms George's point that his parents do indeed treat their children inequitably. Finally, there seems to be no theory on which the sister's greater homework burden is a relevant difference. On the contrary, this difference works in George's favor.

Another way to respond to the allegedly similar case is to cite a counterexample, real or hypothetical. For instance, George cites Noah's case as a counterexample to his parents' assertion that the movie is only for thirteen-year-olds and up. As an instance of a hypothetical counterexample, the parents might say, "If we had known that your sister was going to see *that* particular movie, we would never have given our permission."

Much of the dispute centers around the applicability of rules whose predicates are not well defined. The meaning of even a common term like "teenager" in the PG-13 rule depends on the context. Sometimes it means "≥ 13," but sometimes it may also mean "of the level of maturity of at least an average 13-year-old."

One of the ways of arguing about ill-defined predicates is to cite similar cases where the rule applied, or where the rule did not apply but should have if it really meant what the opponent says it means, as part of a justification for applying or not applying the rule to the case at issue. As the boy's impassioned plea, "I am a teenager!" in effect, points out, if he's not a teenager then neither is Noah, but that did not prevent Noah from seeing the show.

Distinguishing and citing counterexamples usually are not the last words. In rebuttal, an arguer may grant the difference but show that it actually leads to the opposite conclusion from that of the distinguisher. For example, the supposed difference in maturity may imply that the sister has greater responsibility, like homework, and drive a factual query whether sister does not have a big report due tomorrow and shouldn't be going to the movies after all. The asserted distinction backfires and actually hurts the distinguisher's position. Or an arguer may distinguish the counterexample. One can almost hear the parents' next response: "Just because Noah's parents allow him to do certain things does not mean that it is OK in our home. Their standards are different." In addition, an arguer may cite a counterexample to the counterexample (e.g., the parents might note that the Cleavers did not allow their twelve-year-old to see the movie).

Case-based arguments can be won or lost. The arguers also share expectations about how to to evaluate the persuasive strength of an argument citing precedents. An arguer strengthens his position to the extent that he cites cases that had favorable outcomes and are the most analogous to the facts at issue (in other words, cases that are the least distinguishable), cites cases for which there are no more analogous counterexamples (no trumping counterexamples), cites more of these untrumped analogous cases than his opponent.

Case-based arguments present strategic choices:

- If possible, sometimes it's better to avoid being drawn into an argument citing cases. Although the parents might have responded simply by saying, "So what? What your sister does is none of your business," by bothering to distinguish the case cited by their son, the parents, in a sense, buy into the game.

- Leading off with a case for which the opponent can cite numerous equally analogous or trumping counterexamples puts one on the defensive. It would have been better not to cite the case.

- Asserting a distinction that can be turned against your position, like the homework argument, makes the arguer and his argument look foolish and inconsistent.

- Selecting cases to cite. Suppose the boy had a twin brother who was allowed to go. That would have been a better case to cite.

Case-based arguments may turn on issues that, in a sense, are orthogonal to the real merits of the dispute, such as how many and how good are the cases that a side cites. The Cleavers may simply be the authorities on parenting in this neighborhood.

By posing analogous precedents, the arguers make their points efficiently and succinctly. Little brother's opening shot puts his case rather neatly. Think how complicated an argument it is to spell out. There may be any number of theoretical justifications on which he could rely, assuming he could think of any at all: some innate universal principle of family life that all siblings are created equal or a manly conviction that he can handle any grossness that big sister can. Using analogies, the arguers do not even need to express the theoretical justifications, much less agree on them or their validity. If a participant in an argument by analogy does spell out the justification, however, the opponent can take issue with the justification, as well as try to distinguish the posed case.

Everyday Example Revisited This everyday example has much in common with the kind of arguing with cases that Hypo performs. Of course, the example involves a much more open-ended domain, and the argument exchanges show greater subtlety than Hypo can produce. From an AI researcher's viewpoint, however, in attempting to model this kind of reasoning, one could very well start with an approach like that of Hypo.

Rather than representing the abstruse theories that appear to guide the arguers' points and responses, one could represent the comparatively concrete observable factors that strengthen or weaken a position. Some factors that matter with regard to the issue of permission to go to the movies are shown below. Parentheticals show each factor's range of magnitudes and the direction that favors parental permission (+) or denying permission (−).

- Chronological-age (older → +)
- Lateness-of-showtime (later → −)
- Movie-rating (XXX → −)
- Emotional-maturity (maturer → +)
- Homework-burden (greater → −)
- Location (farther from home → −)
- Parental-permissiveness (more liberal → +)
- School-night (Fri. or Sat. → +)

Having defined these factors, good and bad cases, distinctions and counterexamples can be represented quite simply. For instance, in each of the following examples, the sense in which a case is a good or bad one for a side, or a counterexample, may be represented in terms of comparing the overlaps and magnitudes of factors that apply to the cases.

Two good cases for George to cite are the following:

>a. George's twin brother, Skippy, was permitted to see *Rocky Horror* despite its weekday-night showing.
>
>b. His 10-year-old sister was permitted to see the 1:00 a.m. Times Square showing of *Flesh Gordon*.

Case (a) is exactly on point. Case (b) is a strong case for George because his parents permitted his sister to go to the movie despite strongly negative factors: she was younger, the time later, the location more distant, and the movie much more risqué. On the other hand, a bad case for George is,

>c. His older brother was forbidden to see the Sat. 8:00 p.m. showing of *Bambi*.

If George's parents cite case (c), he will not easily be able to distinguish it: his brother is older, it is a weekend, and the movie is much more wholesome.

As the example suggests, distinctions that matter can easily be computed given the factors shown above. In the original debate between George and his parents, the fact that Sarah is more mature is a reasonable distinction between her case and that of her brother's. Greater maturity favors permission (+). The fact that she has more homework is not a reasonable distinction. Greater homework favors denying permission (−).

Similarly, good counterexamples may be represented in terms of the factors. If George's parents cite case (c), case (b) would make an excellent counterexample to cite in response. Case (b) is just as on point as (c) in terms of factor overlap, but it is much more extreme in the sense that the applicable factors favor denying permission, yet permission was granted. In Hypo's parlance, (b) is a boundary counterexample with respect to (c). One can also easily explain why, of the two following cases, (e) is a better case for George to cite as a counterexample than (d):

>d. Noah was permitted to see *Cinderella*.
>
>e. Noah was permitted to see *Emanuelle*.

Case (e) is better for George because *Emanuelle* is much more extreme on the rating factor.

Finally, one can also see how cases can be good to cite to show how to resolve factor conflicts. If in a few years George's homework burden is high, but so is his emotional maturity, the case of his older sister, Sarah, would become a good one for him to cite:

> f. Sarah is fifteen and has lots of homework but was permitted to see *Rocky Horror*.

Case (f) helps an older George because it shows that maturity outweighs homework, it is a case where the parents granted permission despite the homework factor.

11.1.2 Examples from Other Domains

Adversarial, case-based reasoning is important in political decision making. In their book *Thinking in Time*, Neustadt and May describe a methodology for decision making that makes an intelligent use of historical experience. One of their primary interests is protecting against a too facile use of historical analogies to justify a decision. They offer three "minimethods" for critically analyzing the applicability of a proposed analogy by focusing on (1) what is "known, unclear and presumed" about the problem, (2) the relevant "likenesses and differences" between the problem and proffered analogies, and (3) the analogies' sometimes misleading sources of appeal [Neustadt and May 1986, pp. 89-90].

They report a good example of "subjecting analogies to serious analysis," which looks remarkably like the kind of distinguishing that Hypo performs. At the time of the Cuban missile crisis, former secretary of state Dean Acheson is reported to have advised President Kennedy to authorize a quick air strike to destroy the missiles. Acheson attempted to debunk a claim that such a strike would be analogous to "Pearl Harbor in reverse":

> He told the President that there were no points of similarity and many points of difference, to wit: "[A]t Pearl Harbor the Japanese without provocation or warning attacked our fleet thousands of miles from their shores. In the present situation the Soviet Union had installed missiles ninety miles from our coast—while denying they were doing so—offensive weapons that were capable of lethal injury to the United States. This they were doing a hundred and forty years after the warning given in [the Monroe Doctrine]. How much warning was necessary to avoid the stigma of 'Pearl Harbor in reverse?'" [Neustadt and May 1986, p. 7]

The authors believe that critically focusing on the likenesses and differences between the problem and the situation deepens the analysis of the problem. According to the authors, critically focusing on the differences between Pearl Harbor and the current problem convinced the president's brother that in one significant sense, the two were analogous: they were both sneak attacks, a course of action unworthy of the United States.

This emphasis on distinguishing is consistent with the thrust of the Hypo research. One can easily conceive of the factors that would be relevant for making the kind of factual comparisons that Acheson did. At the same time, the example shows a deeper level of analogizing that Hypo does not capture, the lesson of a past example (for example, "sneak attacks are abhorrent"). That is a limitation that needs to be addressed to improve Hypo's model of legal reasoning as well.

Another kind of decision making where adversarial case-based reasoning is important is appraising property: assigning a monetary value to something, for example, real estate, a business, or a business proposal. In appraisals, there often is no substitute for a case-based method for assigning values.

Real estate appraisal is a classic domain for case-based argument. It involves two adversaries (buyer and seller) and prior cases (past sales of real estate). The expert appraiser's goal is to find comparable recent sales transactions from which to extrapolate a price. One can readily imagine the factors for comparing houses for sale, for example, recentness of sale, number of rooms, number of bathrooms, and proximity to good schools. The appraiser estimates a value by finding the most similar recent sale on the block and, for example, adding or subtracting a few thousand to make up for the fact that the prior sale was three months ago or had only one bathroom or was on the sunnier side of the street. Prior cases can even give one an understanding of how to evaluate the factors. If one can find two previously sold houses that were the same but for the number of bathrooms, that is evidence of the worth of an extra bathroom.

11.2 The Adversarial Case-Based Reasoning Process

In various domains, more sophisticated, stylized, or unconstrained versions of the same kind of adversarial case-based reasoning performed in Hypo are actually used in the decision-making process. Arguments citing analogous prior cases as justifications are made for and against assigning an outcome to a problem situation.

The reasoning process in these diverse domains is some variation on Hypo's adversarial case-based reasoning process:

- The new fact situation is analyzed by comparing it to relevant prior cases or precedents.

- Each precedent is used as the basis of a justification that the new case should be treated in the same way as the precedent. The justification is made by drawing the analogy between the new case and the precedent by focusing on their important similarities. In addition, the differences between the new case and the precedent are used as the basis of a justification why the new case should not be treated like a given precedent.

- Since there may be many relevant precedents, some of which may lead to conflicting results, one makes the strongest arguments on all sides of the issue of how to decide the case. The arguments are generated by combining the justifications for treating the new case like various precedents with the justifications for not treating it like the conflicting precedents.

- A decision is made by evaluating the competing arguments and, where possible, selecting the strongest.

- The decision is explained in terms of the supporting argument by discussing the case precedents relied upon and distinguishing the alternative precedents.

11.3 Characteristics of Good Domains for Adversarial Case-Based Reasoning

As an AI methodology, an adversarial case-based reasoning process is appropriate for domains characterized by lack of a strong domain model, competing viewpoints and reasonable alternative competing answers to most questions, and experts' actually using cases in arguments, as test cases, for making ballpark estimates, in teaching, in explanations, and in planning.

Adversarial case-based reasoning may be the only kind that works in domains that do not have strong models. A domain does not have a strong model if any of the following are true:

- It lacks any theory from which to deduce an answer to the problem situation.

- Although it has such a theory, the theory is partial in the sense that the predicates of the theory are not well enough defined to deduce whether they apply to the problem situation. This is the problem of *open-textured* predicates. In many domains, at some level of grain size, the predicates are not or cannot be further defined in terms of rulelike definitions. There may be little consensus about what those definitions should be, the range of novel fact situations the definitions have to encompass may simply be too great or unpredictable, or there may be strong institutional reasons for leaving the predicates ambiguous.

- There are many competing theories, some of which lead to conflicting conclusions about the problem situation. There may be a number of authoritative experts who profess different, possibly conflicting, partial theories about a domain or a class of problems.

Cases play an important role in domains that are primarily adversarial. Where viewpoints clash and there is no method for demonstrating the one right answer, the winner is the one who can persuade the listener that his or her position is the best of a number of competing reasonable alternatives. Often persuasion is a matter of citing the best or most case examples. Attorneys, debaters, philosophers, and ethicists bombard each other with real and hypothetical cases to illustrate the consequences of and alternatives to their and their opponents' positions. By comparing and distinguishing the cases, the arguers lay out the comparative strengths and weaknesses of the alternatives.

Finally, in many domains experts use cases as an integral part of problem solving. In some domains experts regularly consult standard indexed collections of cases. The experts may use the cases in a number of ways:

- As a standard component of expert arguments, as in law [Levi 1949] and historical political analysis [Neustadt and May 1986, Alker and Christensen 1972]

- As test cases. For example, in mathematics or scientific inquiry (domains with strong theoretical models where the primary mode of justifying a conclusion is through the methods of logical inference) experts pose real and hypothetical cases as counterexamples to test and modify hypotheses. See [Kuhn 1970, Lakatos 1976].

- For estimation. Experts may scope out a range of plausible decisions or generate quick estimates by comparing the problem situation to prior cases, without doing the detailed analysis that applying a theoretical analysis entails. There may be a microeconomic theory for determining the market price of a three-bedroom home in Amherst, Massachusetts, but for ease of estimate, and in this example, for accuracy too, there is no substitute for comparing the home to other recent sales on the block.

- In teaching. Business and law schools commonly use case methods and case books. Law school professors in particular typically pose hypotheticals to test students' knowledge of the law.

- In explanations. Comparisons to other examples make good explanations. We expect experts to explain their analysis of a situation by giving case examples and to pose hypotheticals to illustrate the dire consequences of not following their advice.

- In strategic planning. We expect experts to plan for contingencies by posing hypothetical scenarios (worst, best, most recent, most likely cases, etc.) that illustrate the consequences of and alternatives to a given course of action.

11.4 Computationally Implementing Adversarial Case-Based Reasoning

The adversarial case-based reasoning process connects descriptions about the world with judgments of value. The link is by arguments comparing the problem to prior relevant cases. As we have seen, the process is most appropriate where deductive reasoning does not work well, that is, where logical definitions, for a variety of reasons, are ineffective to bridge the gap between empirical descriptions and conclusory judgments.

As with other AI techniques, controlling inference is the greatest problem for implementing adversarial case-based reasoning. Given a problem situation α, finding or generating relevant cases, β's, with which to make or respond to arguments in favor of a position, and selecting from among them the best β's to cite are computational problems of potentially great complexity.

Indexing is the key to computationally implementing this complex kind of search. The index must relate features of cases with their uses as justifications in arguments and facilitate comparing the cases easily. The index enables the program to identify which of the possible factual comparisons make a difference in terms of justifications for treating cases analogously, how those similarities and differences tie in to the justifications, what outcomes they tend to support, and how to assess the strength of the combined justifications.

Even with an index there are problems of complexity. The issue is how much the system should have to analyze α to access the index to find β's. To what extent should it look at only surface-level facts of the cases (if only surface-level facts, which ones), facts and relationships inferable from surface-level facts, the reasoning process used or espoused by the deciders of those cases?

Where the number of features of cases that are represented is large and the possible inferences from the features great, the depth of inference needed to access the index should be kept shallow. *Depth of inference* means the difference between the level at which a case is described and the level of description of the index entries in the light of the possible alternative inferences that could be drawn from the description of the case. It is meant as a rough, qualitative measure of how much inference a program has to perform to match a case to an index.

In essence, Hypo's use of factors and Dimensions to implement arguing by analogy controls the inferencing problem by flattening out the depth of inferencing needed to come up with precedential justifications. The Dimensions are predefined for the system and used as entries in the index of cases. Dimension prerequisites and the language for describing problems are kept relatively close to restrict the amount of inference associated with matching a problem to relevant cases.

Hypo's factors and Dimensions are designed so that much of the comparison or manipulation of cases can be performed within the index. Each Dimension has information about what outcome the associated factor favors and how changes in a factor's magnitude strengthen or weaken its support for an outcome. Thus, making a case more extreme or comparing how on-point cases are can be performed using only the information contained in the Dimension Index.

The problem of controlling inferencing comes up in another context: *explaining* the reasoning. It is not enough for a program to compare cases; it must also be able to explain the comparison in terms of the similarities, differences, and justifications. To get a sense of how complicated a process this might be, consider what explaining a comparison of cases would mean in the Mycin paradigm. Any comparisons would have to be of the results of running the program on each case separately. Comparing the explanations, consisting basically of the trace of inferences augmented with certainty factors and, possibly, references to the goals served by selected inferences in the chain [Clancey 1983], would require a tedious exegesis.

In Hypo's factor-oriented approach, although the depth of inference is shallow, the depth of analysis is not by virtue of the breadth of the index, the size and diversity of the knowledge base of cases, and the schemes for selecting best cases to use as precedents, comparing cases, and hypothetically modifying them.

11.5 Adversarial Case-Based Reasoning in AI

Although adversarial case-based reasoning has not received a great deal of attention in artificial intelligence, a number of lines of AI research bear in some way on the theoretical and practical aspects of such reasoning.

11.5.1 Argument Discourse

Researchers in argument discourse have focused on the problem of reducing undirected inferencing in connection with argument understanding and planning argument responses.

McGuire, Birnbaum, and Flowers have described various ways of coordinating knowledge of the domain, of how to reason and of how to argue in an attempt to reduce undirected inferencing in the tasks of understanding arguments and planning argument responses. They correctly distinguish between the explicit content of a proposition and its force in terms of the argument. They use argument graphs to represent the relationships of support and attack among the individual propositions of an argument and have identified patterns of support and attack relations in arguments, such as the "stand-off" argument molecule and the "contrastive positions" structure, that, once recognized, guide generating responses [McGuire et al. 1981, Birnbaum 1982]. The structures assign argument roles to the various component propositions and lay out rebuttal options so that the reasoning system can select which propositions in the structure need to be, or safely can be, supported or attacked. For example, the system can decide to avoid using a tactic, like attacking the main point, that it has already tried, trying to attack evidence if the evidence was previously verified, or hurting its own position as it would if, having identified a stand-off, it stuck to its claim.

In addition to identifying structures in argument that are useful in directing inferencing, McGuire, Birnbaum, and Flowers maintain that memory (a term that means the organization of the database) should be designed to support the higher-level argument structures. The authors propose to use the structures, for example, to generate rebuttals to arguments, like citing counterexamples, on the fly as a by-product of the "understanding" process [McGuire et al. 1981]. Unfortunately, it is not at all clear that their specific memory organization (about which the authors are somewhat vague) is strong enough to support adversarial reasoning in a robust manner. Although they speak of storing "expectation failures" in memory as hints for subsequently generating counterexamples on the fly [Flowers et al. 1982], they do not explain how inferential memory is informed about the goals of the arguer so that it realizes that any evidence it uncovers that contradicts a particular position will be useful as a counterexample and should be saved. One would expect that as there are more and more senses in which expectations fail from differing points of view, memory would become mired in complexity. Moreover, the selection among response options is more complex than the authors allow. Choosing to attack a point of evidence may have undesirable repercussions on other aspects of a party's argument not represented in the local pattern of support and attack relations represented by a single argument molecule. One needs a more comprehensive model of the overall effects of possible argument moves in order to make more global strategic choices.

Cohen's computational model of argument, with its interesting representation of arguments as trees in which claims are fathers to evidential propositions, also shows the utility of tracking support relations [Cohen 1983]. She wisely focuses on the different kinds of evidential support relations between propositions and a claim in an argument including inductive inference and the "partial" support provided by examples and counterexamples. Yet her main definition of an evidential relationship, namely the existence of logical inference chains, is much too fine grained for any hope of effectively controlling inferencing even with her reliance on a collection of semantic, syntactic, and pragmatic methods like the use of inferencing frames to cope with missing information and with common erroneous inference rules.

By contrast, [Reichman-Adar 1984] emphasizes the use of much-larger-scale structures to guide inferencing in the task of understanding argument discourse (larger scale even than those proposed by McGuire, Birnbaum, and Flowers). Reichman-Adar presents a tantalizingly rich but nonoperational computational model of natural language discourses in which context spaces are used to represent the topics of *groups of propositions* and the roles those groups play in a dialog. A conversation is viewed as a series of conversational moves, each of which corresponds to a particular functional relation between the utterances generated and those of a preceding context space. The moves may be to present, explain, support, and challenge claims, shift topics, or resume a suspended discourse. The moves have preconditions and effects. They set up expectations in the system about what appropriate conversation moves may follow (expectations include resuming a context space, returning to what initiated an analogy, further challenging a claim, or counterchallenging a challenge) and how ensuing statements should be interpreted. The moves thus assist in focusing an inference mechanism or an understanding module. By keeping track of items in focus in particular context spaces, the program theoretically can resolve ambiguous references and determine relevance.

Reichman-Adar recognizes the variety of support and attack relations possible in an adversarial discourse. For example, she describes the process of using an analogy in an argument to support a general principle common to the target and analogous situations [Reichman-Adar 1984]. She leaves a slot for a mapping between features of the target and goal and allows for attacking an analogy by criticizing the mapping or showing that a principle applies to the analogy that undermines application of the target's principle to it. Unfortunately, although Reichman-Adar's "system" is a fecund source of ideas, it also is an example of elaborating knowledge representation schemes without clearly delineating the tasks they are supposed to perform. In the absence of a working system, one cannot judge the efficacy of the finer distinctions among her context spaces.

In summary, the argument discourse research provides the following insights: Propositions should be seen in the light of the roles they play in an argument, and their "meanings" should be expanded to include their force in an argument. Arguments can be schematized in terms of support and attack relations among their components. There are many kinds of support and attack relations among propositions in an argument beside those that involve logical chains of inference. Larger-scale structures in arguments can be identified that elucidate these support and attack relations and can be used to guide inference. Memory should be organized to accommodate the larger-scale structures.

In general, the argument discourse researchers have not gone far enough in organizing database or memory structures that will support realistic argument making in a particular domain. They do not identify crucial domain-specific knowledge such as what constitute acceptable justifications in an argument, detailed models of support and attack relations among the justifications, and criteria for evaluating competing arguments.

The memory structures that they propose will not generate realistic arguments in the domain. Nor are the argument researchers' inference mechanisms computationally tractable. Most rely on *modus ponens*. Some, like [McGuire et al. 1981], speak of generating counterexamples on the fly but do not tell how the indexing schemes would work as the number and complexity of past experiences increase. By contrast, Hypo's model of the support and attack relations among precedents—3-Ply Arguments consisting of points, responses, and rebuttals where responses distinguish and cite various kinds of counterexamples to the cases cited in points—allows it to make realistic arguments.

Stronger, more domain-specific memory structures, like those in Hypo, are required to deal with the problem of controlling inference. Computationally implementing argument requires organizing the knowledge in a way that reflects the criteria for making and evaluating arguments in the specific area of expertise. Where examples and counterexamples are going to be used in argument, they will have to be filed in indexes that reflect their dialectical significance.

Researchers should take their cues from the specific bibliographic tools and indexes employed by experts in the domain. For example, in essence, a legal library is a compilation of past cases indexed especially for use in making arguments. The actual bibliographic indexes and source materials in the law organize the cases for retrieval in terms of how they can be used to support or attack positions in legal arguments about various stereotypical fact situations. Hypo's organization of cases mimics the bibliographic tools of the legal domain while improving their ease and speed of application.

Once a system is developed that has a robust capability for case-based inference, models of argument discourse could be *implemented* as well as described. A case-based reasoner could drive a working discourse program that argues about legal cases. The program's control mechanism could plan the construction of arguments and counterarguments in the light of its case-based inferences about who has the stronger argument. Reichman-Adar's model of discourse moves, like flat denial, *modus ponens*, or analogy, would, of course, be relevant, but the expectations of arguers who make and respond to case-based points would also be explicitly represented so as to guide the choice and application of the moves. One could then perhaps implement a program that demonstrated the insights of Perelman and Toulmin [Perelman 1982, Toulmin 1958].

11.5.2 Analogical Reasoning

The approach taken in Hypo differs from that of other AI research in analogical reasoning in a number of respects. Hypo performs a highly constrained kind of matching, does not use a static hierarchy among features, does not assume a strong model of the domain, combines information from the most analogous cases, and symbolically compares the most analogous cases and counterexamples.

AI systems differ in the kinds of matching they perform. At one extreme is the simple matching performed by the program described in [Winston 1980]. In trying to decide if a problem situation is analogous to a target situation, the program attempts to place the parts of the situations into correspondence by matching up the objects, their classes and properties, and the relations among objects. Points are scored for successful matches. The match with the highest total points is deemed to indicate an analogous base situation [Winston 1980, pp. 693–697]. As the fact situations become more complex, the combinatorics of the matching scheme become unworkable. In order to reduce the number of possible matches that need to be considered, some relations–those that involve causation and temporal relations–are considered to be more important; other relations among the objects are ignored [Winston 1980, pp. 695–696]. Other efforts to deal with the combinatorics of the matching process by imposing general constraints are those of Gentner, Holyoak, and Thagard. Their work focuses on identifying general constraints on matching descriptions of analogs involving predicates and constants. [Gentner 1983] employs syntactic criteria involving the order of relations of the features to be matched. [Holyoak and Thagard 1987] identifies five constraints: logical kind, uniqueness, sameness of relations, similar meanings, and role identity.

At the other extreme in terms of kind of matching performed are the problem-solving programs described in [Carbonell 1982, Carbonell 1983a, Carbonell 1983b]. A key component of this approach is to examine the underlying structure of past solutions to problems that can be thought of as proofs, plans, or justifications for the results. In transformational analogy, solutions to previous problems are indexed according to goals achieved; they are retrieved for use as target models for solving a new problem. Operators like insertion, deletion, splicing in, and reordering are used to transform the targeted past solutions into a solution of the new problem. The transformational approach foundered on the obstacle of recognizing analogous problems despite apparent differences in the language or levels of abstraction used to represent the problems and the solutions. In the subsequent work on derivational analogy, one examines the reasoning that resulted in a prior solution as well as the solution. Successful and unsuccessful solution paths, and the reasons that the paths were taken or aborted, are recorded. As an attempt is made to solve a new problem, matchings are attempted between the evolving path of reasoning steps and those of previous problems. The solution process of a problem deemed similar is applied to the new problem. Decisions made in similar solutions are reevaluated in the light of the new problem's facts.

A somewhat more tractable, purpose-driven problem-solving approach is that taken by [Hammond 1986a, Hammond 1986b]. In his Chef program, recipes are the cases. In the course of encountering planning failures in solving a problem, Chef generalizes descriptions of combinations of features that lead to the failures in order to predict future failures before they happen. The recipes are indexed by both the gastronomical goals they satisfy and the problems they avoid. The program took a problem description including surface features like ingredients and goals to be satisfied and inferred likely goal conflicts to retrieve recipes that avoided the conflict. Burstein also used a purpose- and failure-driven matching to link information in the problem situation, involving the use of programming variables, with that of the target domain of manipulating boxes and objects [Burstein 1983a].

Similarly, Kedar-Cabelli has tried to address reasoning with the purposes underlying an analogy. She suggests, for example, that the purpose of a statute can be used to select the kind of analogy to draw to show that the statute has or has not been violated [Kedar-Cabelli 1984]. Unfortunately, it is well known that the purposes of statutes are notoriously difficult to ascertain.

Hypo differs from each of these AI approaches to analogical reasoning. It employs a highly constrained matching process. The constraints are not general types but capture specific factors that courts have said were important in deciding previous cases. With this more constrained matching, Hypo can deal with larger numbers of cases; it now has 30 cases in the CKB. In addition, having made matches, Hypo can reason about cases by comparing them in terms of the matched factors, magnitudes, and unmatched factors.

Hypo avoids relying on an a priori static hierarchy for determining the relative importance of features or for selecting the best matches. The relations among the features frozen into such hierarchies do not take into consideration the effects that the presence of other features or different magnitudes may have on their significance in specific circumstances. Moreover, the decision of each new case affects the assessment of relative importance in ways not reflected in the hierarchy. Hypo's method for choosing most analogous cases promotes cases in terms of their overlaps of factors. Which factors are more important in a given fact situation depends on the differences among the most analogous cases and their counterexamples relative to the specific problem situation.

Hypo differs from the problem-solving analogical reasoners in the following respects.

- The problem-solving researchers tend to assume that there is a strong model for solving problems in a domain. For example, Hammond's Chef needs a strong causal theory for purposes of credit assignment and explanation so that the program can make predictions about potential planning problems from the surface features of problem situations.

- They assume that target cases are fully worked out or explained examples in the light of the strong model, and the structure of their solutions can be mapped more or less directly onto the problem situation. Once a match is made, the systems attempt to map the model of the target case's solution onto the problem. The structure of the explanation of the target case is used to guide inferencing about the problem, to structure a similar explanation of it, and to fill in missing information.

- And finally, they assume that each target case was correctly decided and has only one explanation.

By contrast, Hypo avoids assuming a strong domain theory with which to structure explanations of either the target cases or the problem situation. Hypo does not assume that the target cases have a unique, structured explanation but that they may have multiple interpretations depending on the particular features, similarities, and differences that become salient in the light of the comparisons among the competing precedents relative to the problem situation.

Unlike most of the AI analogical problem solvers, Hypo does not treat a precedent as a fully worked out model of an answer to the problem situation. Instead, the most analogous precedents are treated as justifications that are combined into arguments. Hypo combines information from the most analogous cases. In Hypo, the configurations of competing most analogous cases relative to the problem situation represent important information. Hypo compares the most analogous cases symbolically and draws inferences from the results of the comparisons. Hypo can also extrapolate from nearby cases by posing hypotheticals.

In the other programs, the differences between nearly analogous cases are translated into point differentials in the matcher; the losers are discarded. No information is extracted from the fact that they were close cases. In Hypo, the differences among the most analogous cases, just like the similarities, have symbolic significance.

Hypo's differences make it much more appropriate for the kind of analogical reasoning performed in the law where there is no strong model of the domain sufficient to determine how a case should be decided or to explain uniquely how a case was decided.

11.5.3 Case-Based Reasoning and Memory Organization

One way that analogical reasoning programs can increase the range of analogies they can draw, and the work they can do with them, is to become more case based, that is, to accommodate large numbers of cases and adopt indexing schemes to retrieve and reason about relevant cases. Recent research in case-based reasoning (CBR) on memory organization, most notably by Kolodner and colleagues, bears on the problem of retrieving relevant cases through the use of indexing schemes. In the question-answering system Cyrus, Kolodner used a database that reorganized its indexing scheme and representations of events as new information is added [Kolodner 1983a, Kolodner 1983b]. The system indexes events, "E-mops," according to the aspects of an event that differ from the norms of the conceptual category of the event (for example, whether they violate expectations).

Building on this memory scheme, Simpson and Kolodner developed a case-based reasoning program, Mediator, that solved problems in the domain of dispute mediation [Kolodner et al. 1985]. Mediator's case base contained information on physical, economic, and political disputes and common mediation tactics, their failures, and corrections for those failures. Cases were indexed by their features (the disputants, their goals, disputed objects), in particular, by those causing dispute mediation failure. A classic example involved a dispute between two sisters over an orange and the failure of the tactic of dividing it equally because one sister wanted the fruit and the other the rind. In connection with a physical dispute where "divide equally" fails, the case of the orange would be recalled and lead Mediator to try the alternative fruit-and-rind solution.

Having access to more potential analogues, however, poses the problem of selecting among them. In Cyrus and Mediator, as distinguished from Hypo, the evaluation function for selecting a most-on-point case from the many retrieved by the reminding process takes into account only the closeness of fit to selected features, which is determined by an a priori ranking of features types. In Hypo, on the other hand, the ranking of features is performed dynamically in the light of the particular combination of features that appear in the case at hand. Prior cases are promoted according to how great a subset they share of those features. Hypo then looks for configurations of counterexamples among the most analogous cases. These configurations, or their absence, dynamically determine which features are most important given the specific facts of the problem situation.

A recent paradigm example of a case-based reasoning program that assesses relevant case similarities within context is MBRTalk by Stanfill and Waltz [Stanfill and Waltz 1986, Stanfill 1987]. MBRTalk "pronounces" novel words based on comparing inputs to information contained in its case base of over 4,000 words. Each "case" associates a letter and a pronunciation. The authors provide an elegant computational definition of dissimilarity, which weights features in context by computing conditional probabilities. The computational requirements are enormous, however, and the authors rely on a Connection Machine to perform computations in parallel. Even with such a capability, however, the program compares cases statistically, not symbolically. The approach will not lead to generating symbolic arguments that compare cases.

Another recent CBR program that does symbolically compare cases is Casey by Koton [Koton 1988a, Koton 1988b]. Casey analyzes patient descriptions and produces a causal explanation of the patient's symptoms of heart disease. The program has a database of 45 solved patient descriptions and a detailed causal model of heart disease embodied in another program, Heart Failure, which uses computationally expensive causal, probabilistic, and heuristic reasoning to generate causal explanations. Casey achieves significant efficiencies by comparing new patient descriptions to prior solved cases, which it has indexed using causal explanations for problems solved by Heart Failure. Casey selects a best matched case and modifies its causal explanation to explain the new patient's symptoms. Casey employs a justified matching procedure to deal with partial matches. The program reasons about the differences between a retrieved case and a new problem in the light of its causal model to determine if the differences warrant rejecting the case. Although Casey's justified matching compares cases symbolically, its reasoning depends on the availability of the causal model. Such models are not generally available for legal domains.

Hypo uses symbolic case comparisons to provide a meaning for the concept of a trade secrets misappropriation claim, a concept for which there is no adequate logical definition. Another approach employing cases to provide meanings for terms is embodied in Protos by Bareiss and Porter [Bareiss et al. 1987, Bareiss 1988]. Like Casey, Protos employs explained examples or exemplars in classifying new problems. Given a new case's features, the program uses remindings to list possible classifications, determines the best classification using various heuristics, and selects an exemplar of the best classification. Then Protos assesses the similarity of the new case using the exemplar's explanation. It attempts to show that unmatched new case features are equivalent to exemplar features or do not matter. If the new case is dissimilar from the exemplar, Protos retains it as a new exemplar and asks a human teacher for an explanation associating the features and the classification. These associations are the basis for new remindings. Applying the approach in Protos to a legal case would require representing an explanation for a decision of the case. Such explanations, however, are complex and controversial, and usually any legal case has a number of conflicting but valid explanations.

11.5.4 Example-Based Reasoning

Reasoning with a knowledge base of cases in CBR was foreshadowed by Rissland's earlier work on example-based reasoning (EBR), which employs a "space" of examples, an Examples Knowledge Base from which to retrieve relevant examples and then manipulate them. In a process called constrained example generation (CEG), modifications of existing examples are undertaken with the goal of making the retrieved example satisfy needed constraints, for instance, those needed to create a counterexample to a conjecture. Rissland's "retrieval-plus-modification" idea in CEG and McCarty's "prototype-plus-deformation" idea, described below, are quite similar [Rissland 1980, McCarty 1980b]. In CEG, selection of techniques for modifying an example is done in a means-ends manner. The modifications are indexed on the attribute they effect.

A fundamental difference between CBR and EBR is that cases or examples in CBR are the foundation of justification. That is, to justify an analysis or argument in CBR, one cites and reasons with cases. In particular, for the cases that support the analysis or argument, one explains the connections, often analogical, and for the troublesome cases, one distinguishes them using legally important dissimilarities as a wedge. In CBR, one does not rely solely on rule-based chaining, *modus ponens*, universal specialization, or other essentially logical techniques as the primary tools. In EBR, on the other hand, although examples are important components of expertise and reasoning [Rissland 1978], they are not necessarily the basis of justification. (For instance, mathematics does not recognize proof by example although examples may play a central role in mathematical reasoning involved in the discovery, formulation, and debugging of a proof, which ultimately must cite definitions, axioms, and theorems.)

11.5.5 Explanation

Clancey addresses the problem of controlling inference in explanation in connection with two insights: the importance of (1) abstraction in explanation and (2) distinguishing between the meaning of a proposition and the role or use that its invocation plays in some broader context such as a diagnostic inquiry (or argument). In his seminal research on explanation, Clancey adopted a useful methodological perspective: to study how well a reasoning system explains, examine what would have to be changed to turn it into a tutorial program. Clancey identified deficiencies in Mycin's rules that prevent it from being easily transformed into a tutorial program, in other words, that limit the ability to generate convincing explanations of Mycin's decisions beyond a trace of the program's backchaining through its rules. The order of invocation of the rules is arbitrarily defined in Mycin; the rules are not tied to justifying principles; and there is no explicit representation of the strategies for invoking the rules [Clancey 1983].

Clancey focuses on the inference control problem when he argues that to explain a rule, one needs to know the intermediate steps from which the conclusion is derived from the premises. Since there may be many of these—the refinement of grain size is unlimited—one must choose which steps in the reasoning need to be explained. The purpose of the explanation and the amount of prior knowledge of the user are important in making the choice.

Clancey offers two solutions for the problem of controlling inference in explaining a rule. The first method is to relate the rule to an abstraction, to a generalized pattern of reasoning. He argues that key concepts in rule explanations are abstractions connecting the rules to familiar patterns of reasoning we have encountered previously and premises that we readily accept [Clancey 1983, pp. 226–226]. For example, a top-level explanation of a causal rule relates the rule's predicates to a general idea of the process being explained as represented by scripts. The second method is to relate the rule to the strategic role that invoking the rule plays in the diagnostic inquiry. Clancey recommends making strategic principles explicit (for example, common, or frequent, causes of a disorder should be considered first; if nothing has been observed, consider situations that have no visible manifestations; if unable to make a deduction, assume the most probable situation; if there is evidence for two hypotheses, A and B, that tend to be confused, then try to rule out B). This allows separating what a heuristic is from how it will be used and is reminiscent of the lesson from argument discourse research that a proposition's meaning should be distinguished from its force in argument.

Researchers have adopted a variety of other specialized knowledge representation techniques for accomplishing Clancey's goal of abstracting the right information for accomplishing the strategic purpose of the explanation. For example, [McKeown et al. 1985] describes a system that advises students about what courses to take. The program uses a rule-based system to answer yes or no questions about the courses the student can take and a trace of the rule invocations to provide a supporting explanation. The program infers the perspective of the student's question and tailors the explanation accordingly by allowing rules relevant to that perspective to be invoked. The program represents each different perspective (prerequisites, scheduling, etc.) with separate but intersecting concept hierarchies. To construct the explanation, the system determines the questioner's goal, selects the appropriate hierarchy, and puts the information about the object inquired of from that perspective into working memory. The information extracted from one hierarchy will allow a different set of rules to fire than will information extracted from another, producing a different explanation.

Clancey sees a connection between argument and explanation in the distinction between the reasoning process with which an expert comes to a conclusion and the process of explaining the conclusion. He observes that diagnostic rules are arguments that a process has occurred in a particular way [Clancey 1983, p. 230] and that the abstract concepts useful for providing good explanations may not necessarily be useful for driving the diagnostic reasoning process:

As we discovered when explaining the rules, not all of the causal steps of the process can be directly confirmed; we can only assume that they have occurred. For example, rather than providing diagnostic clues, the concept of "portal of entry and passage" is very often deduced from the diagnosis itself.

According to this view, principles are good for summarizing arguments, and good to fall back on when you've lost grasp on the problem, but they don't *drive the process* of medical reasoning. [Clancey 1983, p. 233]

After the diagnosis has been constructed, a causal argument is used to "prove" that the diagnosis is correct. "Thus causal knowledge can be used to provide feedback that everything fits." "But [a student] will be an inefficient problem solver if he always attempts to directly convert that [causal] model to a subgoal structure for solving ordinary problems" [Clancey 1983, p. 233].

The insight that principles useful in explanations may not drive the reasoning process is certainly applicable in domains like the law. Rule-like principles of law, for example, are frequently invoked to rationalize decisions made on the basis of other (including case-based) considerations.

The connection between explanation and argument, however, is much stronger than Clancey allows. Playing out alternative sides of an argument is a good way to make an explanation. Most diagnoses can be argued more than one way. Arguing about the rejected alternatives, even if only to discount them, is an effective way of justifying and explaining the alternative that was adopted.

Clancey has also missed the fact that citing well-selected case examples is another good way to illustrate and explain a point. Human experts frequently cite similar cases as a way of persuading us to believe their analysis. They also use hypothetical cases as a way of illustrating how the analysis depends on certain crucial facts that, if altered as in the hypothetical, would lead to other conclusions. Much as in explaining with rules, the trick in explaining with case examples is abstracting the right features of the case example to accomplish the strategic purpose of the explanation. In Hypo, Dimensions are used to focus on the features of a case that are relevant in citing that case as a predicate in an argument supporting a claim. Hypo's Dimensions are its special-purpose knowledge representation structure designed to abstract the facts relevant from the perspective of a particular claim.

Adversarial case-based methods of explanation surely pass muster given Clancey's methodological interest in explanation as tutoring. Good tutors pose training case examples to their students and invite them to argue all sides of the issue of how to decide them. Tutors often modify the examples hypothetically, sometimes posing extreme cases, to get their students to realize the limits of their positions.

Case examples play an especially important role in domains that do not have a strong model. Much has been made recently of explanation-based learning systems. As Doyle has argued, the ability of such systems to "learn" from examples depends on the existence of consistent domain theories [Doyle 1986]:

In these *explanation-based learning* methods ... , an explanation derived from a domain theory shows why a particular example is an instance of some concept. After the critical constraints in the explanation are determined, its components are generalized while maintaining these constraints; the result is a generalized recognition rule for examples of the given concept.

[The approach is well understood for domain theories assumed to be consistent.] Explanations derived and generalized from consistent domain theories constitute *proofs* which can be taken to be correct in the context of all reasoning tasks they may subsequently support.

However, most domain theories are not consistent–they incorporate defaults, they omit details, or they otherwise abstract away from a complete account of the constraints which may be relevant to the reasoning tasks to which they are applied. Explanations derived and generalized from inconsistent domain theories cannot be assumed to be always correct; their inherent abstractions may manifest when inferences derived from them are not corroborated. [Doyle 1986, p. 538]

Doyle recognizes the need for a different kind of explanation capability in domains that do not have consistent domain theories. In Doyle's domain, explaining how physical mechanisms work in terms of commonsense theories of causal mechanisms, the theories may be inconsistent because of approximations that suppress potentially relevant detail. Doyle constructs multiple layers of explanation to guide the process of elaborating an explanation. A failure to plan a plausible causal explanation at one level motivates descending to a more detailed level in search of more detailed building blocks with which to construct a plausible causal explanation of the effect. Each layer is more abstract than that below in the sense that it ignores constraints that are relevant at the lower level or assumes they are satisfied. Besides approximation, Doyle identifies a number of types of abstraction between the explanation layers, including qualitization in which a continuous description is collapsed into a discrete one (for example, on-off barriers become variable) and aggregation in which complex structures are subsumed under simpler ones (for example, gas as molecules in motion vs. as volume, temperature, pressure). Doyle points out that even the lowest levels of explanation can use abstractions, which imply missing knowledge. One possible way to access usable knowledge, he suggests, but does not develop, is through analogy [Doyle 1986].

Extrapolating from analogous case examples is a way of supplying knowledge missing because the rule-based explanatory mechanisms of a system have bottomed out. A system that has knowledge of how cases associated with a concept can be changed hypothetically to make the arguments that they are instances of the concept stronger or weaker can infer whether a new case is an instance of the concept by comparing it with previous cases. In effect, the system makes inferences by extrapolating from precedents. In Hypo, Dimensions provide the knowledge of how to strengthen and weaken cases.

The exigencies of argument drive an arguer to find counterexamples or ways to distinguish cases in much the same sense that explanation failures drive an explainer to descend to a lower level of explanation. The dialectical necessities of bringing a fact situation within a rule or avoiding the rule completely lead an attorney to delve into the particulars and make detailed factual comparisons to analogize the problem situation to some precedents and distinguish it from others.

12 Extending Hypo's Model of Case-Based Legal Argument

12.1 Other AI Models of Legal Reasoning

Since adversarial case-based reasoning is so important in law, AI research in the legal area could be expected to have examined the issues of argumentation, case comparison, and analogical legal reasoning. To some extent, it has.

McCarty addressed argumentation and case comparison in his research on legal reasoning. The object of his Taxman II project was to produce a formal theory of legal argument. McCarty presented a three-part scheme of prototypes and deformations for representing legal concepts, including a logical template or invariant that specifies the necessary but not sufficient conditions for the concept to apply; a set of exemplars or cases, real or hypothetical, where the concept does or does not apply; and a set of transformations that specify how to get from one exemplar to another and what features of the exemplars can be compared.

The prototypes and deformations were designed to model the rhetorical strategy of arguing that a disputed case was an instance of a particular concept by constructing a sequence of mappings or invariance-preserving transformations from a prototypical case exemplar of the concept to the disputed case [McCarty and Sridharan 1982]. McCarty's legal domain was an area of corporate tax law involving determining whether corporate distributions are taxable. The concepts represented included taxable and nontaxable transactions. The exemplars ranged from the clearly taxable cases of a distribution of a cash dividend or of stock of another corporation to the clearly untaxable case of unrealized appreciation in the stock of a corporation. The disputed case (*Eisner v. Macomber*) involved a distribution of the stock of the same company.

McCarty's hand simulation showed how the arguers (the majority and dissenting opinions in the case) could make the disputed case "like" or "unlike" exemplars of either concept by performing transformations that preserved various properties of the stockholder-corporate relationship such as the before and after ratios of stock owned by the distributees.

McCarty proposed criteria of coherence in a legal domain and described how in a legal argument arguers select "moves in the space of possible concepts" that induce coherence in the arguer's position and reduce coherence in the opponent's. Coherence reflected in part consistency with exemplars of the concept. Moves included constructing invariants and transformations for a concept that could be attacked or confirmed by reference to exemplars [McCarty and Sridharan 1982]. The goal of the arguers, in McCarty's view, was to minimize inconsistency, to find the right transformations that successfully linked the disputed case to positive exemplars of the desired concept without also linking it to any of the negative exemplars of the concept.

More recently McCarty has worked on a theory of permissions and obligations to represent the legal effects of actions [McCarty 1985]. He hopes to design a logic for specifying in detail the rights and duties associated with various legal relationships, such as that of a stockholder and the corporation. In this way, he hopes to expand and systematize a description of a transaction so that there are more possible transformations and invariants for the rhetorical process to work with.

McCarty's focus on modeling adversarial reasoning in law and on reasoning by comparing prototypical cases of concepts is a significant advance. He also points the way toward integrating case-based argument and logical methods in law. There are problems, however:

- The work is largely an exercise in knowledge representation. McCarty does not set forth a control or process model that clarifies how a program would actually generate a legal argument [McCarty and Sridharan 1981, 1982]. The reported research involves a hand simulation of the arguments in one U.S. Supreme Court case and work done on hand simulations of several subsequent cases.

- McCarty's mechanism for controlling the complexity of inference is that the positive and negative exemplars of the concept guide the search for mappings. But how much inference is needed to find useful mappings that discriminate between positive and negative exemplars in a consistent way for a side? As the numbers of exemplars, possible transformations, and invariants grow, so does the complexity of comparing the exemplars and finding useful matchings, especially assuming that the mappings have to be assessed for consistency with other possible mappings. In addition, his space of possible concepts is small.

Extending Hypo's Model of Case-Based Legal Argument   225

- Legal arguers make other kinds of comparisons of cases not handled in Taxman II. They compare cases in terms of the relative strengths and weaknesses of the plaintiffs' positions and how close an analogy a precedent case is to the disputed case. Taxman II has no mechanisms for comparing cases in terms of how on point they are, for distinguishing cases, or for selecting the best precedents.

- McCarty's model assumes a much neater domain than exists in law. He assumes that in reality, legal cases are consistently allocated as positive and negative exemplars of concepts. They are not. He assumes that there is a neat match between concepts and the features of a case that are relevant to the concept. There is not. He assumes a domain of "sanitized" positive and negative exemplars of a concept whose relevant differences with respect to the concept are readily compared because other differences that affect the strength of the overall argument are ignored. Thus cases are compared as if all other things were equal, when they are not.

- His efforts to define a set of primitives in terms of permissions and obligations place the cart before the horse. Far from being primitives, the effect of a legal action on permissions and obligations is an arguable legal conclusion requiring the same kind of arguments he is trying to model.

Of the researchers who have focused on modeling reasoning with legal rules, Gardner has taken the most realistic view of the limitations of legal rules and has recognized the role of case-based argument in dealing with those limitations. [Gardner 1987] developed a system to identify legal issues in the analysis of law school examination fact patterns involving the contracts law of offer and acceptance. The program's legal knowledge of contracts law consisted primarily of twenty if-then rules, positive and negative examples of some of the predicates employed in the rules, and an augmented transition network. The rules defined such domain concepts as offer, acceptance, counteroffer, and rejection. The program had a number of heuristics for distinguishing "hard" and "easy" legal issues that were encountered in determining if the rules applied. The question was treated as hard if any of the following occurred: Contradictory rules applied. The rules "ran out" (were inconclusive or had unresolved predicates), and the situation matched both positive and negative example cases of the predicate. The rules ran out, and there was no match to an example case to resolve the predicate.

Although the heuristics are an important advance, an attorney distinguishes hard from easy questions in terms of comparing the strengths of the best argument he or she can make with the best arguments an opponent can make. Gardner's program provides no measure for evaluating the strengths of competing arguments. Gardner referred to, but did not implement, a final stage of reasoning that would have produced arguments on both sides of hard questions. Hypo does make arguments citing cases on both sides of an issue and compares arguments by comparing the most analogous precedents that can be cited on either side of the issue.

Even if Gardner's program evaluated case-based arguments, it could not do so very realistically given the way cases are represented. Distinguishing, for example, is not possible because there is nothing to distinguish. Although Gardner's examples were abstracted from actual cases and indexed by the legal predicates they exemplified, they consisted of simple rulelike patterns including only the generalized facts relevant to satisfying the predicate and eliminating features inconsistent with or extraneous to interpreting the case according to the program's rules.

Other memory organizations have been proposed for relating cases to the legal concepts they supposedly exemplify. Goldman et al. are exploring the use of special memory structures to index and organize cases according to legal concepts like legal-offer or conditional-offer [Goldman et al. 1987]. In their explanation-based STARE program, positive and negative case examples of the concept are indexed according to their conceptual differences, for example, a failed precondition that causes one example to be a legal offer and the other not or differing surface features. This memory structure may impose more conceptual coherence on the cases than is warranted in that it appears to assume the existence of a strong theory for explaining why a case is a negative instance of a concept and for determining which differences are relevant in that connection. In real legal domains, there may be no such theory or, worse, several. In any event, the memory structures for legal acts and relations are intended to enable the program to interpret natural language descriptions of legal fact situations. Like McCarty, Goldman and Dyer propose to define legal primitives. The problem with such primitives, if they are taken too seriously as a means for defining concepts, is that they assume what is to be shown. Far from being a primitive, that someone has a right or duty in a given fact situation is an arguable legal conclusion that must be justified by citing authorities. On the other hand, legal primitives may play an important role if the program uses them as a means for identifying the tentative legal conclusions for which it should seek to make case-based arguments.

Hafner has proposed a different kind of concept/case organization, an issue/case discrimination tree, to structure a collection of legal cases for purposes of conceptual text retrieval [Hafner 1987]. The tree organizes positive and negative case examples of a concept according to issues and factors that positively or negatively affect the outcome. Hafner's factors are based on Dimensions as described in this book and discussed in [Ashley 1986]. Hafner apparently foresees incorporating such trees into the organization of a database of cases.

Other research focuses on rule-based models of legal reasoning without attempting to model adversarial reasoning or to address the problems of reasoning with rules that case-based reasoning does. For example, Waterman and Peterson employed a classic rule-based approach in implementing a model of how lawyers estimate the value of products liability and negligence cases [Waterman and Peterson 1981]. The model, part of a planned larger system for settlement negotiations, used if-then rules to model the substantive law. Waterman estimated that it would take thousands of rules to model estimating the value of products liability suits resulting from auto accidents. Although he recognized the problem of using rules to represent the meanings of ill-defined predicates like "unreasonably dangerous" and "foreseeability of injury," he suggested using ever more refined rules to show how the terms were applied in particular contexts or simply asking the user [Waterman and Peterson 1981]. As Gardner points out, the lessons of jurisprudence imply that the former tack, definitional backchaining, often fails. And while the latter certainly resolves an ill-defined predicate, it also casts doubt on the program's level of expertise. At least a program should guide the user's choice by showing positive and negative examples of the predicate.

In an early work that also emphasized representing substantive rules, Meldman developed a system to analyze fact situations involving intentional tort claims like assault and battery [Meldman 1977]. The program had two kinds of rules: general rules defining the elements of the claims and more specific rules defining when the elements were satisfied. The latter, in effect, were structured examples abstracted from the facts and holdings of real cases. The program attempted to match the case at hand to the elements of a claim by matching facts to the structured examples. A match entailed finding common facts or common ancestors in a generalization hierarchy. Meldman's use of rules (to define the elements of a claim) and that of Gardner (to define the ingredients of contract law) were similar. Also Meldman's use of cases as rule abstractions was somewhat similar to Gardner's use of case examples to resolve ill-defined predicates in the general rules. Meldman, however, treated each case as having a unique holding and dealt only with positive examples of a claim. He did not attempt to model arguing the analysis both ways.

Some more recent proponents of rule-based expert systems in the legal domain, including Schlobohm and Michaelsen, have attempted to find tasks and domains where the costs of rule-based approaches are acceptable given the routine nature of the fact situations, more detailed statutory definitions of the predicates, or greater acceptability of asking the user. Michaelsen's program makes liberal use of asking the user to draw complex tax conclusions for which it provides no explanation or guidance [Michaelsen 1984]. Schlobohm has attempted to expand the ability of his program to explain concepts to a naive user by attaching textual definitions to various rules and frames; the program does not utilize case examples and hypotheticals to explain what would have caused a different decision to have been made [Schlobohm and Waterman 1987].

Far more extreme are the proponents of logic representation schemes for reasoning about statutes. Sergot et al. and Bench-Capon et al. have represented fragments of the British Nationality Act and the Supplemental Benefits Law as "logical models" [Sergot et al. 1986, Bench-Capon et al. 1987]. The models are unable to deal with alternative interpretations of the statute and make no provision for employing cases to supplement the ambiguous, ill-defined predicates of the statutes. Instead they apparently ask the user to decide whether a predicate applies or provide ad hoc definitions for the predicates, definitions that are not sanctioned by any legal authority like a legislature or a court but are introduced only to make the system work.

Such logic-based attempts have also ignored the ambiguities introduced by the logical connectors in the statutes. "Simple" connectors like "and," "or," "unless," and "except" introduce myriad alternative interpretations of the logical structure of even the simplest statutes [Allen and Saxon 1987].

12.2 Jurisprudential Debate about Analogical Reasoning

The variety of AI approaches to modeling legal reasoning reflects some deep-set divisions in jurisprudence and legal practice: civil law versus common law traditions, logic versus experience, rules versus cases, corporate practice versus litigation. Jurisprudential theory about analogical legal reasoning is an intellectual battleground where these competing forces meet.

As described in [Burton 1985, p. 40], what might be called the standard model of analogical legal reasoning requires three steps:

1. Identifying a proper base point or precedent

2. Identifying factual similarities and differences between a base point and a problem situation, or analyzing the facts to compare and contrast the precedent with the problem case

3. Determining whether the factual similarities or the differences are more important under the circumstances or deciding whether to follow or distinguish the precedent

The most famous account of analogical legal reasoning is in [Levi 1949]. Although Levi characterizes the second and third steps as a process of identifying in the precedent the "inherent" rule of law that is applied to the second case, he also says that "in an important sense legal rules are never clear" [Levi 1949, p. 1] and that "the rules change as the rules are applied. More important, the rules arise from a process that, while comparing fact situations, creates the rules and then applies them" [Levi 1949, pp. 3–4]. Other accounts are referred to in [Wellman 1985].

The standard model of analogical reasoning in law has been criticized on two scores. First, the account does not provide guidance for determining in step 3 what similarities and differences are more important. Burton says: "But the crucial third step in such reasoning is left unguided. Judging what facts are more important under the circumstances remains mysterious activity, subject to little apparent governance by the analogical form or the rules of the common law" [Burton 1985, p. 40]. Second, the account fails to specify how to evaluate competing analogies. Wellman says: "What makes an analogical argument valid? What are the criteria by which we could evaluate any given use of analogy by a judge? Consider the situation in which a problematic legal dispute is similar to two (or more) different precedents. There is some analogy to be drawn between the case at hand and each of the precedents. Which analogy is preferable?" [Wellman 1985, p. 83].

Hypo's model of analogical legal reasoning meets both of these criticisms of the traditional model of analogical legal reasoning. First, it provides a justifiable means for specifying what similarities and differences are more important. The set of similarities and differences that are important is defined in terms of shared and unshared factors. For each factor (represented in Hypo by a Dimension) there is at least one case where a court said that the factor was important and decided the case either because, or in spite, of that factor. Hypo determines which of the similarities and differences are more important with respect to a particular problem situation when it selects the best precedents to cite, distinguish, and pose as counterexamples or targets for hypotheticals and when it determines the salient features of those precedents. The similarities and differences associated with the definitions of the best cases and salient features are more important. (Expressions for the best cases and salient features are set forth in chapter 9.)

Second, it follows that there are criteria in Hypo's account of analogical legal reasoning for evaluating competing analogies. The specific criteria for evaluation of arguments, including criteria for choosing among the most analogous precedents, are presented in chapters 4 and 9. The criteria prefer cases that are more on point to the problem situation and arguments that cite precedents that cannot be trumped.

Although the theory of precedential reasoning implemented in Hypo answers questions that the traditional model of analogical legal reasoning leaves open, these answers are not complete. We expect more from law students' explanations of why a precedent should or should not be followed than a discussion of the superficial, factual similarities and differences associated with factors. We expect their explanations to invoke some principled analysis of why the similarities and differences matter and to structure their explanations to reflect the relevant statutes and court-made rules. Thus, at first glance, Hypo's approach to identifying important similarities and differences may not seem philosophically satisfying. But consider the alternatives.

An alternative answer that does seem to have philosophical appeal is that judges do or should resort to generally agreed-upon legal rules or principles to determine what similarities and differences are more important in drawing the analogy. [Dworkin 1977] describes a coherence view of legal reasoning that posits the existence of generally agreed-upon principles that best justify existing precedents. These principles are worked into a general theory that can be used to decide novel disputes. [Rawls 1971] presents a similar coherence theory of moral reasoning. See the characterization of Dworkin's and Rawls's theories as coherence theories in [Stick 1986, notes 43, 66]. Coherence theories are interesting in that they anticipate that the general principles will conflict in specific fact situations, that at least some of the principles will be modified in the light of those conflicts, and that some cases will simply be decided wrongly. Coherence theories do not necessarily involve analogical reasoning—Dworkin believes that the resulting general theory is sufficient to lead the judge to the one right answer in any legal case [Dworkin 1978]—but they do suggest an answer to the first criticism. The antecedents of the possibly conflicting general principles would focus the judge on particular features of the cases that are the basis of similarities and differences most significant in the light of the principles.

The problem with this view is that in the context of a lawsuit, even a generally agreed upon principle will not be agreed to by the party against whom it is going to be used. What is the principle? How can one tell? What does it mean? How does it apply in the problem situation? Where principles conflict, how should the conflict be resolved? The parties will have to make arguments to the judge justifying that a particular principle should or should not be relied upon in determining the similarities and differences that are important.

The preferred way to make those arguments is to cite and distinguish yet other cases where a previous court said that it applied the given principle in determining that particular similarities or differences were more significant and to argue by analogy that the same principle should be applied in the current case. But that means one again must draw an analogy between the current fact situation and those other cases, which involves us in the same question of how to determine which similarities and differences are more important for drawing those analogies, an infinite regress.

When dealing with justifications, one has to start somewhere. Generally accepted principles are an option, but where, as in law, the meanings of the principles are not well defined except by reference to the cases decided under them, a different starting point is necessary.

Hypo starts with precedential justifications that are expressed in terms of factors and cases represented as collections of factors and an outcome. The factors are collections of superficial empirical facts about cases. Unlike legal principles or rules, one can assert that a factor applies to a case without having to cite yet another case in support.

Whereas other researchers have attacked the problem of modeling principled analogical legal analysis from the law side, the research described in this book attacks it from the facts side. Hypo's assumptions about defining similarities and differences in terms of factors and its criteria for evaluating legal arguments are empirically realistic simplifications that allow a computer program, in a legally reasonable way, to justify conclusions by citing analogous cases, draw simple factual analogies, and respond by distinguishing and citing counterexamples.

Undoubtedly fundamental legal principles play a role in legal analogical reasoning. They are invoked regularly in legal arguments, and their use in case-citing arguments is complex and pervasive. But one cannot hope to model that kind of adversarial reasoning until one understands the simpler, more factual analogical comparisons among precedents described in this book.

12.3 The Importance of Modeling Hypothetical Reasoning

Hypothetical reasoning is a key to exploring the dialectics between cases and principles or between cases and rules. It is no accident that the classic method for teaching law, the Socratic method, involves a professor's posing hypotheticals to test a student's understanding.

Advocates and judges often pose hypotheticals to analyze or argue about legal disputes. The hypotheticals are usually designed in such a way that if they were to be decided by a court, they would present some interesting quandaries, the resolution of which would have a significant effect on how to decide the case at hand. For some examples, let us look at hypotheticals posed in oral arguments before the U.S. Supreme Court. The recorded oral arguments before the Court, and the written briefs and opinions, are a repository of case-based argument.

Supreme Court justices are particularly famous for posing hypotheticals as both analytical and rhetorical tools to expose the strengths and weaknesses of a legal position. To the chagrin of counsel before the bar of the Supreme Court, the justices frequently interrupt an attorney's oral presentation to pose hypothetical fact situations to which the attorney must respond.

Like other judges, lawyers and law professors, the justices pose hypotheticals for a variety of purposes in legal argument:

- To compare a fact situation to significant cases from past experience

- To factor a complex situation into component parts (e.g., by exaggerating strengths, weaknesses, or by hypothetically eliminating features)

- To create a test case that puts an issue or pits competing features against each other

- To present, support, and attack positions in an argument (e.g., by testing consequences of a tentative conclusion, pressing an assertion to its limits and exploring the meaning of a concept)

- To control the course of an argument (e.g., by focusing attention of participants in a discussion on particular issues)

- To explain the meaning of a statute or rule by augmenting an existing case base with meaningful test or training cases

12.3.1 Relating Fact Situation to Past Cases

A good example primarily of the first purpose of hypotheticals, to relate a fact situation to past cases, is found in the oral argument of *Lynch v. Donnelly*, 104 S. Ct. 1355 (1984). The issue was the constitutionality under the First Amendment of the city of Pawtucket, Rhode Island's, display of a Christmas time crèche on municipal land. The First Amendment of the U.S. Constitution says that "Congress shall make no law respecting an establishment of religion, or prohibiting the free exercise thereof." The justices posed the following hypotheticals:

To the attorney for the city:

Q: Do you think... that a city could display a nativity scene alone without other displays such as Santa Claus and Christmas trees...?

Q: [C]ould the city display a cross for the celebration of Easter, under your view?

To the attorney opposing the display:

Q: [S]upposing the creche were just one ornament on the Christmas tree and you could hardly see it unless you looked very closely, would that be illegal?

Q: What if they had three wisemen and a star in one exhibit, say? Would that be enough?... What if you had an exhibit that had not the creche itself, but just three camels out in the desert and a star up in the sky?

Q: Well, the city could not display religious paintings or artifacts in its museum under your theory.

Q: There is nothing self-explanatory about a creche to somebody... who has never been exposed to the Christian religion.

Q: Would the display up on the frieze in this courtroom of the Ten Commandments be unconstitutional then, in your view?

Q: Several years ago... there was a ceremony held on the Mall, which is federal property of course.... [T]here were 200,000 or 300,000 people... and the ceremony was presided over by Pope John Paul II. Would you say that was a step toward an establishment of religion violative of the religion clauses? ... Then you think it would be all right to put a creche over on the Mall? ... How do you distinguish a high mass from a creche?... [T]here was a considerable involvement of government in that ceremony, hundreds of extra policemen on duty, streets closed for traffic control purposes, and all that sort of thing. That was a considerable governmental involvement, was it not? [*SUP Lynch v. Donnelly*, Case No. 82-1256, Fiche No. 5, pp. 9, 11, 32, 37-45]

In these questions, the justices were modifying the fact situation along various dimensions: changing the location, focus, size, and symbolic religious content of the display, the nature of the viewer, and the degree of government involvement.

The purpose of some of the modifications is to compare the fact situation to actual cases previously decided by the Court to test whether the current situation presents stronger or weaker facts. See e.g., *Stone v. Graham*, 449 U.S. 39 (1980): Posting copies of Ten Commandments in schools held unconstitutional; *Gilfillan v. City of Philadelphia*, 637 F.2d 924 (CA3 1980): City-financed platform and cross used by Pope John Paul II to celebrate public mass held unconstitutional; *McCreary v. Stone*, 575 F. Supp. 1112 (SDNY 1983): Not unconstitutional for village not to refuse permit to private group to erect crèche in public park. Each of these cases has facts similar to those of the hypotheticals posed by the justices. One may infer that the justices had those specific cases in mind from the fact that they were cited in various of the appellate briefs with which the justices would be familiar by the time of the oral argument [Kurland and Casper 1985]. The last hypothetical, regarding the pope's mass, is interesting because there the actual "case" is significant because it did *not* give rise to litigation.

12.3.2 Argument Testing and Rhetorical Uses of Hypotheticals

Hypotheticals are also used as analytical and rhetorical tools to test the consequences of a proposed holding, test the limits of a definition, simplify complicated fact situations for analysis, and as rhetorical tools to control argument.

Frequently the justices use the hypothetical to apply pressure to the rule proposed by an attorney for deciding the case. That can be seen in the mall example and in the following example from *New Jersey v. T.L.O.*, 105 S. Ct. 733 (1985), a case involving the constitutionality of a high school vice-principal's search of a female student's handbag for cigarettes after a teacher reported that she had been smoking in the girls' room. A justice asked, "Do you think then that a male teacher could conduct a pat-down search of a young woman at age sixteen to find the cigarettes?" In response, the attorney for the state took the position that the Fourth Amendment of the U.S. Constitution, which has been interpreted as prohibiting unreasonable searches by law enforcement authorities, does not apply to high school administrators. The justice rejoined, "And does that mean that their authority then to make searches, if the Fourth Amendment is completely inapplicable, extends to any kind of search, strip search or otherwise?" [*SUP New Jersey v. T.L.O.*, 1984 Term, Fiche No. 5, pp. 13–22].

In the argument of *Sony Corp. v. Universal City Studios*, 464 U.S. 417 (1984), an attorney argued for the plaintiff that if Sony sold video recorders while knowing that consumers would use them to copy copyrighted materials, then Sony should be legally responsible to the owners of the copyrights. The technical issue was whether Sony was liable for contributory infringement (responsible for someone else's direct copyright infringement) despite the fact that the recorders had a "substantial noninfringing use" (were capable of being used without necessarily infringing someone's copyright.) The following interchange occurred:

Q: Suppose... that about ten percent of all programming could be copied without any interference by the producer or whoever owned the program....
A: I don't think that would make any difference. I think ten percent is too small of an amount.
Q: Well, what about 50?

The attorney for the Studios asserted that even if there were only one television program that was copyrighted, if Sony knew the program would be copied, it would be legally responsible. Finally, the justice asked,

Q: Under your test, supposing somebody tells the Xerox people that there are people who are making illegal copies with their machine and they know it.... But your view of the law is that as long as Xerox knows that there's some illegal copying going on, Xerox is a contributory infringer?
A: To be consistent, Your Honor, I'd have to say yes.
Q: A rather extreme position. [*SUP Sony Corp. v. Universal City Studios*, Case No. 81-1687, Fiche No. 2, pp. 21–25]

In the last two examples, although the altered fact situations posed by the justice are still covered by the proposed rule, it is progressively harder for the attorney to justify applying the rule to the hypotheticals because the latter present progressively weaker facts. The justice stacks the hypothetical with more extreme facts that weigh against the party in the hypothetical who corresponds to the attorney's client. The attorney is forced to distinguish the hypothetical, to come up with some alternative explanation for why the hypothetical and the current fact situation need not be decided the same way. The pressure on the attorney to distinguish is especially strong if the hypotheticals are closely based on actual cases that the Court has decided or for which there are strong reasons to decide, contrary to the way it would be decided if the proposed rule were followed.

12.3.3 Supreme Court Hypotheticals Revisited

Any model of principled legal analysis needs to model the process of posing hypotheticals. Posing hypotheticals is a way of probing the meanings of the principles and rules invoked as rationalizations for a result. Those meanings cannot adequately be expressed in terms of a logical statement of necessary and sufficient conditions. But the meanings, at least, can be probed, manipulated, stretched, and broken by the methodology of posing hypotheticals. In this sense, the process of posing hypotheticals is the best link we have between the possible facts of legal disputes and legal conclusions.

Hypo makes a start at modeling arguing with hypotheticals. Like the justices and arguers before the Court, Hypo poses hypotheticals to compare a fact situation to past precedents and to show how arguments can be strengthened and weakened. In addition, Hypo's model of Dimensions and heuristics for building hypotheticals is general enough to analyze the sequence of hypotheticals posed by the justices in the *Lynch* and *Sony* cases.

The hypotheticals about the civic crèche display from the *Lynch* case oral argument can be analyzed in Dimensional terms. The justices make the basic fact situation weaker and stronger along a Dimension that might be called *focus-of-attention*: they remove all of the secular images, leaving only the religious one; they physically shrink the symbol to an extreme and relegate it to a corner; or they remove the religious symbols and leave the secular ones. They weaken plaintiff's case along the Dimension of *civic-content-message* by moving it to a municipal art museum or the frieze of a courtroom. They compare the case along the Dimension of *government-involvement* to an extreme example, the pope's mass on the mall.

Similarly, the hypotheticals of the *Sony* case oral argument can be analyzed in terms of houristic moves along Dimensions. There the Court repeatedly weakened the case for the plaintiff along the Dimension of *possible-noninfringing-use*, changing the values of the focal slot, percentage of uncopyrighted sources of the work, from 10 percent to 50 percent. The attorney took the final step of weakening it further to an extreme case, 99.99 percent of the programs being uncopyrighted, as a means of rhetorically underscoring the significance of strengthening the case along a conflicting Dimension *known-infringing-uses* by posing that the defendant knew that 0.01 percent of programs that were copyrighted were being infringed.

12.4 Extending Hypo

In this section, I briefly sketch the promise and problems of extending the research methodology described in this book in six ways to build an extension of Hypo (Extended Hypo or Hypo-XL) that could perform one or more of the following tasks: reason with abstract legal predicates, pose sophisticated hypotheticals to test predicates' meanings, tutor with hypotheticals, argue by analogy from other kinds of claims, connect with existing legal databases, learn Dimensions.

12.4.1 Reasoning with Abstract Legal Predicates

Statutes and other express rules from constitutions and regulations, court-made rules for deciding claims, and general principles propounded by courts as decisional guides can be seen as theoretical rationales for legal conclusions. They employ abstract theoretical terms, legal predicates like "reasonable time," "ordinary care," or "substantial noninfringing use." The predicates are not adequately defined to enable deductively inferring whether they apply to a fact situation, and there may be disagreements among courts as to which rationales to apply, how to formulate them, and what they mean.

To suggest what such a rationale for a legal conclusion might look like in the context of a now-familiar example, consider how Hypo-XL might reformulate the point and response in Argument [1] of the *Crown* Extended Example from chapter 5:

> ↪ Point for Side 1, the defendant:
>
> Hypo-XL cites *Midland Ross* for the proposition that, after disclosing its information to outsiders, plaintiff Crown could no longer satisfy the "Secrecy" element of a trade secrets misappropriation claim.
>
> ↪ Response for Side 2, the plaintiff:
>
> Hypo-XL responds that plaintiff Crown does not need to satisfy any Secrecy element. Crown has as much of a secret after disclosing its confidential information to just 5 people as the plaintiff in *Data General* had after disclosing its information to 6,000 people, which is to say, no secret at all.

In this example, the more abstract legal predicate at the focus of the dispute is Secrecy. Although there is disagreement as to what the elements of a trade secrets claim are, there is no dearth of court opinions or legal treatises that purport to define a trade secret. Secrecy is on almost everybody's list of elements, although usually the authorities do not purport to define Secrecy beyond making the generally unhelpful distinction between "absolute" and "relative" secrecy. See [Milgrim 1985] and [Nimmer 1985]. Hypo-XL's argument on behalf of Side 2 is that 6,000 is such a large number of disclosees that the court in *Data General*, in effect, has waived, or at least weakened, any requirement of Secrecy.

An extended Hypo would need a more extensive vocabulary of abstract legal predicates. Its current vocabulary of abstract legal predicates is very limited, comprising basically only the legal claims with which it deals: trade secrets misappropriation and breach of contract, especially breach of nondisclosure and noncompetition agreements.

Extending Hypo's vocabulary of abstract legal predicates entails dealing with the problem that the predicates are not well defined. Just as with Hypo's claims, the theoretical concepts employed in express legal rules frequently have no definitions sufficient to deduce whether the terms apply to a fact situation. The meanings of the abstract terms, like the meanings of claims, come from the cases, in particular from the holdings of courts as to whether the term was satisfied in a given fact situation, and the methods for analogizing from one fact situation to another. Thus, an attorney will need to cite cases to support an assertion that a particular legal predicate is satisfied, just as he or she would to support an assertion that a particular party should win a claim. In addition, the methods of response—distinguishing and citing counterexamples—still apply.

In extending Hypo's vocabulary of abstract legal terms, the same approach would be employed to represent the terms' meanings as has been used in Hypo to represent the meanings of claims. An Extended Hypo would tag certain important predicates with cases where the issue was litigated of whether the predicate was satisfied. Just as Dimensions in Hypo represent factors that affect claims, in an Extended Hypo, Dimensions would represent factors that affect other legal predicates like the elements of claims. Cases where courts held that a particular predicate was or was not satisfied would be indexed by both the predicate and the

Dimensions along which they are stronger and weaker examples of the predicate.

There would still be some difficult problems to solve before an Extended Hypo could reason effectively with more abstract legal predicates. These problems include selecting the right predicates, representing the rationale espoused by a court in a precedent, supporting multiple alternative rationales of a precedent, dealing with interactions among factors and predicates, and dealing with the logic of the predicates.

Selection If one is to represent more abstract legal terminology, one must choose which theoretical terms to represent. The goal is to pick terms that tend to be litigated. This may be quite controversial in dealing with court-made rules. Substantially different formulations of a rule may appear in different opinions or even in the same opinion.

Augmenting Case Representation Hypo's representation of how a case is decided will need to be augmented to reflect the court's rationale for deciding the case. The predicates applied by the court and its holding as to whether a predicate is satisfied will have to be identified. This also is not uncontroversial. Courts may not state clearly what issues they are deciding, what the criteria for decision are, or how they decided the issue. Thus the process of entering cases into the CKB will require considerably more interpretation.

Multiple Interpretations To be faithful to the way legal argument is performed, an extension of Hypo should deal with at least some of the alternative rationales that have currency in the domain. Thus, in addition to representing the rationale that the court did apply in a precedent, it is also necessary for the program to reinterpret the case in terms of at least some of the alternative rationales that the court chose not to apply. There usually is an alternative; if the court had come to the opposite result, it probably would have said that it was employing a different test. Different principles, statutes, rules, or formulations of rules would have been applied to rationalize the result. The alternative rationales are found in other lines of precedents.

Interactions Among Factors and Predicates As one starts to deal with theoretical components of claims, one will not be able to avoid dealing with the theoretical interactions among the factors. Facts that are strengths for one component of a claim may be weaknesses for another. Although this problem exists for Hypo now, it is ameliorated by Hypo's focus on claims. The potentially complex detailed interactions among factors tend to be lumped together in the court's final decision of the claim. Although facts that are strengths for one claim may be weaknesses for another claim, Hypo's criteria for evaluating arguments do not take those more complex strategic interactions into account. Since a legal claim is a basic and important unit—lawyers tend to consider individual claims independently even though they also care about the overall lawsuit—this oversimplification has not posed major problems.

Logic of the Predicates Another complication is the logical interaction among the predicates. Although the predicates are not well enough defined to allow one to deduce whether they apply, they are defined to some extent, if only by their common nontechnical usage. Arguments that describe precedents in terms of abstract theoretical predicates will thus have to deal with avoiding or exploiting apparent inconsistencies in terms. In addition, these predicates are embedded in statutes and rules that have a logical structure which must be taken into account. The logical connectors "and," "or," and "unless" introduce their own ambiguities of scope with which the program must deal [Allen and Saxon 1987].

12.4.2 Pose Sophisticated Hypotheticals to Test Predicates' Meanings

Although arguing about the meanings of predicates is beyond Hypo's present capabilities, with some modifications, an Extended Hypo could pose a series of hypotheticals to stretch a predicate's meaning. For example, Hypo does "know" that *Data General* is an extreme case for the plaintiff in some sense. It is a boundary case for plaintiff along the *Secrets-Disclosed-Outsiders* Dimension; it is the case involving the most disclosures of the secret to outsiders where the plaintiff still won. By linking the legal predicate, the element of Secrecy in a trade secrets case, to that Dimension, an Extended Hypo would "know" that moving to an extreme along the Dimension could put pressure on the meaning of Secrecy.

It might invoke the stretching strategy in a case, like *Data General* itself, where the plaintiff has made the point that although it has disclosed its allegedly confidential information to 6,000 outsiders, the information still satisfies the element of Secrecy because all of the outsiders agreed to maintain confidentiality.

An extended Hypo could pose successive hypotheticals to show that one cannot draw a rational line between what is and is not a secret and therefore that plaintiff's information is not secret. The following example uses this rather sophisticated way of arguing that confidentiality restrictions on disclosures should not save a plaintiff's trade secret:

How Hypo-XL Might Pose Line-Drawing Hypotheticals

↪ Point for Side 1, the defendant:

Hypo-XL would cite *Midland Ross* for the proposition that, after disclosing its information to 6,000 outsiders, plaintiff Data General could no longer satisfy the Secrecy element of a trade secrets misappropriation claim.

↪ Response for Side 2, the plaintiff:

Hypo-XL responds that plaintiff's information still satisfies the element of Secrecy despite the disclosures because all of the outsiders agreed to maintain confidentiality.

↪ Rebuttal for Side 1, the defendant:

Hypo-XL poses series of hypotheticals:

(1) What if Data General made 10 million disclosures, all subject to restrictions. Would they be a secret? No!

(2) One hundred thousand disclosures. Still a secret? No!

(3) Ten thousand? Where does one draw the line?

Modeling more sophisticated kinds of argument is computationally more complex because arguers have more options. If an arguer cites a precedent in support of an assertion that the precedent's legal rationale should be applied to decide the problem situation, an opponent may attack the precedent on either the facts or the law. Instead of just responding to a precedent by distinguishing its facts or citing a more-on-point counterexample, an arguer may also be able to attack the rationale applied in the precedent.

An arguer may attack the rationale of a precedent in at least two ways: by arguing that a legal predicate should not even be part of the proposed rule for decision or that the predicate, though part of the rule, is not satisfied. The examples of more sophisticated arguments illustrate the two possibilities. In the first, the arguer, in effect, asserts that the rule for deciding a trade secrets case should not even require the Secrecy element. In the second, the arguers dispute whether the element of Secrecy is satisfied.

12.4.3 Tutoring with Hypotheticals

Getting a computer program to pose more sophisticated hypotheticals in arguments raises problems of complexity. One area where these problems may be manageable is in devising a computerized tutor.

A facility for posing tough hypotheticals is a great asset for those who teach law or ethics. Tough hypotheticals pose moral dilemmas, pitting one general principle against another. They force students to penetrate the bland generalities of legal or ethical rules and confront the hard problems of applying general rules to specific contexts.

As a computerized tutor, an Extended Hypo could pose hypotheticals to teach students legal or ethical principles or rules. The program would introduce the rules by posing clear cases satisfying or violating the rules. Then the system would hypothetically modify the cases by exaggerating or ameliorating factors or by combining conflicting factors of positive and negative examples. The goal of the modifications might be to change a clear case into one where rules or principles conflict. The system would ask the students how the changes strengthened or weakened the analysis of the case in terms of the rules and what new arguments could be made.

From the viewpoint of complexity, a computerized tutor could be a good research vehicle. For a given lesson, the tutor could work with fewer cases chosen for didactic effect. The program could deal with richer representations of the factors along which a case can be modified and richer representations of the rules and principles to be taught.

12.4.4 Arguing by Analogy from Other Kinds of Claims

A somewhat simpler extension of Hypo's adversarial case-based methodology would be to get Hypo to argue by analogy from other kinds of claims. When, in searching for precedents that support a client's position, a lawyer cannot find any that deal with the same claim, he or she may resort to cases dealing with similar fact situations in other claims.

In effect, the attorney relaxes the criteria of what constitutes an analogous case to accept cases that at least favor the right side in similar circumstances, even if not under the right rubric. Courts actually do apply cases from one kind of claim to another. For example, in deciding in favor of the defendant Sony on the copyright claim in *Sony Corp. v. Universal City Studios*, 464 U.S. 417,456 (1984), the Supreme Court cited patent cases that raised the same factual issue of the existence of a substantial noninfringing use.

An Extended Hypo could import arguments from one claim to another by looking for analogous cases to cite for a side in Claim Lattices for other claims that it constructs for a current fact situation. For example, in Argument [5] of the *Crown* Extended Example, Hypo-XL could respond to citation of the *Data General* case, cited on a claim for trade secrets misappropriation, in a way that would be appropriate for a contracts claim. It could raise the issue of whether the outsider's contractual obligations not to disclose the secrets could be enforced where there is no evidence that the contracts were supported by consideration. If the nondisclosure agreements between plaintiff and its outside disclosees are not enforceable, then plaintiff has failed adequately to protect its secrets.

There are two key elements to this kind of reasoning: (1) Hypo-XL's failure to make an argument response drives it to consider cases from different domains that are further afield. (2) Hypo-XL must appropriately relax the criteria of analogy to unearth cases that are still useful for the argument.

For example, in its attempt to find a way to respond to the point citing the *Data General* case in Argument [5] on behalf of defendant as Side 2, the 3-Ply Arguer would be frustrated because there are no more-on-point counterexamples in the Claim Lattice. As a result, Hypo-XL would check lattices dealing with other claims. Since the current fact situation involves an agreement between plaintiff and disclosees to keep the disclosures confidential, Hypo-XL would also construct around the cfs a Claim Lattice for a contracts claim. It would determine that there is a pro-defendant contracts most-on-point case, *Dougherty v. Salt* (227 N.Y. 200 1919), which held against the party trying to enforce the contract where the other party received nothing of value for entering into the agreement (the contract was held to be unenforceable for lack of consideration). Since there is no information in the problem situation that the disclosees received any consideration either, Hypo-XL would cite the *Dougherty* case in response. In this example, relaxing the criteria of analogy meant treating a weakness in a hypothetical contracts claim of plaintiff against its disclosees as a weakness of plaintiff's trade secrets claim against the defendant.

There is no guaranty that such a response, imported from another claim, will be meaningful. But as a general heuristic, when the underlying facts of cases are similar, so are the legal considerations despite the difference in formal claims. For example, the nonenforceability of nondisclosure agreements is suggested as a threat to protecting trade secrets in [Gilburne, 1982, p. 231].

12.4.5 Connecting with Legal Databases

Hypo presents the possibility of a considerable advance over current means of access to the existing legal databases, Lexis and Westlaw, which now require cumbersome keyword searches and whose ranking of returned cases is based on statistical criteria that do not adequately capture the relevance of the cases to the attorney user's inquiry. The fact that Hypo performs sophisticated argument tasks using a simple Dimensional scheme for representing and reasoning about the argument significance of case features suggests that its basic mechanisms of case-based reasoning could also be used to order cases returned by database queries more intelligently in terms of their real relevance to an attorney's problem.

A simple link between the current version of Hypo and these databases would allow an attorney to conduct research in the following way. The attorney would describe the fact situation to the program. Hypo would conduct its analysis, retrieve cases from its CKB, and present them to the attorney in the form of 3-Ply Arguments and Claim Lattices. If the attorney wanted to examine the text of the cases, he or she would be able to retrieve them on the basis of the citation information contained in the Hypo version of the case. The top-level case frames of cases in the CKB contain the citation to where the actual text of the opinions may be found. With that information, a Lexis or Westlaw search could be conducted on the citation fields of cases in their case databases. Thus, the attorney could have not only Hypo's summary of the cases and how they may be used but the full text of the actual decision.

A more sophisticated link between an Extended Hypo and these databases offers the promise of making available their enormous databases of cases. An Extended Hypo program could be used to help prune the cases returned by a Lexis or Westlaw search so that only the best cases (in Hypo's more intelligent sense of "best") are presented first to the attorney. Since it is unlikely that one can restructure the way cases are represented in Lexis or Westlaw, this would entail being able to reexpress the thousand or so cases returned by Lexis or Westlaw in a Hypo-type representation scheme, a sophisticated natural language problem. The problem may be simplified somewhat by the fact that West's key numbering scheme with its abstracts of the cases is also on line. Those abstracts and the key numbering scheme correspond, to some extent, to Hypo's Dimensions, offering the possibility of filling out a legal case frame representation from the abstracts. An Extended Hypo could then select the most-on-point or troublesome cases to present to the attorney.

12.4.6 Learning Dimensions

Of the variety of learning tasks that an Extended Hypo might perform, the hardest and most important is learning new Dimensions. Two cornerstones of the current Hypo program will be very important for that difficult task: comparing arguments and posing hypotheticals.

An Extended Hypo would determine that it needs to learn a new Dimension by comparing the best arguments it can make about a case with the actual decision of the court. If Hypo-XL's strongest arguments favored one side but the court decided in favor of the other side, that would present an anomaly indicating the need to learn something new. For example, if the *Outsider-Disclosures-Restricted* Dimension had been unknown at the time *Data General* was entered into the CKB, the circumstance that plaintiff won the case despite the fact that Hypo-XL could only make pro-defendant arguments is an anomaly. It would alert a learning module to the need to acquire knowledge of a yet unknown, pro-plaintiff Dimension associated with *Data General*.

Learning Dimensions presents hard problems of credit assignment. An anomaly like the above would have a number of possible explanations. The case may present factors unknown to Hypo-XL's library of Dimensions. These factors would be the basis of new Dimensions. The court may not have resolved conflicting, existing factors in the same way that Hypo-XL did. The court may have applied argument evaluation criteria that were different from Hypo-XL's.

An Extended Hypo's ability to pose hypothetical test cases would be essential for testing what the correct resolution of the anomaly should be. By posing hypothetical variants of the case that add, subtract, or exaggerate factors, the program would have some tools with which to address the credit assignment problem.

13 Conclusion

This book has described a working model of the way attorneys argue with legal cases and hypotheticals. The model is embodied in Hypo, a computer program that analyzes problem disputes dealing with trade secrets, retrieves relevant legal cases from its Case Knowledge Base, and cites them in reasonable legal arguments for and against both sides in the dispute. Hypo's arguments demonstrate its ability to reason symbolically with past cases, to draw simple factual analogies among cases, to cite and distinguish precedents, and to pose counterexamples and hypotheticals.

13.1 A Model of Adversarial Case-Based Reasoning

Hypo's reasoning, and the kind of legal argument it simulates, are examples of adversarial case-based reasoning, a general kind of reasoning from experience as represented by specific past cases. Basically the reasoner

- analyzes a problem situation by comparing it to past cases;
- justifies deciding the problem like a particular precedent by drawing an analogy or justifies not deciding the problem like the case by distinguishing them and drawing competing analogies to counterexamples, real and hypothetical;
- makes the strongest possible arguments citing precedents on all sides of the issue;
- evaluates the competing arguments, deciding the problem situation accordingly, if possible, and explaining the decision by discussing the competing arguments.

The partial theory of adversarial case-based reasoning set forth in this book deals with a simplified kind of legal argument from precedents. It assumes that a past case can be represented abstractly as a collection of possibly conflicting factors, and factor magnitudes, tending to favor, or not favor, a particular outcome and an actual outcome assigned to the case by an authoritative decision maker, the judge. According to the theory, an arguer justifies a decision in a new case by citing a precedent with the desired outcome and as close to the same factors and magnitudes as possible. The precedent justifies resolving the problem's conflicting factors in the same way that they were resolved in the precedent.

The theory provides computational definitions regarding the roles that precedents play in case-based arguments. Specifically, the theory defines the following concepts in terms of set theory notation and factors:

- Relevant similarities and differences among cases

- Most analogous precedents

- Roles of precedents in arguments as cited cases, distinguished cases, counterexamples, and targets for hypotheticals

- Four kinds of counterexamples: trumping, as on point or partial, boundary and potentially trumping

For each argument role, the theory provides definitions of the best precedents to cite given a problem dispute and the features of a precedent that are salient when cited in that role. The theory also provides rudimentary criteria for evaluating conflicting precedent-citing arguments.

Hypo, in effect, implements the partial theory of adversarial case-based reasoning using four basic knowledge sources: (1) a Legal Case Frame language for representing information about a legal case similar to that found in a law school student's brief; (2) a Case Knowledge Base for collecting actual and hypothetical cases; (3) Dimensions, a general scheme for representing factors; and (4) standards for evaluating arguments citing cases. There are thirteen implemented Dimensions and thirty legal cases in Hypo's Case Knowledge Base.

Five basic operations of case-based reasoning, which, in effect, implement the definitions of the partial theory, have been described in detail. These basic operations are ordering analogous cases, selecting most-analogous cases, identifying configurations of counterexamples among the most-analogous cases, posing hypotheticals to explore connections to neighboring cases, and comparing case-based analyses of different problem situations.

Adversarial case-based reasoning is not just for attorneys. It applies to a variety of domains where experts argue with or extrapolate from case examples. Examples of similar reasoning have been drawn from everyday discourse, political decision making, and appraising values.

13.2 Contribution to AI

The work contributes to research in artificial intelligence not only as an example of a case-based reasoner that works but as an example of an expert system that (1) presents alternative answers, not just the one "right" answer, (2) argues in favor of the alternatives, and (3) models intelligent behavior in a messy domain that lacks a strong theoretical model.

The research addresses five general issues that are of central concern to AI: relevance, credit assignment, inference control and indexing, analogical reasoning, and explanation.

Relevance Hypo employs its model of the way cases are used in arguments to make assessments of the relevance of cases and of the aspects of a case that are salient within the context of the argument. In assessing relevance and salience, Hypo's computational definitions and procedures take the following contextual circumstances into account:

- Purpose of the arguer in citing the case as a justification, in particular, the claim asserted and the side the arguer takes

- Role of the precedent in an argument. Relevance and salience depend on whether the arguer needs the precedent to make a point or respond to one, to draw an analogy to the precedent or distinguish it, to cite a counterexample to it, or to cite it as a counterexample. If the precedent is cited as a counterexample, relevance and salience depend on the kind of counterexample.

- Facts of the problem situation. A precedent's relevance depends on the features (in Hypo, the factors) it shares or does not share with the problem situation.

- Other precedents. Relevance depends on the existence of other, possibly contradictory, precedents that may be as or more analogous to the problem. As counterexamples, these precedents may diminish a precedent's significance.

Since Hypo takes context into account, it is able to assess relevance and salience dynamically. It flexibly interprets the significance of a precedent and the salience of its features in the light of the side and claim argued for, the precedent's role in the argument, the specific facts of the problem situation, and the other precedents in the CKB. In effect, Hypo reciprocally views a problem in the light of the precedents in the Case Knowledge Base and views the precedents in the context of the problem. As a result, Hypo's descriptions of the salient aspects of a single precedent differ depending on the context.

Credit Assignment Assigning credit or blame among the competing factors in a problem is hard for two reasons. First, the cases are not neat. When comparing the problem to precedents, all other things are not equal. In most instances, the competing most analogous cases do not differ relative to the problem situation and to each other in only one respect but in several. Their factors overlap to various extents. The magnitudes of the factors vary widely. Second, the relative significance of competing factors is highly contextual. Although one factor may usually be more significant than another, in a given case, due to the presence of other factors or extreme differences in factor magnitudes, the opposite may be true.

Knowledge engineers should avoid using a priori hierarchies to select the best matches among the most analogous cases or weighting schemes to combine the effects of competing factors. Such schemes do not account for context; they ignore the effects that the presence of other factors or different magnitudes may have on their significance in specific circumstances. Moreover, the decision of each new case affects the assessment of relevance in ways not necessarily reflected in the hierarchy or combining function.

Hypo deals realistically with the problems of credit assignment: (1) it avoids static feature hierarchies; (2) it deals with factor weights symbolically (its arguments play out alternative interpretations of the significance of competing factors in the light of the precedents); and (3) its tools for generating hypotheticals point to ways of making controlled comparisons among cases. Hypotheticals can be designed to vary just one factor at a time for testing its significance where all other things are kept equal.

Inference Control and Indexing Hypo's facility for making arguments demonstrates the utility of adopting strong, domain-dependent indexes for controlling inference. The Dimensional Index reflects the specific ways that knowledge is organized in the legal domain to facilitate making arguments. The Dimensional Index supports reasoning about cases within the index, in particular, comparing the cases that make stronger or weaker justifications for a given outcome. At the same time, the Dimensional Indexing method is general enough to be useful in nonlegal domains where case comparisons are important.

Analogical Reasoning Hypo provides a mechanism for analogical transfer where there is no strong domain theory for structuring explanations of prior cases that can be mapped to a problem situation. Hypo does not assume that a strong domain theory exists.

Other analogical reasoning programs assume that there will be a best-matched case that is a model for deciding the problem. They transform the differences among nearly analogous cases into point differentials in a matcher. The losers are discarded, and information is lost. By contrast, Hypo makes the comparisons among the best cases symbolically, draws inferences from them, and transforms them into arguments. It also combines information from competing analogous cases.

Explanation Hypo's arguments explain alternative ways to decide the problem by drawing factual analogies to competing cases. Its hypotheticals demonstrate crucial features of the problem and how they affect the decision. Adversarial case-based methods help to explain decisions in domains where explanations are primarily by example and where there is no unique theory for explaining the example. This research goes beyond deductive reasoning domains, with their provably right answers, well-defined predicates, and back-chaining explanations. It also goes beyond explanation-based learning domains with their neat invertible operators.

13.3 Contribution to Legal Philosophy

The partial theory of case-based argument performs a classic function of a theory of argument or rhetoric. It provides a practical and realistic scheme for ordering statements about values, even in the absence of logical deduction. In precedential reasoning, the ordering reflects experience. The more relevantly similar is a past experience and the less that other similar experiences lead to contrary outcomes, the more persuasive is the conclusion.

The theory is only a start at explaining analogical legal argument. Its computational definitions of relevance and on pointness represent a first cut at ordering arguments about value judgments, such as who should win a legal claim. The work is a basis for further research to account for the role of legal principles in selecting among analogies.

Whatever the strengths or weaknesses of Hypo's theory of precedential argument, the research demonstrates a new, contemporary medium for doing jurisprudence. Using artificial intelligence techniques, a legal scholar does not test theoretical constructs on only one or two manually worked out examples. Instead, he or she implements a theory in a computer program that runs not only on the illustrative examples but on other examples as well. Even an only partially successful computational theory of jurisprudence may still prove useful. For example, Lexis and Westlaw represent a theory about legal reasoning: that relevance can be assessed by the appearance of keywords in past cases. No one would accept that theory as adequate, and yet it yields a practical tool.

Finally, the research focuses on appropriate goals for a jurisprudential theory of analogical legal argument. If lawyers argue with precedents precisely because it is not feasible to prove the right answer by deductive logic, then the goal of a theory of analogical legal argument should not be to explain what the right answer is. Precedential reasoning is interesting precisely because, even without logical necessity, there still may be an ordering to the persuasiveness of arguments. The appropriate goal for a theory of arguing from precedents is to describe that order accurately. The theory's success should be measured by the comprehensiveness of the kinds of reasonable legal arguments for which it accounts, its ability to order the arguments according to their persuasiveness, and the extent to which it explains how to generate novel, reasonable arguments, even for a losing side. Hypo is a step toward such a theory.

A. The Uniform Trade Secrets Act

Section 1. [Definitions]

(1) "Improper means" includes theft, bribery, misrepresentation, breach or inducement of a breach of a duty to maintain secrecy, or espionage through electronic or other means;

(2) "Misappropriation" means:

(i) acquisition of a trade secret of another by a person who knows or has reason to know that the trade secret was acquired by improper means; or

(ii) disclosure or use of a trade secret of another without express or implied consent by a person who

(A) used improper means to acquire knowledge of the trade secret; or

(B) at the time of disclosure or use, knew or had reason to know that his knowledge of the trade secret was

(I) derived from or through a person who had utilized improper means to acquire it;

. . .

(4) "Trade secret" means information, including a formula, pattern, compilation, program, device, method, technique, or process, that:

(i) derives independent economic value, actual or potential, from not being generally known to, and not being readily ascertainable by proper means by, other persons who can obtain economic value from its disclosure or use, and

(ii) is the subject of efforts that are reasonable under the circumstances to maintain its secrecy.

Commissioner's Comment

. . .

Proper means include:

1. Discovery by independent invention;
2. Discovery by "reverse engineering", that is, by starting with the known product and working backward to find the method by which it was developed. The acquisition of the known product must of course, also be by a fair and honest means, such as purchase of the item on the open market for reverse engineering to be lawful;
3. Discovery under a license from the owner of the trade secret;
4. Observation of the item in public use or on public display;
5. Obtaining the trade secret from published literature.

B A Restatement of Torts—Section 757

Section 757. Liability for disclosure or use of another's trade secret—General Principle.

One who discloses or uses another's trade secret, without a privilege to do so, is liable to the other if

(a) he discovered the secret by improper means, or

(b) his disclosure or use constitutes a breach of confidence reposed in him by the other in disclosing the secret to him, or

(c) he learned the secret from a third person with notice of the facts that it was a secret and that the third person discovered it by improper means or that the third person's disclosure of it was otherwise a breach of his duty to the other, or

(d) he learned the secret with notice of the facts that it was a secret and that its disclosure was made to him by mistake.

Comment b. Definition of trade secret.

A trade secret may consist of any formula, pattern, device or compilation of information which is used in one's business, and which gives him an opportunity to obtain an advantage over competitors who do not know or use it. It may be a formula for a chemical compound, a process of manufacturing, treating or preserving materials, a pattern for a machine or other device, or a list of customers. . . . A trade secret is a process or device for continuous use in the operation of the business. Generally it relates to the production of goods, as, for example, a machine or formula for the production of an article. It may, however, relate to the sale of goods or to other operations in the business, such as a code for determining discounts, rebates or other concessions in a price list or catalogue, or a list of specialized customers, or a method of bookkeeping or other office management.

The subject matter of a trade secret must be secret. Matters of public knowledge or of general knowledge in an industry cannot be appropriated by one as his secret. Matters which are completely disclosed by the goods which one markets cannot be his secret. Substantially, a trade secret is known only in the particular business in which it is used. It is not requisite that only the proprietor of the business know it. He may, without losing his protection, communicate it to employees involved in its use. He may likewise communicate it to others pledged to secrecy. Others may also know of it independently, as, for example, when they have discovered the process or formula by independent invention and are keeping it secret. Nevertheless, a substantial element of secrecy must exist so that, except by the use of improper means, there would be difficulty in acquiring the information. An exact definition of a trade secret is not possible. Some factors to be considered in determining whether given information is one's trade secret are: (1) the extent to which the information is known outside of his business; (2) the extent to which it is known by employees and others involved in his business; (3) the extent of measures taken by him to guard the secrecy of the information; (4) the value of the information to him and to his competitors; (5) the amount of effort or money expended by him in developing the information; (6) the ease or difficulty with which the information could be properly acquired or duplicated by others.

C A Complete List of Legal Case Frames

Legal

- Case
- Type-Of-Claim
- Party-To-Lawsuit
- Person-Party
- Corporate-Party
- Employee-Party

Actors

- Person
- Corporation

Product-related

- Product
- Knowledge
- Product-Worked-On
- Intrinsic-Similarities
- Security-Breach
- Disclosure-Event

Employment-related

- Employee
- Employment
- Employment-Change

Contracts

- Agreement
- NonCompetition-Cov NonDisclosure-Agreement
- Promise
- Reliance

D Factual Predicates

THERE IS A CORPORATE PLAINTIFF:
   Values: Nil, Corporate-Party, Negative

PLAINTIFF MAKES A PRODUCT:
   Values: Nil, Product, Negative

PLAINTIFF HAS PRODUCT INFORMATION:
   Values: Nil, Knowledge, Negative

THERE IS A CORPORATE DEFENDANT:
   Values: Nil, Corporate-Party, Negative

DEFENDANT MAKES A PRODUCT:
   Values: Nil, Product, Negative

PLAINTIFF AND DEFENDANT COMPETE:
   Values: Nil, Affirmative, Negative

PLAINTIFF'S AND DEFENDANT'S PRODUCTS COMPETE:
   Values: Nil, Affirmative, Negative

THERE IS AN EMPLOYEE DEFENDANT:
   Values: Nil, Employee-Party, Negative

EMPLOYEE WORKED FOR PLAINTIFF:
   Values: Nil, Employment, Negative

EMPLOYEE WORKED FOR DEFENDANT:
   Values: Nil, Employment, Negative

EMPLOYEE WORKED FOR BOTH PLAINTIFF AND DEFENDANT:
   Values: Nil, Affirmative, Negative

EMPLOYEE SWITCHED FROM WORKING FOR PLAINTIFF TO WORKING FOR DEFENDANT:
   Values: Nil, Employment-Change, Negative

EMPLOYEE RECEIVED SOMETHING OF VALUE TO SWITCH EMPLOYMENT:
   Values: Nil, Employment-Change: List of items received, Negative

EMPLOYEE BROUGHT PLAINTIFF'S PRODUCT DEVELOPMENT TOOLS TO DEFENDANT:
Values: Nil, Employment-Change: List of tools brought, Negative

EMPLOYEE WORKED ON PLAINTIFF'S PRODUCT:
Values: Nil, Product-Worked-On, Negative

DEFENDANT HAD ACCESS TO PLAINTIFF'S PRODUCT VIA EMPLOYEE:
Values: Nil, Disclosure-Event, Negative

PLAINTIFF AND EMPLOYEE ENTERED INTO EMPLOYMENT AGREEMENT:
Values: Nil, Agreement, Negative

PLAINTIFF MADE SOME DISCLOSURES TO OUTSIDERS:
Values: Nil, Knowledge: Number of Disclosures, Negative

DISCLOSURES TO OUTSIDERS WERE SUBJECT TO RESTRICTION:
Values: Nil, Knowledge: Percent of Disclosees Restricted, Negative

TYPE OF PRODUCT INFORMATION IS TECHNICAL:
Values: Nil, Product: List of vertical or technical, Negative

DEFENDANT SAVED PRODUCT DEVELOPMENT EXPENSE RELATIVE TO PLAINTIFF:
Values: Nil, Product: List of development times and expenses, Negative

PLAINTIFF ADOPTED SECURITY MEASURES:
Values: Nil, Product: List of security measures, Negative

PLAINTIFF DISCLOSED PRODUCT INFORMATION TO DEFENDANT IN NEGOTIATIONS:
Values: Nil, Disclosure-Event: How disclosure made, Negative

DEFENDANT HAD ACCESS TO PLAINTIFF'S PRODUCT INFORMATION VIA COMMON EMPLOYEE OR NEGOTIATIONS:
Values: Nil, List of Disclosure-Events, Negative

DEFENDANT OR EMPLOYEE ENTERED INTO NONDISCLOSURE AGREEMENT WITH PLAINTIFF:
Values: Nil, Nondisclosure-Agreement, Negative

EMPLOYEE ENTERED INTO NONCOMPETITION AGREEMENT WITH PLAINTIFF:
Values: Nil, Noncompetition-covenant, Negative

Nondisclosure agreement specifically covered plaintiff's product:
Values: Nil, Nondisclosure-Agreement: Specific re info, Negative

Employee was sole developer of plaintiff's product:
Values: Nil, Product-Worked-On: Employee development role, Negative

There is a contract plaintiff:
Values: Nil, Agreement, Negative

There is a contract defendant:
Values: Nil, Agreement, Negative

Case involves some contractual agreement:
Values: Nil, Agreement, Negative

E Cases in the Case Knowledge Base

Amoco Production Co. v. Lindley, 609 P.2d 733 (Okla. 1980) (Defendant won trade secrets misappropriation claim where plaintiff's former employee was sole developer of plaintiff's product and nondisclosure agreement did not specifically refer to it.)

Analogic Corp. v. Data Translation, Inc., 358 N.E.2d 804 (Mass. 1976) (Plaintiff won trade secrets misappropriation claim where defendant gained competitive advantage, plaintiff's employee brought product-related tools to defendant, and employee entered into nondisclosure agreement.)

Automated Systems, Inc. v. Service Bureau Corp., 401 F.2d 619 (10 Cir. 1968) (Defendant won claim for trade secrets misappropriation where secrets about vertical business information and disclosures made to defendant in negotiations.)

Black, Sivalls & Bryson, Inc. v. Keystone Steel Fabrication, Inc., 584 F.2d 946 (10th Cir. 1978) (Where defendant's access to plaintiff's coefficient saved defendant development time and uncertainty, directed verdict for defendant on trade secrets misappropriation claim reversed even though plaintiff published paper on related topic.)

Com-Share, Inc. v. Computer Complex, Inc., 338 F. Supp. 1229 (E.D. Mich. 1971) (Plaintiff won preliminary injunction on claim for breach of nondisclosure agreement where defendant disclosed information to third parties.)

Crown Industries, Inc. v. Kawneer Co., 335 F. Supp. 749 (N.D. Ill. 1971) (Defendant won claim for trade secrets misappropriation where plaintiff disclosed secrets to seven outsiders.)

Data General Corp. v. Digital Computer Controls Inc., 357 A.2d 105 (Del. Ch. 1975) (Plaintiff won claim for trade secrets misappropriation even though plaintiff disclosed secrets to 6,000 outsiders where disclosures covered by nondisclosure agreements.)

Dougherty v. Salt, 227 N.Y. 200, 125 N.E. 94 (1919) (Aunt's estate not liable on aunt's note to nephew where contract not supported by consideration.)

Eastern Marble Products Corp. v. Roman Marble, Inc., 364 N.E.2d 799 (Mass. 1977) (Plaintiff won trade secrets misappropriation claim where adequate security measures taken and defendant entered into nondisclosure agreement.)

Hancock Bank & Trust Co. v. Shell Oil Co., 309 N.E.2d 482 (Mass. 1974) (Lease on property purchased by bank in foreclosure sale not void where supported by consideration of mutual obligations under the lease.)

J.T. Healy & Son, Inc. v. James A. Murphy & Son, Inc., 357 Mass. 728 (1970) (Defendant won trade secrets misappropriation claim where plaintiff took insufficient measures to protect secrets.)

Kirksey v. Kirksey, 8 Ala. 131 (1845) (Contract was a gift not supported by consideration despite donee's reliance and donor's partial performance.)

Kewanee Oil Co. v. Bicron Corp., 416 U.S. 470, 94 S. Ct. 1879, 40 L. Ed. 2d 315 (1974) (Plaintiff won trade secrets misappropriation claim where there was nondisclosure agreement covering defendant's access.)

Laff v. John O. Butler Co., 381 N.E.2d 423, 64 Ill. App. 3d 603 (1978) (Plaintiff won contracts claim for breach of agreement to license trade secret even though third parties could legally learn secret through reverse engineering.)

Midland-Ross Corp. v. Sunbeam Equipment Corp., 316 F. Supp. 171 (W.D. Pa. 1970) (Defendant won claim for trade secrets misappropriation where plaintiff disclosed secrets to 150 outsiders.)

Midland-Ross Corp. v. Yokana, 293 F.2d 411 (3 Cir. 1961) (Defendant won claim for trade secrets misappropriation where plaintiff disclosed secrets to outsiders.)

Modern Controls Inc. v. Andreadakis, 578 F.2d 1264 (8 Cir. 1978) (Plaintiff won claim for breach of noncompetition agreement.)

Motorola, Inc. v. Fairchild Camera and Instrument Corp., 366 F. Supp. 1173 (D. Arizona 1973) (Defendant won trade secrets misappropriation claim where nondisclosure agreements did not specifically refer to plaintiff's product.)

Peggy Lawton Kitchens, Inc. v. Hogan, 466 N.E.2d 138 (Mass. App. 1984) (Plaintiff won trade secrets misappropriation claim where adequate security measures taken.)

Plant Industries, Inc. v. Coleman, 287 F. Supp. 636 (C.D. Cal. 1968) (Plaintiff won trade secrets misappropriation claim where adequate security measures taken.)

Pressure Science Inc. v. Kramer, 413 F. Supp. 618 (D. Conn. 1976) (Defendant won trade secrets misappropriation claim even though it gained competitive advantage.)

Raycorp v. Tronic (Hypothetical Case) (Defendant won trade secrets misappropriation claim even though there was an express noncompetition agreement.)

Schnell v. Nell, 17 Ind. 29 (1861) (Contract promise to make payment of money not supported by consideration despite previous moral obligation.)

Schulenburg v. Signatrol, Inc., 212 N.E.2d 865, 33 Ill. 2d 379 (1965) (Plaintiff won trade secrets misappropriation claim where defendant gained competitive advantage and paid plaintiff's former employee to switch employers.)

Space Aero Products Co. v. R. E. Darling Co., 208 A.2d 74 (Md. Ct. App. 1965) (Plaintiff won trade secrets misappropriation claim where defendant gained competitive advantage, bribed plaintiff's employee, and brought product-related tools to defendant even though plaintiff disclosed secrets to defendant in negotiations.)

Speedry Chemical Products, Inc. v. Carter's Ink Co., 306 F.2d 328 (2d Cir. 1962) (Defendant won trade secrets misappropriation claim where plaintiff disclosed secrets to defendant in negotiations.)

Sperry Rand Corp. v. Pentronix, 311 F. Supp. 910 (E.D. Pa. 1970) (Plaintiff won claim of breach of nondisclosure agreement where defendant induced plaintiff's former key employees to switch employ by offering high salaries and bonuses and defendant's competing product took only five months to develop.)

Structural Dynamics Research Corp. v. Engineering Mechanics Research Corp., 401 F. Supp. 1102 (E.D. Mich. 1975) (Plaintiff won claim for trade secrets misappropriation where employees entered into nondisclosure agreements covering product of which they were sole developers.)

Telex Corp. v. IBM Corp., 367 F. Supp. 258 (N.D. Okl. 1973); aff'd in part, mod. in part, 510 F.2d 894 (10 Cir. 1975) (Plaintiff won claim for trade secrets misappropriation where defendant bribed plaintiff's employees to switch employers and gained competitive advantage.)

Trilog Associates, Inc. v. Famularo, 314 A.2d 287 (Pa. 1974) (Defendant won trade secrets and breach of contract claims where information provided by plaintiff's former employee was generally known and noncompetition agreement was not sufficiently limited.)

USM Corp. v. Marson Fastener Corp., 379 Mass. 90 (1979) (Plaintiff won trade secrets misappropriation claim where adequate steps taken to protect secrets.)

Wexler v. Greenberg, 160 A.2d 430 (Pa. 1960) (Defendant won trade secrets misappropriation claim where plaintiff's former employee was sole developer of plaintiff's product.)

Widget-King v. Cupcake (Hypothetical Case) (Plaintiff won trade secrets misappropriation claim even though defendant gained competitive advantage.)

Squib for *Data General* **Case**

Title: Data General Corp. v. Digital Computer Controls, Inc.

Cite: 357 A.2d 105 (Del. Ct. Chanc. 1975)

Date: November 7, 1975

Parties: Plaintiff: Data Gen.; Defendant: Digital

Claim: Trade Secrets Misappropriation

Procedural Setting: Plaintiff denied preliminary injunction; seeks permanent injunction after trial.

Decision: Judgment for plaintiff

Facts: Data General manufactured the Nova 1200 minicomputer. Digital ordered a Nova 1200 from a third-party supplier. From the supplier, it also secured one of plaintiff's maintenance manuals with design drawings from the supplier, which it copied and returned. The drawings bore a proprietary legend prohibiting copying, and the contract for the machine included a confidentiality agreement prohibiting use of the drawings for manufacture. Digital used the drawings to produce its D-116 minicomputer, which was substantially identical to the Nova 1200. Plaintiff distributed the same drawings, bearing the same restrictive legend, to some 6,000 customers, users, vendors and trainees. Plaintiff's sales contracts all prohibited the use of the drawings for manufacturing. Data General took measures to protect its trade secrets, including plant security, trainee confidentiality agreements, and stamping restrictive legends.

Issues: Did plaintiff lose its trade secret rights to the drawings by distributing them to 6,000 outsiders?

Holding: For plaintiff: No. The restrictive legends were sufficient to preclude disclosure to the public.

Squib for *Amoco* Case

Title: Amoco Production Co. v. Lindley

Cite: 609 P.2d 733 (Sup. Ct. Okla.)

Date: 1980

Parties: Plaintiff: Amoco; Defendant: Lindley

Claim: Breach of Nondisclosure Agreement, Trade Secrets Misappropriation

Procedural Setting: Defendant appeals from lower court's granting plaintiff a temporary injunction against defendant's use or disclosure of information in connection with computer system developed by defendant.

Decision: In favor of defendant lifting the injunction.

Facts: In 1964, Lindley, a well log analyst, entered into an employment agreement with Amoco to perform research related to oil and gas exploration. The agreement contained a provision under which Lindley agreed to disclose all inventions or discoveries to Amoco and not to disclose them to others. Starting in 1971, on his own time, Lindley developed a computer system (the "Lindley System") for analyzing well logs. Amoco refused to approve his development of the Lindley System in favor of another system ("AMS"), although they did order him to incorporate its features into the AMS system in 1973. In 1975, Amoco officially recognized the Lindley System when it was found responsible for discovering a large field of hydrocarbons. Ten months later, Lindley left Amoco in a dispute over the program. Amoco did not take any extraordinary measures to protect secrecy of Lindley System, such as controlling documents to maintain confidentiality.

Issues: (1) Was the Lindley System covered by the nondisclosure agreement? (2) Did Lindley have right to use or disclose information connected with Lindley System?

Holding: (1) Held for defendant: Lindley system was not an invention and not covered by contract. (2) Held for defendant: Plaintiff did not take adequate measures to protect secret. Lindley developed system on his own.

Cases cited: re (2): *Telex Corp. v. IBM Corp.*, 367 F. Supp. 258 (N.D. Okla. 1973), rev'd on other gnds, 510 F.2d 894 (10th Cir.

1975); *Com-Share, Inc. v. Computer Complex, Inc.* 338 F. Supp. 1229 (E.D. Mich. 1971); *Structural Dynamics Research Corp. v. Engineering Mechanics Research Corp.*, 401 F. Supp. 1102 (E.D. Mich. 1975).

F Implemented Dimensions in Hypo

Competitive-Advantage-Gained

Short Name: Competitive-Advantage

Claim: Trade Secrets Misappropriation

Generalization: Plaintiff is strengthened the greater the competitive advantage gained by the defendant.

Focal Slot Prerequisites: "Defendant saved product development expense relative to plaintiff"

Focal Slots:
Plaintiff's Product: Development time
Plaintiff's Product: Development cost
Defendant's Product: Development time
Defendant's Product: Development cost

Comparison Type: Computed

Ranges: 2–60 months
$10,000–$10,000,000
1 to 99 percent (Defendant's to plaintiff's time or cost)

Pro-Plaintiff Direction: Greater savings

Vertical-Knowledge

Short Name: Vertical-Knowledge

Claim: Trade Secrets Misappropriation

Generalization: Plaintiff is strengthened if knowledge does not pertain to customer business methods (i.e., if it is technical, not vertical, knowledge).

Focal Slot Prerequisites: "Type of product information is technical"

Focal Slots: Plaintiff's Knowledge: Type of knowledge

Comparison Type: Binary

Range: Vertical or Technical

Pro-Plaintiff Direction: Technical

Secrets-Voluntarily-Disclosed

Short Name: Secrets-Disclosed-Outsiders

Claim: Trade Secrets Misappropriation

Generalization: Plaintiff is strengthened the fewer disclosures to outsiders it has made of confidential information.

Focal Slot Prerequisites: "Plaintiff made some disclosures to outsiders"

Focal Slots: Plaintiff's Product: Number of Disclosures

Comparison Type: Greater-than versus less-than

Range: 0–10,000,000

Pro-Plaintiff Direction: 0 disclosures

Disclosures-Subject-To-Restriction

Short Name: Outsider-Disclosures-Restricted

Claim: Trade Secrets Misappropriation

Generalization: Plaintiff is strengthened to extent that any disclosees are restricted from disclosing confidential information to others.

Focal Slot Prerequisites: "Disclosures to outsiders were subject to restriction"

Focal Slots: Plaintiff's Product: Percentage of disclosees restricted

Comparison Type: Binary

Range: 0 or 100 percent

Pro-Plaintiff Direction: 100 percent

Agreement-Supported-By-Consideration

Short Name: Consideration

Claim: Breach of Contract

Generalization: Plaintiff is strengthened to extent that defendant received something of value for entering into contract.

Focal Slot Prerequisites: "Case involves some contractual agreement"

Focal Slots: Agreement: Contract defendant's consideration received

Comparison Type: Something versus Nothing

Range: Nothing or Something (e.g., Promise, Money)

Pro-Plaintiff Direction: Something

Common-Employee-Paid-To-Change-Employers

Short Name: Bribe-Employee

Claim: Trade Secrets Misappropriation

Generalization: Plaintiff is strengthened the more defendant paid plaintiff's former employee to switch employment.

Focal Slot Prerequisites: "Employee received something of value to switch employment"

Focal Slots:
Employment-Change: List of items received

Comparison Type: Something versus Nothing

Range: Nothing or Something (i.e., Promise of higher salary, Promise of promotion, Promise of stock, Promise of bonus)

Pro-Plaintiff Direction: Something

Exists-Express-Noncompetition-Agreement

Short Name: Noncompetition-Agreement

Claim: Trade Secrets Misappropriation, Breach of Noncompetition Agreement

Generalization: Plaintiff is strengthened if employee entered noncompetition agreement.

Focal Slot Prerequisites: "Employee entered into noncompetition agreement with plaintiff"

Focal Slots: Noncompetition-Covenant

Comparison Type: Something versus Nothing

Range: Nothing or Noncompetition-Covenant

Pro-Plaintiff Direction: Noncompetition-Covenant

Common-Employee-Transferred-Product-Tools

Short Name: Brought-Tools

Claim: Trade Secrets Misappropriation

Generalization: Plaintiff is strengthened if former employee brought product-related tools to defendant.

Focal Slot Prerequisites: "Employee brought plaintiff's product development tools to defendant"

Focal Slots:
Employment-Change: List of tools brought

Comparison Type: Something versus Nothing

Range: Nothing or Something (i.e., Development Notes, Source Code, Copy of Product)

Pro-Plaintiff Direction: Something

Nondisclosure-Agreement-Re-Defendant-Access

Short Name: Agreed-Not-To-Disclose

Claim: Trade Secrets Misappropriation, Breach of Nondisclosure Agreement

Generalization: Plaintiff is strengthened to extent defendant entered into a nondisclosure agreement.

Focal Slot Prerequisites: "Defendant or employee entered into nondisclosure agreement with plaintiff"

Focal Slots: Nondisclosure-Agreement

Comparison Type: Something versus Nothing

Range: Nothing or Nondisclosure-Agreement

Pro-Plaintiff Direction: Nondisclosure-Agreement

Common-Employee-Sole-Developer

Short Name: Employee-Sole-Developer

Claim: Trade Secrets Misappropriation

Generalization: Plaintiff is strengthened if defendant was not sole developer of the confidential information.

Focal Slot Prerequisites: "Employee was sole developer of plaintiff's product"

Focal Slots:
Product-Worked-On: Employee development role

Comparison Type: Binary

Range: Negative or Affirmative

Pro-Plaintiff Direction: Negative

Nondisclosure-Agreement-Specific

Short Name: Nondisclose-Agreement-Specific

Claim: Trade Secrets Misappropriation, Breach of Nondisclosure Agreement

Generalization: Plaintiff is strengthened if nondisclosure agreement specifically referred to plaintiff's product.

Focal Slot Prerequisites: "Nondisclosure agreement specifically covered plaintiff's product"

Focal Slots: Nondisclosure-Agreement: Specific re info

Comparison Type: Binary

Range: Affirmative or Negative

Pro-Plaintiff Direction: Affirmative

Disclosure-In-Negotiations-With-Defendant

Short Name: Disclosure-in-Negotiations

Claim: Trade Secrets Misappropriation

Generalization: Plaintiff is strengthened to extent that it did not disclose secret to defendant in negotiations.

Focal Slot Prerequisites: "Plaintiff disclosed product information to defendant in negotiations"

Focal Slots:
Disclosure-Event: How disclosure made

Comparison Type: Binary

Range: Negative or Affirmative

Pro-Plaintiff Direction: Negative

Security-Measures-Adopted

Short Name: Security-Measures

Claim: Trade Secrets Misappropriation

Generalization: Plaintiff is strengthened the more security measures it took to protect its confidential information.

Focal Slot Prerequisites: "Plaintiff adopted security measures"

Focal Slots: Plaintiff's Product: Security measures list

Comparison Type: More versus Less

Range:
Minimal measures
Access to premises controlled
Restrictions on entry by visitors
Restrictions on entry by employees
Product marked confidential
Employee trade secret program exists
Restrictions on hardcopy release
Employee nondisclosure agreements

G Argument Evaluation Criteria

1. Minimum criteria for citing a precedent: To be "citable" in support of legal conclusion that a side in a fact situation should win a claim, a precedent should involve the same claim, have been won by that side, be relevantly analogous, have not been overruled.

2. Comparing precedents in terms of how on point they are: If precedent [a] is more on point than precedent [b], precedent [a] is better.

3. Comparing precedents in terms of how distinguishable they are: If precedent [a] and precedent [b] are equally on point and precedent [a] is not distinguishable, precedent [a] is better.

4. Comparing points and responses: A response that cites a more-on-point counterexample is stronger than the point to which it responds (i.e., the "trumped" point) and a response to the same point that does not.

5. Comparing points: A point to which there is no response citing a more-on-point counterexample (i.e., a "nontrumped" point) is stronger than one to which there is.

6. Minimum criteria for reasonable argument on claim: There must be at least one nontrumped point for a side on the claim. (There may, however, be a response citing an as-on-point counterexample.)

7. Improving an argument: The more nontrumped points there are, the better for a side's argument.

8. Comparing opposing sides in one argument: If all of the nontrumped points favor Side 1 and there are no nontrumped points for Side 2, Side 1's argument is stronger.

9. Comparing same side in two arguments: If there are more nontrumped points favoring Side 1 in argument [b] than in argument [a], argument [b] is stronger for Side 1 than argument [a].

H Sample Hypo Outputs

This appendix shows Hypo's actual outputs for three sample fact situations: *Amexxco*, *Structural Dynamics*, and *USM*. All three examples are based on the fact situations of actual legal cases. It is as if an attorney for one of the parties to the lawsuit were consulting Hypo for help in planning arguments to make in court. By using actual cases, Hypo's arguments can be compared with those that the lawyers and judges made in the cases. Hypo's arguments and hypotheticals compare favorably with those actually made in the briefs submitted to the court and in the court's opinions.

A fourth example, *Crown*, was presented in chapter 5. That chapter discussed Hypo's processing of the *Crown* example step by step. The *USM* example is discussed in detail in chapters 6 through 8. The *Amexxco* example was introduced in chapter 2 and discussed in chapters 4 and 6. The *Structural Dynamics* example is discussed in some detail in chapter 8.

Hypo Outputs for the *Amexxco* Example

The first example involves the *Amexxco* fact situation of chapter 2 in which G. Whiz, an Amexxco employee, came up with an oil drill analysis program that Exxssinc has its eye on. Chapter 2 contains a summary of the fact situation.

Hypo's Citation Summary for *Amexxco* shows that there are strong arguments on both sides. Arguments [1] through [3] are the arguments that Hypo makes spontaneously from the list of best cases. Arguments [4] and [5] were made by Hypo from cases selected by the attorney from the Claim Lattice to illustrate how the responses to the cases both distinguish them and cite a trumping counterexample to each, the *Structural Dynamics* case.

Citation Summary in *Amcxxco*

> **3-Ply Arguments for Best Cases to Cite on Claim of Trade Secrets Misappropriation in Fact Situation of Amexxco:**
>
> On a claim for Trade Secrets Misappropriation, both sides can make a strong argument.
>
> Plaintiff can cite the following cases for which there are no more-on-point counterexamples:
>
> Structural Dynamics Research Corp. v. Engineering Mechanics Research Corp. 401 F. Supp. 1102 (E.D. Mich., 1975)

Defendant can cite the following cases for which there are no more-on-point counterexamples:

Amoco Production Co. v. Lindley 609 P.2d 733 (Okla. 1980)

3-Ply Arguments in *Amexxco*

[1]

$\Longrightarrow$ Point for Plaintiff as Side-1:

Where: Plaintiff and defendant entered into a nondisclosure agreement. Plaintiff adopted security measures.

Plaintiff should win a claim for Trade Secrets Misappropriation.

Cite: Eastern Marble Products Corp. v. Roman Marble, Inc. 364 N.E.2d 799 (Mass. 1977).

$\Longleftarrow$ Response for Defendant as Side-2:

Eastern Marble Products Corp. v. Roman Marble, Inc. is distinguishable because:

In Eastern-Marble, plaintiff adopted more security measures than in Amexxco

In Amexxco, employee defendant was sole developer of plaintiff's product. Not so in Eastern-Marble.

Counterexamples:

Amoco Production Co. v. Lindley 609 P.2d 733, is more on point and held for defendant where it was also the case that: Employee defendant was sole developer of plaintiff's product.

$\Longrightarrow$ Rebuttal for Plaintiff as Side-1: None.

[2]

$\Longrightarrow$ Point for Plaintiff as Side-1:

Where: Plaintiff and defendant entered into a nondisclosure agreement.

Even though: Employee defendant was sole developer of plaintiff's product.

Plaintiff should win a claim for Trade Secrets Misappropriation.

Cite: Structural Dynamics Research Corp. v. Engineering Mechanics Research Corp. 401 F. Supp. 1102 (E.D. Mich., 1975).

$\Longleftarrow$ Response for Defendant as Side-2:

Sample Hypo Outputs

Structural Dynamics Research Corp. v. Engineering Mechanics Research Corp. is distinguishable because:

In Structural Dynamics, defendant received something of value for entering into the agreement. Not so in Amexxco.

In Structural Dynamics, plaintiff's former employee brought product development information to defendant. Not so in Amexxco.

In Structural Dynamics, the nondisclosure agreement specifically referred to plaintiff's product. Not so in Amexxco.

$\implies$ Rebuttal for Plaintiff as Side-1: None.

[3]

$\implies$ Point for Defendant as Side-1:

Where: Employee defendant was sole developer of plaintiff's product.

Even though:

Plaintiff and defendant entered into a nondisclosure agreement. Plaintiff adopted security measures.

Defendant should win a claim for Trade Secrets Misappropriation.

Cite. Amoco Production Co. v. Lindley 609 P.2d 733.

$\impliedby$ Response for Plaintiff as Side-2: None.

$\implies$ Rebuttal for Defendant as Side-1: None.

3-Ply Arguments in *Amexxco* for Cases Selected by Attorney

3-Ply Argument for Selected Case to Cite on Claim of Trade Secrets Misappropriation in Fact Situation of Amexxco:

[4]

$\implies$ Point for Defendant as Side-1:

Where:

Even though:

Plaintiff and defendant entered into a nondisclosure agreement.

Defendant should win a claim for Trade Secrets Misappropriation.

Cite: Motorola, Inc. v. Fairchild Camera and Instrument Corp. 366 F. Supp. 1173 (D. Ariz., 1973).

⇐ Response for Plaintiff as Side-2:

Motorola, Inc. v. Fairchild Camera and Instrument Corp. is distinguishable because:

In Amexxco, plaintiff adopted more security measures than in Motorola.

Counterexamples:

Structural Dynamics Research Corp. v. Engineering Mechanics Research Corp. 401 F. Supp. 1102 (E.D. Mich., 1975), is more on point and held for plaintiff where it was also the case that:
Employee defendant was sole developer of plaintiff's product.

⟹ Rebuttal for Defendant as Side-1:

Structural Dynamics Research Corp. v. Engineering Mechanics Research Corp. is distinguishable because:

In Structural Dynamics, defendant received something of value for entering into the agreement. Not so in Amexxco.

In Structural Dynamics, plaintiff's former employee brought product development information to defendant. Not so in Amexxco.

In Structural Dynamics, the nondisclosure agreement specifically referred to plaintiff's product. Not so in Amexxco.

[5]

⟹ Point for Defendant as Side-1:

Where: Employee defendant was sole developer of plaintiff's product.

Defendant should win a claim for Trade Secrets Misappropriation.

Cite: Wexler v. Greenberg 160 A.2d 430 (Sup. Ct. Pa., 1960).

⇐ Response for Plaintiff as Side-2:

Wexler v. Greenberg is distinguishable because:

In Amexxco, plaintiff and defendant entered into a nondisclosure agreement. Not so in Wexler.

In Amexxco, plaintiff adopted more security measures than in Wexler.

Counterexamples:

Structural Dynamics Research Corp. v. Engineering Mechanics Research Corp. 401 F. Supp. 1102 (E.D. Mich., 1975), is more on

Sample Hypo Outputs

point and held for plaintiff where it was also the case that: Plaintiff and defendant entered into a nondisclosure agreement.

⟹ Rebuttal for Defendant as Side-1:

Structural Dynamics Research Corp. v. Engineering Mechanics Research Corp. is distinguishable because:

In Structural Dynamics, defendant received something of value for entering into the agreement. Not so in Amexxco.

In Structural Dynamics, plaintiff's former employee brought product development information to Defendant. Not so in Amexxco.

In Structural Dynamics, the nondisclosure agreement specifically referred to plaintiff's product. Not so in Amexxco.

Suggested Hypotheticals in *Amexxco*

Hypotheticals to Consider on Claim of Trade Secrets Misappropriation in Fact Situation of Amexxco:

Plaintiff's position would be strengthened in following situations:

Suppose:

Defendant's access to plaintiff's product information saved it time or expense. Plaintiff's former employee brought product development information to defendant.
Cf. Analogic Corp. v. Data Translation, Inc. 358 N.E.2d 804 (S.J.C. Mass., 1976)

Defendant's access to plaintiff's product information saved it time or expense. Defendant paid plaintiff's former employee to switch employment. Plaintiff's former employee brought product development information to defendant.
Cf. Space Aero Products Co. v. R. E. Darling Co. 208 A.2d 74 (Ct. App. Md., 1965)

Defendant's access to plaintiff's product information saved it time or expense. Defendant paid plaintiff's former employee to switch employment.
Cf. Telex Corp. v. IBM Corp. (1) 510 F.2d 894 (10 Cir., 1975)

Plaintiff's former employee brought product development information to defendant.
Cf. Structural Dynamics Research Corp. v. Engineering Mechanics Research Corp. 401 F. Supp. 1102 (E.D. Mich., 1975)

Defendant's position would be strengthened in following situations: Suppose:

Plaintiff disclosed its product information in negotiations with defendant. Plaintiff disclosed its product information to outsiders.
Cf. Crown Industries Inc. v. Kawneer Co. 335 F. Supp. 749 (N.D. Ill., 1971)

Plaintiff disclosed its product information to outsiders.
Cf. Midland-Ross Corp. v. Yokana 293 F.2d 411 (3 Cir. 1961)

Plaintiff disclosed its product information in negotiations with defendant. Plaintiff's product information was about customer business relations.
Cf. Automated-Systems v. Service-Bureau 401 F.2d 619 (10 Cir., 1968)

Plaintiff disclosed its product information to outsiders.
Cf. Midland-Ross Corp. v. Sunbeam Equipment Corp. 316 F. Supp. 171 (W.D. Pa., 1970)

Hypo Outputs for the *Structural Dynamics* Example

This extended example shows Hypo's arguments for one of the cases cited in the preceding *Amexxco* example, *Structural Dynamics*. Chapter 8 contains the squib of the case and a discussion of the best case selection process.

Hypo makes arguments for two different legal claims in this example; a trade secrets claim and a claim for breach of a nondisclosure agreement. Arguments [4] through [6] and a Citation Summary show how Hypo argues the claim for breach of the nondisclosure agreement, including distinguishing the citation of a classic contracts case, *Dougherty v. Salt*.

Citation Summary re Trade Secrets Claim in *Structural Dynamics*

3-Ply Arguments for Best Cases to Cite on Claim of Trade Secrets Misappropriation in Fact Situation of Structural Dynamics:

On a claim for Trade Secrets Misappropriation, both sides can make a strong argument.

Plaintiff can cite the following cases for which there are no more-on-point counterexamples:

Analogic Corp. v. Data Translation, Inc. 358 N.E.2d 804 (S.J.C. Mass., 1976)

Defendant can cite the following cases for which there are no more-on-point counterexamples:

Amoco Production Co. v. Lindley 609 P.2d 733 (Okla. 1980)

3-Ply Arguments for Trade Secrets Claim in *Structural Dynamics*

[1]

⟹ Point for Plaintiff as Side-1:

Where: Plaintiff and defendant entered into a nondisclosure agreement. Plaintiff's former employee brought product development information to defendant.

Plaintiff should win a claim for Trade Secrets Misappropriation.

Cite: Analogic Corp. v. Data Translation, Inc. 358 N.E.2d 804 (S.J.C. Mass., 1976).

⟸ Response for Defendant as Side-2:

Analogic Corp. v. Data Translation, Inc. is distinguishable because:

In Structural Dynamics, employee defendant was sole developer of plaintiff's product. Not so in Analogic v. Data Trans.

In Analogic v. Data Trans, defendant's access to plaintiff's product information saved it more time or expense than in Structural Dynamics.

⟹ Rebuttal for Plaintiff as Side-1: None.

[2]

⟹ Point for Defendant as Side-1:

Where: Employee defendant was sole developer of plaintiff's product.

Even though: Plaintiff and defendant entered into a nondisclosure agreement.

Defendant should win a claim for Trade Secrets Misappropriation.

Cite: Amoco Production Co. v. Lindley 609 P.2d 733.

⟸ Response for Plaintiff as Side-2:

Amoco Production Co. v. Lindley is distinguishable because:

In Structural Dynamics, defendant received something of value for entering into the agreement. Not so in Amoco.

In Structural Dynamics, plaintiff's former employee brought product development information to defendant. Not so in Amoco.

In Structural Dynamics, the nondisclosure agreement specifically referred to plaintiff's product. Not so in Amoco.

$\Longrightarrow$ Rebuttal for Defendant as Side-1: None.

3-Ply Argument in *Structural Dynamics* for Cases Selected by Attorney

3-Ply Argument for Selected Case to Cite on Claim of Trade Secrets Misappropriation in Fact Situation of Structural Dynamics:

[3]

$\Longrightarrow$ Point for Defendant as Side-1:

Where: Employee defendant was sole developer of plaintiff's product.

Defendant should win a claim for Trade Secrets Misappropriation.

Cite: Wexler v. Greenberg 160 A.2d 430 (Sup. Ct. Pa., 1960).

$\Longleftarrow$ Response for Plaintiff as Side-2:

Wexler v. Greenberg is distinguishable because:

In Structural Dynamics, plaintiff's former employee brought product development information to defendant. Not so in Wexler.

In Structural Dynamics, the nondisclosure agreement specifically referred to plaintiff's product. Not so in Wexler.

In Structural Dynamics, plaintiff and defendant entered into a nondisclosure agreement. Not so in Wexler.

$\Longrightarrow$ Rebuttal for Defendant as Side-1: None.

[4]

$\Longrightarrow$ Point for Plaintiff as Side-1:

Where: Plaintiff and defendant entered into a nondisclosure agreement.

Plaintiff should win a claim for Trade Secrets Misappropriation.

Cite: Telex Corp. v. IBM Corp. (1) 510 F.2d 894 (10 Cir., 1975).

Sample Hypo Outputs

⇐ Response for Defendant as Side-2:

Telex Corp. v. IBM Corp. (1) is distinguishable because:

In Structural Dynamics, employee defendant was sole developer of plaintiff's product. Not so in Telex v. IBM.

In Telex v. IBM, defendant's access to plaintiff's product information saved it more time or expense than in Structural Dynamics.

In Telex v. IBM, defendant paid plaintiff's former employee to switch employment. Not so in Structural Dynamics.

Counterexamples:

Amoco Production Co. v. Lindley 609 P.2d 733, is more on point and held for defendant where it was also the case that: Employee defendant was sole developer of plaintiff's product.

⇒ Rebuttal for Plaintiff as Side-1: Amoco Production Co. v. Lindley is distinguishable because:

In Structural Dynamics, defendant received something of value for entering into the agreement. Not so in Amoco.

In Structural Dynamics, plaintiff's former employee brought product development information to defendant. Not so in Amoco.

In Structural Dynamics, the nondisclosure agreement specifically referred to plaintiff's product. Not so in Amoco.

Suggested Hypotheticals in *Structural Dynamics* for Trades Secrets Claim

Hypotheticals to Consider on Claim of Trade Secrets Misappropriation in Fact Situation of Structural Dynamics:

Plaintiff's position would be strengthened in following situations:

Suppose:

Plaintiff adopted security measures. Cf. Eastern Marble Products Corp. v. Roman Marble, Inc. 364 N.E.2d 799 (Mass. 1977)

Defendant's access to plaintiff's product information saved it time or expense. Cf. Analogic Corp. v. Data Translation, Inc. 358 N.E.2d 804 (S.J.C. Mass., 1976)

Defendant's access to plaintiff's product information saved it time or expense. Plaintiff adopted security measures. Defendant paid plaintiff's former employee to switch employment.

Cf. Space Aero Products Co. v. R.E. Darling Co. 208 A.2d 74 (Ct. App. Md., 1965)

Defendant's access to plaintiff's product information saved it time or expense. Defendant paid plaintiff's former employee to switch employment.
Cf. Telex Corp. v. IBM Corp. (1) 510 F.2d 894 (10 Cir., 1975)

Defendant's position would be strengthened in following situations:

Suppose:

Plaintiff disclosed its product information in negotiations with defendant. Plaintiff disclosed its product information to outsiders.
Cf. Crown Industries Inc. v. Kawneer Co. 335 F. Supp. 749 (N.D. Ill., 1971)

Plaintiff disclosed its product information to outsiders.
Cf. Midland-Ross Corp. v. Yokana 293 F.2d 411 (3 Cir. 1961)

Plaintiff disclosed its product information in negotiations with defendant. Plaintiff's product information was about customer business relations.
Cf. Automated-Systems v. Service-Bureau 401 F.2d 619 (10 Cir., 1968)

Plaintiff disclosed its product information to outsiders.
Cf. Midland-Ross Corp. v. Sunbeam Equipment Corp. 316 F. Supp. 171 (W.D. Pa., 1970)

Citation Summary for Breach of Nondisclosure Agreement in *Structural Dynamics*

3-Ply Arguments for Best Cases to Cite on Claim of Breach of Nondisclosure/Noncompetition Agreement in Fact Situation of Structural Dynamics:

On a claim for Breach of Nondisclosure/Noncompetition Agreement, plaintiff can make a stronger argument. Plaintiff can cite the following cases for which there are no more-on-point counterexamples:

Modern Controls Inc. v. Andreadakis 578 F.2d 1264 (8 Cir., 1978)

3-Ply Arguments for Breach of Nondisclosure Agreement in *Structural Dynamics*

[5]

⟹ Point for Plaintiff as Side-1:

Where: Plaintiff and defendant entered into nondisclosure agreement.

Plaintiff should win a claim for Breach of Nondisclosure/Noncompetition Agreement.

Cite: Modern Controls Inc. v. Andreadakis 578 F.2d 1264 (8 Cir., 1978).

⟸ Response for Defendant as Side-2:

Modern Controls Inc. v. Andreadakis is distinguishable because:

In Modern Controls, defendant received something of value for entering into the agreement. Not so in Structural Dynamics

In Structural Dynamics, employee defendant was sole developer of plaintiff's product. Not so in Modern Controls.

⟹ Rebuttal for Plaintiff as Side-1: None.

[6]

⟹ Point for Defendant as Side-1:

Where: Defendant received nothing of value for entering into the agreement.

Defendant should win a claim for Breach of Contract.

Cite: Dougherty v. Salt 227 N.Y. 200, 125 N.E. 94 (1919).

⟸ Response for Plaintiff as Side-2:

Dougherty v. Salt is distinguishable because:

In Structural Dynamics, plaintiff's former employee brought product development information to defendant. Not so in Dougherty v. Salt.

In Structural Dynamics, the nondisclosure agreement specifically referred to plaintiff's product. Not so in Dougherty v. Salt.

In Structural Dynamics, plaintiff and defendant entered into a nondisclosure agreement. Not so in Dougherty v. Salt.

⟹ Rebuttal for Defendant as Side-1: None.

Hypo Outputs for the *USM* Example

Chapters 6 through 8 treat the *USM* case in detail as an example illustrating Hypo's case representation scheme and reasoning process. The squib and Legal Case Frames are described in chapter 6. Chapter 7 presents the Interpretation Frame and Case Analysis Record. The process of interpreting the Claim Lattice and selecting the best cases is discussed in chapter 8. Chapter 10 compares Hypo's arguments in the *USM* case to those actually made in the counsels' briefs and the court's opinion.

Citation Summary for *USM*

3-Ply Arguments for Best Cases to Cite on Claim of Trade Secrets Misappropriation in Fact Situation of USM v. Marson:

On a claim for Trade Secrets Misappropriation, plaintiff can make a stronger argument. Plaintiff can cite the following cases for which there are no more-on-point counterexamples:

Space Aero Products Co. v. R.E. Darling Co. 208 A.2d 74 (Ct. App. Md., 1965)

Peggy Lawton Kitchens, Inc. v. Hogan 466 N.E.2d 138 (Mass. App., 1984)

Plant Industries, Inc. v. Coleman 287 F. Supp. 636 (C.D. Cal., 1968)

3-Ply Arguments in *USM*:

[1]

⟹ Point for Plaintiff as Side-1:

Where: Defendant's access to plaintiff's product information saved it time or expense.

Plaintiff should win a claim for Trade Secrets Misappropriation.

Cite: Telex Corp. v. IBM Corp. (1) 510 F.2d 894 (10 Cir., 1975).

⟸ Response for Defendant as Side-2:

Telex Corp. v. IBM Corp. (1) is distinguishable because:

In Telex v. IBM, defendant's access to plaintiff's product information saved it more time or expense than in USM v. Marson

Sample Hypo Outputs

In Telex v. IBM, plaintiff and defendant entered into a nondisclosure agreement. Not so in USM v. Marson.

In Telex v. IBM, defendant paid plaintiff's former employee to switch employment. Not so in USM v. Marson.

Counterexamples:

Pressure Science, Inc. v. Kramer 413 F. Supp. 618 (D. Conn., 1976), is as on point and held for defendant.

$\Longrightarrow$ Rebuttal for Plaintiff as Side-1:

Pressure Science, Inc. v. Kramer is distinguishable because:

In USM v. Marson, plaintiff adopted more security measures than in Press Sci v. Kramer.

[2]

$\Longrightarrow$ Point for Plaintiff as Side-1:

Where: Defendant's access to plaintiff's product information saved it time or expense.

Plaintiff should win a claim for Trade Secrets Misappropriation.

Cite: Kewanee Oil Co. v. Bicron Corp. 416 U.S. 470, 94 S. Ct. 1879, 40 L. Ed. 2d 315 (1974).

$\Longleftarrow$ Response for Defendant as Side-2:

Kewanee Oil Co. v. Bicron Corp. is distinguishable because:

In Kewanee v. Bicron, defendant's access to plaintiff's product information saved it more time or expense than in USM v. Marson

In Kewanee v. Bicron, plaintiff and defendant entered into a nondisclosure agreement. Not so in USM v. Marson.

In Kewanee v. Bicron, defendant received something of value for entering into the agreement. Not so in USM v. Marson.

Counterexamples:

Pressure Science, Inc. v. Kramer 413 F. Supp. 618 (D. Conn., 1976), is as on point and held for defendant.

$\Longrightarrow$ Rebuttal for Plaintiff as Side-1:

Pressure Science, Inc. v. Kramer is distinguishable because:

In USM v. Marson, plaintiff adopted more security measures than in Press Sci v. Kramer.

[3]

⟹ Point for Plaintiff as Side-1:

Where: Defendant's access to plaintiff's product information saved it time or expense.

Plaintiff should win a claim for Trade Secrets Misappropriation.

Cite: Analogic Corp. v. Data Translation, Inc. 358 N.E.2d 804 (S.J.C. Mass., 1976).

⟸ Response for Defendant as Side-2:

Analogic Corp. v. Data Translation, Inc. is distinguishable because:

In Analogic v. Data Trans, defendant's access to plaintiff's product information saved it more time or expense than in USM v. Marson

In Analogic v. Data Trans, plaintiff and defendant entered into a nondisclosure agreement. Not so in USM v. Marson.

In Analogic v. Data Trans, plaintiff's former employee brought product development information to defendant. Not so in USM v. Marson.

Counterexamples:

Pressure Science, Inc. v. Kramer 413 F. Supp. 618 (D. Conn., 1976), is as on point and held for defendant.

⟹ Rebuttal for Plaintiff as Side-1:

Pressure Science, Inc. v. Kramer is distinguishable because:

In USM v. Marson, plaintiff adopted more security measures than in Press Sci v. Kramer.

[4]

⟹ Point for Plaintiff as Side-1:

Where: plaintiff adopted security measures.

Plaintiff should win a claim for Trade Secrets Misappropriation.

Cite: Plant Industries, Inc. v. Coleman 287 F. Supp. 636 (C.D. Cal., 1968).

⟸ Response for Defendant as Side-2: None.

⟹ Rebuttal for Plaintiff as Side-1: None.

Sample Hypo Outputs

[5]

$\Longrightarrow$ Point for Plaintiff as Side-1:

Where: Plaintiff adopted security measures.

Plaintiff should win a claim for Trade Secrets Misappropriation.

Cite: Peggy Lawton Kitchens, Inc. v. Hogan 466 N.E.2d 138 (Mass. App. 1984).

$\Longleftarrow$ Response for Defendant as Side-2: None.

$\Longrightarrow$ Rebuttal for Plaintiff as Side-1: None.

[6]

$\Longrightarrow$ Point for Plaintiff as Side-1:

Where: Plaintiff adopted security measures.

Plaintiff should win a claim for Trade Secrets Misappropriation.

Cite: Eastern Marble Products Corp. v. Roman Marble, Inc. 364 N.E.2d 799 (Mass. 1977).

$\Longleftarrow$ Response for Defendant as Side-2:

Eastern Marble Products Corp. v. Roman Marble, Inc. is distinguishable because:

In Eastern-Marble, plaintiff and defendant entered into a nondisclosure agreement. Not so in USM v. Marson.

Counterexamples:

Healy, Inc. v. Murphy, Inc. 357 Mass. 728 (1970), is as on point and held for defendant.

$\Longrightarrow$ Rebuttal for Plaintiff as Side-1: Healy, Inc. v. Murphy, Inc. is distinguishable because:

In USM v. Marson, plaintiff adopted more security measures than in Healy v. Murphy

In USM v. Marson, defendant's access to plaintiff's product information saved it more time or expense than in Healy v. Murphy.

[7]

$\Longrightarrow$ Point for Plaintiff as Side-1:

Where: Plaintiff adopted security measures. Defendant's access to plaintiff's product information saved it time or expense.

Plaintiff should win a claim for Trade Secrets Misappropriation.

Cite: Space Aero Products Co. v. R.E. Darling Co. 208 A.2d 74 (Ct. App. Md., 1965).

⇐ Response for Defendant as Side-2:

Space Aero Products Co. v. R.E. Darling Co. is distinguishable because:

In Space Aero v. Darling, defendant paid plaintiff's former employee to switch employment. Not so in USM v. Marson.

In Space Aero v. Darling, plaintiff's former employee brought product development information to defendant. Not so in USM v. Marson.

⟹ Rebuttal for Plaintiff as Side-1: None.

3-Ply Argument in *USM* for Case Selected by Attorney

3-Ply Argument for Selected Case to Cite on Claim of Trade Secrets Misappropriation in Fact Situation of USM v. Marson:

[8]

⟹ Point for Defendant as Side-1:

Where:

Even though: Plaintiff adopted security measures.

Defendant should win a claim for Trade Secrets Misappropriation.

Cite: Healy, Inc. v. Murphy, Inc. 357 Mass. 728 (1970).

⇐ Response for Plaintiff as Side-2:

Healy, Inc. v. Murphy, Inc. is distinguishable because:

In USM v. Marson, plaintiff adopted more security measures than in Healy v. Murphy

In USM v. Marson, defendant's access to plaintiff's product information saved it more time or expense than in Healy v. Murphy.

Counterexamples:

Plant Industries, Inc. v. Coleman 287 F. Supp. 636 (C.D. Cal. 1968), is as on point and held for plaintiff.

Peggy Lawton Kitchens, Inc. v. Hogan 466 N.E.2d 138 (Mass. App., 1984), is as on point and held for plaintiff.

Space Aero Products Co. v. R.E. Darling Co. 208 A.2d 74 (Ct. App. Md., 1965), is more on point and held for plaintiff where it was also the case that: Defendant's access to plaintiff's product information saved it time or expense.

3-Ply Argument for *Eastern Marble* Case, Selected by Attorney on Subsequent Loop through Basic Processing Loop

[9]

$\Longrightarrow$ Point for Plaintiff as Side-1:

Where: Plaintiff and defendant entered into a nondisclosure agreement. Plaintiff should win a claim for Trade Secrets Misappropriation.

Cite: Structural Dynamics Research Corp. v. Engineering Mechanics Research Corp. 401 F. Supp. 1102 (E.D. Mich., 1975).

$\Longleftarrow$ Response for Defendant as Side-2:

Structural Dynamics Research Corp. v. Engineering Mechanics Research Corp. is distinguishable because:

In Structural Dynamics, defendant received something of value for entering into the agreement. Not so in Eastern-Marble.

In Structural Dynamics, plaintiff's former employee brought product development information to defendant. Not so in Eastern-Marble.

In Structural Dynamics, the nondisclosure agreement specifically referred to plaintiff's product. Not so in Eastern-Marble.

Counterexamples:

Motorola, Inc. v. Fairchild Camera and Instrument Corp. 366 F. Supp. 1173 (D. Ariz., 1973), is as on point and held for defendant.

Amoco Production Co. v. Lindley 609 P.2d 733 (Okla. 1980) is more on point and held for defendant where it was also the case that: Plaintiff adopted security measures.

$\Longrightarrow$ Rebuttal for Plaintiff as Side-1:

Motorola, Inc. v. Fairchild Camera And Instrument Corp. is distinguishable because: In Eastern-Marble, plaintiff adopted more security measures than in Motorola.

Suggested Hypotheticals in USM

Hypotheticals to Consider on Claim of Trade Secrets Misappropriation in Fact Situation of USM v. Marson:

Defendant's position would be strengthened in following situations:

Suppose:

Plaintiff disclosed its product information in negotiations with defendant. Plaintiff disclosed its product information to outsiders.
Cf. Crown Industries Inc. v. Kawneer Co. 335 F. Supp. 749 (N.D. Ill., 1971)

Plaintiff disclosed its product information in negotiations with defendant.
Cf. Speedry Chemical Products, Inc. v. Carter's Ink Company 306 F.2d 328 (2d Cir., 1962)

Plaintiff disclosed its product information in negotiations with defendant. Plaintiff's product information was about customer business relations.
Cf. Automated-Systems v. Service-Bureau 401 F.2d 619 (10 Cir., 1968)

I Excerpts from Opinion and Briefs in the *USM* Case

Opinion

The following excerpts are from the opinion of the court in *USM Corp. v. Marson Fastener Corp.*, 379 Mass. 90, 98–103 (1979):

No general rule may be established to determine whether the security precautions taken by the possessor of a trade secret are reasonable. "Relevant factors to be considered include (1) the existence or absence of an express agreement restricting disclosure, (2) the nature and extent of security precautions taken by the possessor to prevent acquisition of the information by unauthorized third parties, (3) the circumstances under which the information was disclosed... to [any] employee to the extent that they give rise to a reasonable inference that further disclosure, without the consent of the possessor, is prohibited, and (4) the degree to which the information has been placed in the public domain or rendered 'readily ascertainable' by the third parties through patent applications or unrestricted product marketing." [citation of a Michigan appellate court case]...

USM required supervisory, technical, and research personnel, including the defendant Lahnston, to sign nondisclosure agreements... While the nondisclosure agreements did not list the particular information which USM considered secret, such specificity is not required to put employees on notice that their work involves access to trade secrets and confidential information. See *Eastern Marble Prods. Corp. v. Roman Marble, Inc.*, 372 Mass. 835, 840 (1977)... Accord, *Kodekey Elecs., Inc. v. Mechanex Corp.*, 486 F.2d 449, 455 (10th Cir. 1973) (nondisclosure agreements a "primary and essential precaution")...

It is not fatal that the blueprints and parts drawings were not labeled "confidential" or "secret" or that USM had not expressly informed its employees that these part drawings were considered secret by USM. See *A. H. Emery Co. v. Marcan Prods. Corp., supra*...

Similarly, the plant security precautions taken by USM were sufficient to exclude the general public from the production areas of USM's plants, thereby denying access to USM factory equipment, including the USM machine. The fact that USM conducted escorted tours for employees' families and USM product distributors, including certain defendants, does not militate against a finding that USM denied public access to the USM machine. Compare *Plant Indus., Inc. v. Coleman*, 287 F. Supp. 636, 643 (C.D. Cal. 1968) (tours by women's clubs and customers' representatives do not constitute failure to maintain secrecy)... with *Motorola, Inc. v. Fairchild Camera & Instrument Corp.*, 366 F. Supp. 1173, 1186 (D. Ariz. 1973) (security inadequate where competitors toured plant, operated "secret" machine and "observed its 'secret' process in a separate microscope placed there for this purpose")...

We do not require the possessor of a trade secret to take heroic measures to preserve its secrecy... The question whether a plaintiff has taken "all proper and reasonable steps" depends on the circumstances of each case, considering the nature of the information sought to be protected *as well as the conduct of the parties*...

Applying this standard, we denied trade secret protection in *Healy* because the plaintiff had made a conscious policy decision to do nothing to safeguard the confidentiality of its manufacturing processes. *J. T. Healy & Son v. James A. Murphy & Son, supra* at 737-738. In *Healy*, the employees were never informed that any of the manufacturing processes were considered secret; employees were not required to sign nondisclosure agreements... The plaintiff in *Healy*, other than excluding the general public from the manufacturing plant, took no security precautions whatever...

By contrast, in *Eastern Marble Prods. Corp. v. Roman Marble, Inc.*, 372 Mass. 835 (1977), trade secret protection was afforded a plaintiff who ...required all manufacturing employees "to sign an agreement not to disclose the methods and procedures involved in the [plaintiff's] manufacturing processes."...

We think that, considering the character of the information which USM sought to protect, the steps taken by USM to preserve the secrecy of its trade secret were reasonable. Accord, *Eastern Marble Prods. Corp. v. Roman Marble, Inc. supra*... In short, USM's "efforts at secrecy, like the process itself, met the basic criterion of success." *Space Aero Prods. Co. v. R. E. Darling Co.*, 238 Md. 93, 112, cert. denied, 382 U.S. 843 (1965). See Restatement of Torts Sec. 757, Comment b (1939).

Plaintiff's Brief

The following excerpts are from the brief filed by the plaintiff's attorney in the *USM* case:

The Master was in error in his conclusion of law... that USM had not sufficiently guarded the confidential information within its machine so as to qualify that information as a trade secret.... This error was based on a misinterpretation of the language of the Court in *J.T. Healy & Son, Inc. v. James A. Murphy & Sons, Inc.*, 357 Mass. 728, 738 (1970) ("Healy")...

The *Healy* case was, of course, unique in that the owner of the allegedly secret process did absolutely nothing to guard it, and in the course of its opinion the Court described various precautionary measures which the *Healy* plaintiff had not taken, including the failure to enter into non-disclosure agreements or give its employees continual warnings and admonitions of secrecy.... Whatever might or might not be the correctness of the *Healy* decision on its own facts, some of its language was susceptible to the misinterpretation of establishing not only a set of specific secrecy requirements but, under an undefined "eternal vigilance" standard, an artificially extreme level of security which, as a practical matter, would tend to eliminate trade secrets as a viable means of protective development and use of confidential information and processes...

[The Master and the Superior Court (i.e., the court below)] seem to have read the "eternal vigilance" language of "Healy" as establishing a list of precautionary measures, all of which have to be taken in every case in order to have anything qualify as a trade secret in any case... Thus, for example, a predominant concern of both the Master and the Superior Court was with the fact that the USM machine was not kept constantly and carefully concealed from all observation, without paying attention at all to the related fact, ..., that the trade secret could not be in any way determined or duplicated through observation of the machine... The plaintiffs in *Jet Spray* had not complied with all the precautionary measures mentioned in *Healy*, but the Court nevertheless held that their actions "clearly constituted sufficient and appropriate precautions [to maintain secrecy]."... In so holding, the *Jet Spray* Court... stated that "[I]n our view, the result in each case depends upon the conduct of the parties and the nature of the information."... See, also *Eastern Marble Products Corp. v. Roman Marble, Inc....*

The undesirable effect of any such artificial approach... would be as a practical matter to encourage theft and other improper commercial practices by supporting the proposition that if a manufacturer's confidential information can be somehow misappropriated by improper means, it is not sufficiently safeguarded to qualify as a trade secret.

Defendant's Brief

The following excerpts are from the brief filed by the defendant's attorney in the in *USM* case:

The court has stated the nature of this burden to maintain secrecy in great detail in *J. T. Healy & Son, Inc. v. James A. Murphy & Son, Inc., supra*:
"If the person entitled to a trade secret wishes to have its exclusive use in his own business, he must not fail to take all proper and reasonable steps to keep it secret... [O]ne who claims that he has a trade secret must exercise eternal vigilance..."...

In all three of these cases [the *Healy, Jet Spray Cooler,* and *Eastern Marble Products* cases], the court applied to the plaintiff's activities a requirement that all proper and reasonable steps be taken to protect the alleged secret process. The differences in result arise because in some instances a plaintiff has been able to meet that burden, while in others, the plaintiff's efforts have fallen short of the required standard...

The findings in this case contain numerous indications of the absence of security and secrecy regarding the USM machine. [Two defendants] each visited the plaintiff's plant and were allowed to observe and examine closely the plaintiff's machine in operation... Cf. *Motorola, Inc. v. Fairchild Camera and Instrument Corp.*, 366 F. Supp. 1173, 1186 (D. Ariz. 1973). Neither they nor anyone else were notified in any manner that the machines they observed were secret or confidential. There was no effective control over plans and drawings at Shelton. Employees could thus easily obtain sepias and blueprints and remove them from the plant...

Although Lahnston was given an agreement to sign it was a form agreement designed primarily for research and development employees... The fact that the agreement signed by Lahnston was a printed form bearing little relation to his actual duties reinforces the impression that USM did not make a serious effort to inform its employees such as Lahnston as to their obligations not to disclose trade secrets...

In *Motorola, Inc., supra* the court held a secrecy agreement invalid and stated:

"While the Motorola employee-defendants had executed the above-mentioned nondisclosure agreement, they were not advised upon execution, either generally or specifically, what, if any, production processes, know-how, or other things plaintiff considered proprietary. At no time during their employment were they so advised."...

Contrast this with the situation in *Eastern Marble Products Corp. v. Roman Marble, Inc.*... wherein the nondisclosure agreement specifically required employees not to disclose the methods and procedures involved in the manufacturing processes of Eastern Marble.

J Implementation of Hypo

Chapter 4 provides a detailed account of Hypo's architecture, modules, data structures, and algorithms. This appendix details some lower-level features of Hypo's implementation, including the programming environment and flavor system modifications.

Programming Environment

The Hypo program runs on a Texas Instruments Explorer and is written in Zetalisp. It comprises approximately 3,500 blocks of VAX storage, which includes both source code and a compiled version of the program. It takes approximately 20 minutes to load the program.

Hypo takes from 2 to 4 minutes to generate a complete set of 3-Ply Arguments and suggestions for hypotheticals from a fact situation already represented in Legal Case Frames. The approximate times for generating 3-Ply Arguments and hypotheticals for the fact situations of the Extended Examples in chapter 5 and appendix H are shown below:

Structural Dynamics, 132 seconds

Amexxco, 183 seconds

Crown, 199 seconds

USM, 278 seconds

These times include the input/output delays for making three or four menu selections and writing the files of outputs. The longer processing times for some cases reflect the fact that for those fact situations, there are multiple best cases to cite for a side, each one of which is the subject of a separate 3-Ply Argument.

Flavor System Modifications

The Hypo program makes extensive use of the flavor facilities available in Zetalisp. As described in chapters 4 and 6, Hypo's language for representing and analyzing cases is implemented in flavors. The Legal Case Frames, Interpretation Frames, Case Analysis Records, Argument Records, Claim Lattice nodes, and Dimensions are defined as flavors.

Hypo's flavors are specially modified to deal with three implementation problems frequently encountered in frame-based representation schemes employing flavors: keeping track of flavor instances, cross-referencing flavor instances, and "copying" flavor instances. The modifications are contained in four mixins that make up Hypo's flavors: self-cataloging, self-naming, postprocessing, and dumping.

Keeping track The self-cataloging mixin facilitates keeping track of flavor instances. Instances with the self-cataloging mixin are automatically cataloged upon instantiation in each of their target catalogs. There are two main catalogs: the Global Catalog and the Post Process Catalog. The Global Catalog contains all of the instances generated in a session with Hypo or their replacements. As described in chapters 4 and 6, it is used as a database for storing and retrieving information about cases in the Case Knowledge Base. The use of the Post Processing Catalog is described below.

Cross-referencing Most Hypo flavor instances cross-reference other flavor instances, that is, the values of some of their slots are other flavor instances. For example, the value of the case slot of each Legal Case Frame associated with a given legal case is the top-level Case frame for that legal case. The self-naming and postprocessing mixins facilitate cross-referencing. By virtue of the self-naming mixin, the value of the string in the instance's name slot is set equal to the instance itself. Any instance with the postprocessing mixin gets cataloged automatically in the Post Processing Catalog.

The utility of the cross-referencing feature is apparent when the Hypo program is loaded. Each legal case has a corresponding file of make-instance forms for its various Legal Case Frames. When the file is loaded, the make-instances are evaluated and the Legal Case Frames are instantiated, their names are set to themselves, and they are cataloged in the Global Catalog and Post Processing Catalog. At that point, their various slots refer to the *names* of other instances rather than to the instances themselves. A call to the postprocessing function replaces the names with the instances. It runs through each of the objects in the Post Processing Catalog, and for each of the slots listed in the object's postp-list, it replaces the name of any instance in that slot with the instance itself.

Copying Instances are copied through the use of the dumping mixin. Instances with the dumping mixin can be "dumped" into files in the sense that make-instance forms are created that can be written to the file. When those make-instances are reevaluated, they create "copies" of the same instances. As described in chapters 4 and 8, copying cases is useful in creating hypothetical variants of a seed case. A copy of a seed case is made by dumping it into a file, in the process of which the modifications are inserted. The make-instances for the variant are then reevaluated, automatically cataloged, and postprocessed. Copying is also useful in permanently storing hypothetical cases generated by Hypo in the course of a session. It is not possible to store the actual instances in a file except in the sense that make-instance forms for the newly created instances are dumped into a file from which they can be "reconstituted."

Glossary

Argument Evaluation Criteria: Standards for evaluating the strength of legal arguments that cite precedents. One of Hypo's basic sources of domain knowledge. See chapter 4.

Argument Record: Basic Hypo data structure for generating 3-Ply Arguments. See chapters 4 and 5.

Basic Processing Loop: The basic control loop in the Hypo program. See chapter 4.

Best Case Selector: Hypo module that selects from among the relevant cases various types of most analogous cases, including the most-on-point cases and best cases for plaintiff and defendant to cite. See chapters 4 and 8.

Boundary counterexample: A precedent whose features favor a particular outcome even more extremely than either the current fact situation or the precedent cited in the point but where a different outcome was reached. See chapters 4 and 8.

Case: In law, a dispute between two parties, a plaintiff and a defendant, arising out of a specific fact situation, a lawsuit. See chapters 2 and 5 and appendix E for sample legal cases.

Case Analysis Record (CAR): Basic Hypo data structure for recording results of Dimensional analysis of a current fact situation and for keeping track of Claim Lattices and arguments made about current fact situation. See chapters 4 and 5.

Case Analyzer: Hypo module that performs Dimensional analysis of a current fact situation to determine the cases that are relevant. See chapters 4 and 5.

Case-Based Reasoning (CBR): A kind of reasoning where cases are employed as justifications for conclusions about or as models for solutions to a problem situation.

Case Editor: Hypo module to assist attorney/user to input new fact situations, modify existing cases, or permanently store cases in the Case Knowledge Base. See chapter 4.

Case Knowledge Base (CKB): Hypo's database of legal cases that are represented in the Legal Case Frame language and indexed by Dimensions. See chapter 6.

Case Positioner: Hypo module that retrieves relevant cases from the Case Knowledge Base and organizes them according to how on point they are with respect to the current fact situation. See chapter 4.

Constrained Example Generation (CEG): A research approach for reasoning by examples in which a "space" of examples is used. Examples are generated by modifying existing examples to meet various useful constraints.

Citable in first instance: Whether a precedent is good enough to cite in an initial point for a side or should be held in reserve to cite only if needed as a counterexample to the opponent's point.

Citation signals: In law, labels for citing precedents that convey to reader how strongly the precedent supports the proposition for which it is cited. See chapter 9.

Cite: In law, to justify a legal conclusion, such as that a party in a case should win a claim, by formally referring to a legal authority such as a prior case, a statute, or a legal reference work.

Cites displays: In Hypo, output lists of cases that inform attorney/user the precedents that can be cited for or against a party on a claim and how strongly they support the party's position. See chapter 5 for examples.

Claim: A recognized kind of legal complaint for which the courts will grant relief (e.g., negligence, malpractice, breach of contract, trade secrets misappropriation).

Claim Lattice: In Hypo, the main tool for organizing relevant cases in the Case Knowledge Base in terms of how analogous or on point they are to a problem situation. See chapters 4, 5, and 8. Claim Lattices are used in selecting the best cases to cite and in locating counterexamples to cited precedents.

Common law: The Anglo-American system of law in which prior cases are a source of law even in the absence of statutory or constitu-

Glossary 309

tional provisions. Distinguished from European civil law in which detailed statutory codes are the primary source of law.

Counterexample: A case that in some sense is as analogous to a problem situation as a given case but had a different outcome. In Hypo, citing cases as counterexamples is a way of responding to points in a legal argument. See chapters 4, 8, and 9.

Current fact situation (cfs): The problem situation that Hypo currently is analyzing, retrieving cases relevant to, or making arguments about.

Decision: In law, the court's selection of the winning party on a claim in a case.

Defendant (Δ, δ): A party to a legal case who is sued by the plaintiff and defends against the claim alleged by the plaintiff.

Dimension: A knowledge representation construct in Hypo for representing factors that make a party's position on a claim in a lawsuit stronger or weaker. Dimensions identify the features that are the bases of important similarities and differences among cases. See chapters 4 and 7. Appendix F contains a complete listing.

Dimension Index: Hypo's primary indexing scheme for retrieving relevant precedents from the Case Knowledge Base. See chapter 7.

Distinguish: In law and Hypo, a way of responding to a point citing a precedent by pointing out the significant differences between the precedent and the current fact situation. See chapters 2 and 4.

Elements of a legal claim: In law, generalized statements of the facts that must be proved in order to prevail on the claim. See chapter 2.

Example-Based Reasoning (EBR): Reasoning that employs retrieval, generation, analysis, modification, or manipulation of examples for explanation, learning, discovery, or debugging.

Example Knowledge Base (EKB): A knowledge base of examples for use in reasoning by example about problem situations.

Explainer: Hypo module that explains Hypo's analysis of the current fact situation by summarizing best cases to cite, making 3-Ply Arguments for and against a side's position, suggesting hypotheticals to strengthen the position, and comparing arguments. See chapters 4 and 9.

Factual Predicates: Generalized factual tests for the existence of legally significant relationships in a case represented in Hypo's Legal Case Frame language. Used in Dimension prerequisites. See chapters 4 and 7. Appendix D provides a complete listing.

Focal slot: In Hypo, the focal slot of the Dimension is the crucial value for comparing cases along a Dimension. In a case to which the Dimension applies, the focal slot value determines where the case lies along the range of the Dimension. See chapters 4 and 7.

Global Catalog: A list of pointers to all of the objects in Hypo sorted by type, such as Case, Product, Employee, Interpretation Frame, Argument Record, etc.

Hold, holding, hold in favor of: In a lawsuit, the court's resolution in favor of one side or the other of their dispute about a particular issue.

Hypo: A computer program that performs case-based reasoning in a legal domain.

Hypo Generator: Hypo module that generates hypothetical variants of the current fact situation or relevant cases to bolster points and responses. See chapters 4 and 8.

Hypothetical: A "made-up" legal dispute that has not been decided by a court but whose fact situation is similar to that of actual legal cases.

Interpretation Frame: A basic Hypo data structure for recording the values in a fact situation of the Factual Predicates. See chapter 4.

Jurisprudence: The philosopy of law.

Legal Case Frames: A frame-based language, implemented in flavors, for representing legal cases. See chapters 4 and 6.

Lines of cases: A series of legal cases presenting similar fact situations that were decided on similar grounds.

Most on point: The most analogous cases to a problem situation as determined by relative degrees of overlap between sets of Dimensions shared by cases and the problem situation. Measured in Hypo by Claim Lattices. See chapters 4, 8, and 9.

Near-miss Dimension: In Hypo, a Dimension is a near miss with respect to a problem situation if all of its prerequisites are satisfied except the one(s) associated with the focal slots of the Dimension. See chapter 7.

On point: A symbolic measure of how analogous or close a prior case is to a given fact situation. In Hypo, a prior case is on point to the extent that it shares the same strengths and weaknesses, as represented by Dimensions, that are present in the current fact situation. See chapters 4, 8, and 9.

Open textured: A predicate in a rule is open textured if it is not further defined by more detailed rules. Predicates in legal rules are commonly open textured. Only the cases that apply the predicates to specific fact situations provide a meaning for the predicates.

Partial counterexample: In Hypo, a precedent that shares some of the same factors of the current fact situation that a cited precedent does but had a different outcome. See chapters 4, 8, and 9.

Plaintiff (Π, π): A party to a legal case who sues the defendant by commencing a lawsuit and alleging a claim against the defendant.

Point: In law, a legal conclusion accompanied by citation to an authority to justify the conclusion. In Hypo, a point is the first ply in a 3-Ply Argument where the legal conclusion is that a side in the current fact situation should win a claim, a prior case is cited, and an analogy is drawn between the current fact situation and the cited case.

Positioning: In Hypo, using Claim Lattices to interpret and assess the relevance of past cases to a current fact situation by seeing them from the viewpoint of the case at hand and finding the most-on-point cases.

Potentially more-on-point counterexample: In Hypo, a precedent that is nearly more on point than a cited case but had a different outcome. See chapters 4, 8, and 9.

Potential most-on-point case: In Hypo, a case that would be more on point than a given case relative to a problem situation if the prerequisites of certain near-miss Dimensions were added to the problem situation. Useful in suggesting hypotheticals to bolster points or responses. See chapters 4, 8, and 9.

Precedent: In law, a prior case that can be cited to justify a legal conclusion.

Prerequisites: In Hypo, a list of Factual Predicates that must be satisfied in a case for a Dimension to apply to that case. See chapter 7.

Rebuttal: In Hypo, the third ply of a 3-Ply Argument in which any counterexample cases cited in the response are distinguished from the current fact situation. See chapter 4.

Response: In Hypo, the second ply of a 3-Ply Argument in which the case cited in the Point is distinguished from the current fact situation and counterexamples are cited. See chapter 4.

Seed case: In Hypo, a case as represented in the Legal Case Frame language that serves as the basis for a hypothetical. A copy of the seed case is modified to produce a hypothetical variant of the seed case. See chapter 8.

Session Manager: Hypo module that keeps track of cases and hypotheticals employed as current fact situations during the course of an attorney/user's session with Hypo. See chapter 4.

Slippery Slope: A kind of argument tactic. One asserts that if a rule applied with a given result to a given fact situation, then it would also necessitate the same results in a series of hypothetical fact situations. Each hypothetical in the series is more exaggerated than the preceding one and demonstrates circumstances in which the result is more and more absurd.

Squib: A structured summary of a legal case (also known as a case brief). Commonly used in legal case books and by law students to summarize important features of cases.

Stare decisis: In law, the doctrine of the common law that a court's decision in a previous case is binding on the same or a lower court in a similar case.

Glossary

Target case: In Hypo, a case various of whose features are incorporated into a hypothetical variant of a seed case. See chapter 8.

3-Ply Arguer: Hypo module that generates 3-Ply Arguments about a current fact situation and suggests hypotheticals for improving the arguments. See chapter 4.

3-Ply Argument: Turn-taking schematic for a legal argument citing cases; consists of a Point for Side 1, Response for Side 2, and Rebuttal for Side 1. See chapters 2, 4, and 5.

Top-level Legal Case Frame: A frame of Hypo's language for representing legal cases that represents a legal case's name, court, date, parties, winner, and claims, as well as indexing information for retrieving the case from the Case Knowledge Base. See chapter 6.

Trade secrets misappropriation: A kind of legal claim usually involving corporate competitors. The plaintiff corporation complains that the defendant corporation has gained access to plaintiff's secret information and used it to obtain an unfair competitive advantage. Most of the cases in Hypo's Case Knowledge Base deal with claims for trade secrets misappropriation. See chapter 2 for a representative fact situation raising a trade secrets claim.

Trumping or most-on-point counterexample: In Hypo, a precedent that is more analogous than the one cited in the Point and that had a different outcome. These are the strongest counterexamples to cite in a Response. See chapters 4, 8, and 9.

Underlying Legal Case Frame: Frames of Hypo's language for representing legal cases that represent the facts of the case. See chapter 6.

Bibliography

[Alker and Christensen 1972] Hayward R. Alker Jr. and Cheryl Christensen. From Causal Modelling to Artificial Intelligence: The Evolution of a UN Peace-Making Simulation. In J. La Ponce and P. Smoker, editors, *Experimentation and Simulation in Political Science*. University of Toronto Press, Toronto, 1972.

[Allen and Saxon 1987] Layman E. Allen and Charles S. Saxon. Some Problems in Designing Expert Systems to Aid Legal Reasoning. In *First International Conference on Artificial Intelligence and Law*, Northeastern University, Boston, 1987.

[Ashley and Rissland 1986] Kevin D. Ashley and Edwina L. Rissland. Toward Modelling Legal Argument. In Antonio A. Martino and F. Socci Natali, editors, *Automated Analysis of Legal Texts, Logic, Informatics, Law*, pages 19–30. Elsevier (North-Holland), 1986.

[Ashley and Rissland 1987a] Kevin D. Ashley and Edwina L. Rissland. But, See, Accord: Generating *Blue Book* Citations in HYPO. In *First International Conference on Artificial Intelligence and Law*, Northeastern University, Boston, 1987.

[Ashley and Rissland 1987b] Kevin D. Ashley and Edwina L. Rissland. Compare and Contrast, A Test of Expertise. In *Proceedings AAAI—87*. American Association for Artificial Intelligence, August 1987. Seattle.

[Ashley and Rissland 1988a] K. D. Ashley and E. L. Rissland. A Case-Based Approach to Modeling Legal Expertise. *IEEE Expert*, 1988.

[Ashley and Rissland 1988b] Kevin D. Ashley and Edwina L. Rissland. Waiting on Weighting: A Symbolic Least Commitment Approach. In *Proceedings AAAI—88*. American Association for Artificial Intelligence, August 1988. St. Paul, MN.

[Ashley 1985] Kevin D. Ashley. Reasoning by Analogy: A Survey of Selected A.I. Research with Implications for Legal Expert Systems. In Charles Walter, editor, *Computing Power and Legal Reasoning*. West Publishing Co., St. Paul, MN, 1985.

[Ashley 1986] Kevin D. Ashley. Modelling Legal Argument: Reasoning with Cases and Hypotheticals—A Thesis Proposal. Project Memo 10, Counselor Project, Department of Computer and Information Science, University of Massachusetts, 1986.

[Ashley 1987] Kevin D. Ashley. *Modelling Legal Argument: Reasoning with Cases and Hypotheticals*. PhD thesis, University of Massachusetts, 1987. COINS Technical Report No. 88-01.

[Ashley 1988] Kevin D. Ashley. Arguing by Analogy in Law: a Case-Based Model. In David H. Helman, editor, *Analogical Reasoning: Perspectives of Artificial Intelligence, Cognitive Science, and Philosophy*. Kluwer, 1988.

[Ashley 1989a] Kevin D. Ashley. Defining Salience in Case-Based Arguments. In *Proceedings IJCAI—89*. International Joint Conferences on Artificial Intelligence, August 1989. Detroit.

[Ashley 1989b] Kevin D. Ashley. Toward a Computational Theory of Arguing with Precedents: Accommodating Multiple Interpretations of Cases. In *Second International Conference on Artificial Intelligence and Law*, University of British Columbia, Vancouver, BC, 1989.

[Bareiss et al. 1987] E. Ray Bareiss, Bruce W. Porter, and Craig C. Wier. Protos: An Exemplar-Based Learning Apprentice. In *Proceedings Fourth International Workshop on Machine Learning*, pages 12–23, University of California at Irvine, June 1987.

[Bareiss 1988] Raymond Bareiss. *Protos: A Unified Approach to Concept Representation, Classification, and Learning*. PhD thesis, University of Texas, 1988. Technical Report CS 88-10, Dept. of Computer Science, Vanderbilt University, Nashville, TN.

[Bench-Capon et al. 1987] T. J. M. Bench-Capon, G. O. Robinson, T. W. Routen, and M. J. Sergot. Logic Programming for Large Scale Applications in Law: A Formalism of Supplementary Benefit Legislation. In *First International Conference on Artificial Intelligence and Law*, Northeastern University, Boston, 1987.

[Berman and Greiner 1980] Harold J. Berman and William R. Greiner. *The Nature and Functions of Law*. Foundation Press, Mineola, NY, 1980.

[Birnbaum et al. 1980] L. Birnbaum, M. Flowers, and R. McGuire. Towards an AI Model of Argumentation. In *Proceedings AAAI—80*, pages 313–315. American Association for Artificial Intelligence, August 1980. Stanford, CA.

[Birnbaum 1982] L. Birnbaum. Argument Molecules: A Functional Representation of Argument Structure. In *Proceedings AAAI—82*, Pittsburgh, August 1982. American Association for Artificial Intelligence.

[Blair and Maron 1985] David C. Blair and M. E. Maron. An Evaluation of Retrieval Effectiveness for a Full-Text Document-Retrieval System. *Communications of the ACM*, 28(3):289–299, March 1985.

[BlueBook 1986] *BlueBook: A Uniform System of Citation*. Harvard Law Review Association, Cambridge, MA, 14th edition, 1986.

[Buchanan and Headrick 1970] Bruce G. Buchanan and Thomas E. Headrick. Some Speculation about Artificial Intelligence and Legal Reasoning. Project Memo AIM 123, Stanford Artificial Intelligence Project, 1970.

[Burstein 1983a] M. H. Burstein. A Model of Learning by Incremental Analogical Reasoning and Debugging. In *Proceedings AAAI—83*, Washington, DC, August 1983. American Association for Artificial Intelligence.

[Burstein 1983b] M. H. Burstein. Concept Formation by Incremental Analogical Reasoning and Debugging. In *Proceedings International Machine Learning Workshop*, Monticello, IL, June 1983.

[Burton 1985] Steven J. Burton. *An Introduction to Law and Legal Reasoning*. Little, Brown, Boston, 1985.

[Carbonell 1981] J. G. Carbonell. A Computational Model of Problem Solving by Analogy. In *Proceedings IJCAI—81*, Vancouver, BC, August 1981. International Joint Conferences on Artificial Intelligence.

[Carbonell 1982] J. G. Carbonell. Experiential Learning in Analogical Problem Solving. In *Proceedings AAAI—82*, Pittsburgh, August 1982. American Association for Artificial Intelligence.

[Carbonell 1983a] J. G. Carbonell. Derivational Analogy and Its Role in Problem Solving. In *Proceedings AAAI—83*, Washington, DC, August 1983. American Association for Artificial Intelligence.

[Carbonell 1983b] J. G. Carbonell. Learning by Analogy: Formulating and Generalizing Plans from Past Experience. In R. S. Michalski, J. G. Carbonell, and T. M. Mitchell, editors, *Machine Learning, An Artificial Intelligence Approach*. Tioga Press, Palo Alto, 1983.

Bibliography

[Carbonell 1986] J. G. Carbonell. Derivational Analogy: A Theory of Reconstructive Problem Solving and Expertise Acquisition. In R. S. Michalski, J. G. Carbonell, and T. M. Mitchell, editors, *Machine Learning: An Artificial Intelligence Approach*, Volume 2. Morgan Kaufmann, Los Altos, CA, 1986.

[Clancey 1983] W. J. Clancey. The Epistemology of a Rule-based Expert System: A Framework for Explanation. *Artificial Intelligence*, 20(3):215–251, 1983.

[Clancey 1984] William J. Clancey. Classification Problem Solving. In *Proceedings AAAI—84*, Austin, TX, August 1984. American Association for Artificial Intelligence.

[Cohen 1983] Robin Cohen. Computational Model for the Analysis of Arguments. Technical Report CSRG-151, Department of Computer Science, University of Toronto, 1983.

[De Jong and Mooney 1986] G. De Jong and R. Mooney. Explanation-Based Learning: An Alternative View. *Machine Learning*, 1(2), 1986.

[Doyle 1986] Richard J. Doyle. Constructing and Refining Causal Explanations from an Inconsistent Domain Theory. In *Proceedings AAAI—86*. American Association for Artificial Intelligence, August 1986. Philadelphia.

[Dworkin 1977] Ronald Dworkin. *Taking Rights Seriously*. Harvard University Press, Cambridge, 1977.

[Dworkin 1978] R. Dworkin. No Right Answer? *New York University Law Review*, 53:1–32, 1978.

[Dworkin 1985] Ronald Dworkin. *A Matter of Principle*. Harvard University Press, Cambridge, 1985.

[Evans 1968] T. G. Evans. A Program for the Solution of Geometric Analogy Intelligence Test Questions. In Marvin Minsky, editor, *Semantic Information Processing*. MIT Press, Cambridge, 1968.

[Flowers et al. 1982] M. Flowers, R. McGuire, and L. Birnbaum. Adversary Arguments and the Logic of Personal Attacks. In W. Lehnert and M. Ringle, editors, *Strategies for Natural Language Processing*. Lawrence Erlbaum Associates, Hillsdale, NJ, 1982.

[Gardner 1984] A. Gardner. *An Artificial Intelligence Approach to Legal Reasoning*. PhD thesis, Stanford University, 1984.

[Gardner 1987] A. Gardner. *An Artificial Intelligence Approach to Legal Reasoning*. MIT Press, Cambridge, 1987.

[Gentner 1983] D. Gentner. Structure-Mapping: A Theoretical Framework for Analogy. *Cognitive Science*, 7:155-170, 1983.

[Gewirtz 1981] Paul Gewirtz. The Jurisprudence of Hypotheticals. *American Bar Association Journal*, 67:864–866, 1981.

[Gilburne and Johnston 1982] M. R. Gilburne and R. L. Johnston. Trade Secret Protection for Software Generally and in the Mass Market. *Computer/Law Journal*, 3(3), 1982.

[Goldman et al. 1987] Seth R. Goldman, Michael G. Dyer, and Margot Flowers. Precedent-Based Legal Reasoning and Knowledge Acquisition in Contract Law: A Process Model. In *First International Conference on Artificial Intelligence and Law*, Northeastern University, Boston, 1987.

[Hafner 1987] Carol D. Hafner. Conceptual Organization of Case Law Knowledge Bases. In *First International Conference on Artificial Intelligence and Law*, Northeastern University, Boston, 1987.

[Hammond 1986a] Kristian J. Hammond. CHEF: A Model of Case-based Planning. In *Proceedings AAAI—86*. American Association for Artificial Intelligence, August 1986. Philadelphia.

[Hammond 1986b] Kristian J. Hammond. Learning to Anticipate and Avoid Planning Problems through the Explanation of Failures. In *Proceedings AAAI—86*. American Association for Artificial Intelligence, August 1986. Philadelphia.

[Hammond 1987] Kristian J. Hammond. Explaining and Repairing Plans That Fail. In *Proceedings IJCAI—87*. International Joint Conferences on Artificial Intelligence, August 1987. Milan.

[Hart 1961] H. L. A. Hart. *The Concept of Law*. Clarendon Press, Oxford, 1961.

[Holyoak and Thagard 1987] Keith J. Holyoak and Paul Thagard. Analogical Mapping by Constraint Satisfaction: A Computational Theory. Manuscript, 1987.

[Kedar-Cabelli 1984] S. Kedar-Cabelli. Analogy with Purpose in Legal Reasoning from Precedents: A Dissertation Proposal. Technical Report LRP-TR-17, Laboratory for Computer Science Research, Rutgers University, 1984.

[Kling 1971] R. E. Kling. A Paradigm for Reasoning by Analogy. *Artificial Intelligence*, 2:147–178, 1971.

[Kolodner et al. 1985] Janet L. Kolodner, Robert L. Simpson, and Katia Sycara-Cyranski. A Process Model of Case-Based Reasoning in Problem Solving. In *Proceedings IJCAI—85*, Los Angeles, August 1985. International Joint Conferences on Artificial Intelligence.

[Kolodner 1983a] Janet L. Kolodner. Maintaining Organization in a Dynamic Long-Term Memory. *Cognitive Science*, 7(4):243–280, 1983.

[Kolodner 1983b] Janet L. Kolodner. Reconstructive Memory: A Computer Model. *Cognitive Science*, 7(4):281–328, 1983.

[Kolodner 1988] Janet L. Kolodner. Extending Problem Solver Capabilities through Case-Based Inference. In *Proceedings of the Case-Based Reasoning Workshop*, Clearwater Beach, FL, May 1988. DARPA/ISTO.

[Koton 1988a] Phyllis Koton. Reasoning about Evidence in Causal Explanations. In *Proceedings AAAI—88*. American Association for Artificial Intelligence, August 1988. St. Paul, MN.

[Koton 1988b] Phyllis Koton. *Using Experience in Learning and Problem Solving*. PhD thesis, MIT, 1988.

[Kuhn 1970] T. S. Kuhn. *The Structure of Scientific Revolutions*. University of Chicago Press, 1970.

[Kurland and Casper 1985] Philip B. Kurland and Gerhard Casper, editors. *Landmark Briefs and Arguments of the Supreme Court of the United States: Constitutional Law, 1983 Term Supplement*, volume 151. University Publications of America, Frederick, MD, 1985.

[Lakatos 1976] I. Lakatos. *Proofs and Refutations*. Cambridge University Press, London, 1976.

[Lenat 1977] D. B. Lenat. Automated Theory Formation in Mathematics. In *Proceedings IJCAI—77*, pages 833–841, Cambridge, MA, August 1977. International Joint Conferences on Artificial Intelligence.

[Levi 1949] Edward H. Levi. *An Introduction to Legal Reasoning*. University of Chicago Press, 1949.

[Llewellyn 1930] K. N. Llewellyn. *The Bramble Bush: On Our Law and Its Study*. Oceana Publications, Dobbs Ferry, NY, 1960 edition, 1930.

[Llewellyn 1933] Karl N. Llewellyn. Praejudizienrecht und Rechtssprechung in Amerika, 1933. Section 52, Certainty in Case Law; In Doubtful Cases the Legal Rule Is Not Decisive, pages 72–86.

[Llewellyn 1938] Karl N. Llewellyn. On Our Case Law of Contract: Offer and Acceptance. *Yale Law Journal*, 48, 1938.

[McCarty and Sridharan 1981] L. Thorne McCarty and N. S. Sridharan. The Representation of an Evolving System of Legal Concepts: II. Prototypes and Deformations. In *Proceedings IJCAI—81*, Vancouver, BC, August 1981. International Joint Conferences on Artificial Intelligence.

[McCarty and Sridharan 1982] L. Thorne McCarty and N. S. Sridharan. A Computational Theory of Legal Argument. Technical Report LRP-TR-13, Laboratory for Computer Science Research, Rutgers University, 1982.

[McCarty 1980a] L. Thorne McCarty. A Computational Theory of Eisner v. Macomber. Technical Report LRP-TR-9, Laboratory for Computer Science Research, Rutgers University, 1980.

[McCarty 1980b] L. Thorne McCarty. Example Generation. In *Third Biennial Conference of the Canadian Society for Computational Studies of Intelligence*, University of Victoria, Victoria, BC, 1980.

[McCarty 1985] L. Thorne McCarty. Permissions and Obligations. In Charles Walter, editor, *Computing Power and Legal Reasoning*. West Publishing Co., St. Paul, MN, 1985.

[McDonald and Pustejovsky 1985] D. D. McDonald and J. Pustejovsky. Multi-level, Description-Directed, Goal-Driven Natural Language Generation. In *Proceedings IJCAI—85*, Los Angeles, August 1985. International Joint Conferences on Artificial Intelligence.

[McGuire et al. 1981] R. McGuire, L. Birnbaum, and M. Flowers. Opportunistic Processing in Arguments. In *Proceedings IJCAI—81*, pages 58–60, Vancouver, BC, August 1981. International Joint Conferences on Artificial Intelligence.

[McKeown et al. 1985] Kathleen R. McKeown, Myron Wish, and Kevin Matthews. Tailoring Explanations for the User. In *Proceedings IJCAI—85*, Los Angeles, August 1985. International Joint Conferences on Artificial Intelligence.

[Meldman 1977] Jeffrey A. Meldman. A Structural Model for Computer-Aided Legal Analysis. *Journal of Computers and the Law*, 6:27–71, 1977.

[Michaelsen 1984] R. H. Michaelsen. An Expert System for Federal Tax Planning. *Expert Systems*, 1(2), October 1984.

[Milgrim 1985] Roger M. Milgrim. *Business Organizations, Milgrim on Trade Secrets*, volume 12. Matthew Bender, New York, 1985.

[Mitchell et al. 1983] T. M. Mitchell, P. E. Utgoff, and R. B. Banerji. Learning by Experimentation: Acquiring and Refining Problem-Solving Heuristics. In R. S. Michalski, J. G. Carbonell, and T. M. Mitchell, editors, *Machine Learning, An Artificial Intelligence Approach*, pages 163–190. Tioga Press, Palo Alto, 1983.

[Murray 1982] Murray. The Role of Analogy in Legal Reasoning. *UCLA Law Review*, 29:833, 1982.

[Neustadt and May 1986] R. E. Neustadt and E. R. May. *Thinking in Time*. Free Press, New York, 1986.

[Nimmer 1985] Raymond T. Nimmer. *The Law of Computer Technology*. Warren, Gorham, & Lamont, Boston, 1985.

[Perelman 1982] C. Perelman. *The Realm of Rhetoric*. University of Notre Dame Press, Notre Dame, IN, 1982.

[Polya 1973] G. Polya. *How To Solve It*. Princeton University Press, Princeton, 2d edition, 1973.

[Radin 1933] Max Radin. Case Law and Stare Decisis. *Columbia Law Review*, 33:199, 1933.

[Rawls 1971] John Rawls. *A Theory of Justice*. Harvard University Press, Cambridge, 1971.

[Reichman-Adar 1984] R. Reichman-Adar. Extended Person-Machine Interface. *Artificial Intelligence*, 22:157–218, 1984.

[Reichman 1981] R. Reichman. Modeling Informal Debates. In *Proceedings IJCAI—81*, Vancouver, BC, August 1981. International Joint Conferences on Artificial Intelligence.

[Rissland and Ashley 1986] Edwina L. Rissland and Kevin D. Ashley. Hypotheticals as Heuristic Device. In *Proceedings AAAI—86*. American Association for Artificial Intelligence, August 1986. Philadelphia.

[Rissland and Ashley 1987] Edwina L. Rissland and Kevin D. Ashley. A Case-Based System for Trade Secrets Law. In *First International Conference on Artificial Intelligence and Law*, Northeastern University, Boston, 1987.

[Rissland and Ashley 1989] E. L. Rissland and K. D. Ashley. HYPO: A Precedent-Based Legal Reasoner. In Guy Vandenberghe, editor, *Recent Advances in Computer Science and Law*. Kluwer, 1989.

[Rissland et al. 1986] Edwina L. Rissland, Bruce G. Buchanan, Paul Rosenbloom, and H. T. Ng. Intelligent Example Selection: Empirical Experiments with Near-Misses. Unpublished manuscript, 1986.

[Rissland 1978] Edwina L. Rissland. Understanding Understanding Mathematics. *Cognitive Science*, 1(4), 1978.

[Rissland 1980] Edwina L. Rissland. Example Generation. In *Third Biennial Conference of the Canadian Society for Computational Studies of Intelligence*, University of Victoria, Victoria, BC, 1980.

[Rissland 1982] Edwina L. Rissland. Examples in the Legal Domain: Hypotheticals in Contract Law. In *Fourth Annual Cognitive Science Society Conference*, University of Michigan, Ann Arbor, 1982.

[Rissland 1983] Edwina L. Rissland. Examples in Legal Reasoning: Legal Hypotheticals. In *Proceedings IJCAI—83*, Karlsruhe, Germany, August 1983. International Joint Conferences on Artificial Intelligence.

[Rissland 1984] Edwina L. Rissland. Hypothetically Speaking: Experience and Reasoning in the Law. In *Proceedings First Annual Conference on Theoretical Issues in Conceptual Information Processing*, Georgia Institute of Technology, Atlanta, March 1984.

[Rissland 1985] Edwina L. Rissland. AI and Legal Reasoning, Panel Report. In *Proceedings IJCAI—85*, Los Angeles, August 1985. International Joint Conferences on Artificial Intelligence.

[Samuel 1963] A. Samuel. Some Studies in Machine Learning Using the Game of Checkers. In E. A. Feigenbaum and J. Feldman, editors, *Computers and Thought*, pages 71–105. McGraw-Hill, New York, 1963.

[Schlobohm and Waterman 1987] Dean A. Schlobohm and Donald A. Waterman. Explanation for an Expert System That Performs Estate Planning. In *First International Conference on Artificial Intelligence and Law*, Northeastern University, Boston, 1987.

[Sergot et al. 1986] M. J. Sergot, F. Sadri, R. A. Kowalski, F. Kriwaczek, P. Hammond, and H. T. Cory. The British Nationality Act as a Logic Program. *Communications of the ACM*, 29(5):370–386, May 1986.

[Sprowl 1976a] James A. Sprowl. Computer-Assisted Legal Research—An Analysis of Full-Text Document Retrieval Systems, Particularly the Lexis System. *American Bar Foundation Research Journal*, 1976:175.

[Sprowl 1976b] James A. Sprowl. The Westlaw System—A Different Approach to Computer-Assisted Legal Research. *Jurimetrics*, 16(3), 1976.

[Stanfill and Waltz 1986] Craig Stanfill and David Waltz. Toward Memory-Based Reasoning. *Communications of the ACM*, 29(12):1213–1228, December 1986.

[Stanfill 1987] Craig W. Stanfill. Memory-Based Reasoning Applied to English Pronunciation. In *Proceedings AAAI—87*, pages 577–581. American Association for Artificial Intelligence, August 1987. Seattle.

[Stick 1986] John Stick. Can Nihilism Be Pragmatic? *Harvard Law Review*, 100(2): 332–401, December 1986.

[SUP 1988] SUP. The Complete Oral Arguments of the Supreme Court of the United States. University Publications of America, Frederick, MD, 1988.

[Toulmin 1958] Stephen Toulmin. *The Uses of Argument*. Cambridge University Press, 1958.

[Utgoff 1983] Paul E. Utgoff. Adjusting Bias in Concept Learning. In *Proceedings of the International Machine Learning Workshop*, pages 105–109, Monticello, IL, 1983.

[Waterman and Peterson 1980] D. A. Waterman and M. Peterson. Rule-Based Models of Legal Expertise. In *Proceedings AAAI—80*, Stanford, CA, August 1980. American Association for Artificial Intelligence.

[Waterman and Peterson 1981] D. A. Waterman and M. Peterson. Models of Legal Decisionmaking. Technical Report R-2717-1CJ, Rand Corporation, Santa Monica, CA, 1981.

[Wellman 1985] Vincent A. Wellman. Practical Reasoning and Judicial Justification: Toward an Adequate Theory. *University of Colorado Law Review*, 57:45–115, 1985.

[Winston 1980] Patrick H. Winston. Learning and Reasoning by Analogy. *Communications of the ACM*, 23(12):689–703, 1980.

[Yu et al. 1984] Victor L. Yu, Lawrence M. Fagan, Sharon W. Bennett, William J. Clancey, A. Carlisle Scott, John F. Hannigan, Robert L. Blum, Bruce G. Buchanan, and Stanley N. Cohen. An Evaluation of MYCIN's Advice. In Buchanan, Bruce G. and Shortliffe, Edward H., editor, *Rule-Based Expert Systems*, pages 589–596. Addison-Wesley, Reading, MA, 1984.

Index

Adversarial case-based reasoning, 1, 3–4, 25–26, 31, 33-34, 36, 195, 199, 202–205, 249–250
  application outside the law, 195–202
  hallmarks of, 195–199
  Hypo's model of, 4, 249
  strategic choices in, 198
  suitable domains for, 204
Alker, H. R., 205
Allen, L., 228–229, 241
Amexxco case
  case representation of, 94–98
  comparing Hypo's and court's analyses of, 188–190
  Interpretation Frame for, 101–102
  scenario, 9–10
Analogical reasoning, 2, 6, 211, 213, 215, 231, 253
Analogical legal reasoning, 13, 229, 232
  Hypo's model of, 230–231
  standard model of, 229–230
Analogous, definition of, 136
Analogy, 212
Analyzer. *See* Case Analyzer
Arguer. *See* 3-Ply Arguer
Arguing with cases. *See* Adversarial case-based reasoning
Argument. *See also* 3-Ply Argument
  computational theory of case-based, 157–167, 249–250
  context of, 6, 32–33
  theory of, 6
Argument discourse models, 207–211
Argument Evaluation Criteria, 36, 38, 127, 145, 166
  list of, 279–280
Argument graph, 208
Argument Record, 42, 63–70, 80–81, 84–85, 120–121
  examples of, for *Crown* case, 64–65, 72–74
  slots of, 63
Argument roles, 161–166
  example of case described in various, 167–174
Aristotle, 6
As-on-point or partial counterexample, 69, 145–147, 164
Authority, citation of, in legal argument, 11–12

Bareiss, E. R., 217

BCX. *See* Boundary counterexample, definition of
Bench-Capon, T. J. M., 228
Best Case Selector, 39, 42, 57, 60–62, 143–144
Best case to cite. *See also* Best untrumped case to cite, definition of
  definition of, 31, 60, 142
  example of, for *Crown* case, 60–62
  selecting, 39, 61–62, 144
  use of, 64, 75–76
Best untrumped case to cite, definition of, 162
Bibliographic tools, 18–19, 210. *See also* Lexis; Westlaw
Birnbaum, L., 207–208
Blair, D. C., 19
Blue Book, 7, 80, 178–180
Boundary counterexample, 69–70, 145–146, 165, 174, 200
  definition of, 69, 164–165
Briefs, in *USM* case, 184, 302–304
BUC. *See* Best untrumped case to cite, definition of
Burstein, M. H., 213
Burton, S. J., 229, 230

Carbonell, J. G., 212
Case Analysis Record
  creation/filling out, 40, 42, 51, 99
  example of, for *Crown* case, 54, 60
  slots of, 51–52
  use of, 62, 64, 66, 68–69, 75, 80–81, 85
Case Analyzer, 39–40, 52–54, 99, 103, 116–117
Case-based argument, 9, 197–198, 227. *See also* Adversarial case-based reasoning
  partial theory of, 174–175, 253–254
Case-based reasoning. *See also* Adversarial case-based reasoning
  basic operations of, in Hypo, 25, 127
  other approaches to, 215
Case Editor, 39–40, 46, 102
Case Knowledge Base, 25, 35–37, 87
  accessing cases in, 103–104 (*see also* Indexing)
  implementation of, 102
  list of cases in, 265–268
Case Positioner, 39–40, 55, 103, 129
Case Positioning, 35–36, 39
Case Representation Language, 36, 105

Cases. *See also* Case Knowledge Base; Legal cases; Legal precedents
  representing, 28–33, 36–37, 87, 240, 265 (*see also* Legal Case Frames; Factual Predicates)
  representing cases in Gardner's program, 226
  use of, in human problem solving, 5, 204–205
Casey, 216
Cataloging flavor instances, 306
Causal model, 125, 217, 220. *See also* Domain model
Cfs. *See* Current fact situation
Cfs spinoff, 148, 152, 154
Chef, 212–213
Christmas crèche hypotheticals, 233–235, 237
Citable Case, definition of, 60
Citable in first instance, 61. *See also* Best case to cite, selecting
  definition of, 60, 122, 142
Citable in Points, 127. *See also* Citable in first instance
Citable in Responses, 127
Citation Labels, 80, 178–180
Citation Summary, 36, 75–76, 83–84, 179–180
  for *Amexxco* case, 20
  for *Amoco* case, 189
Cited case, 161–163, 172, 196
Citing precedents, 12
CKB. *See* Case Knowledge Base
Claim
  analogies from other kinds of claims, 243–244
  claims represented in the Case Knowledge Base, 37, 108
  elements of a claim, 17, 105
  factors associated with, 26–33
  relation between Dimensions and Claims, 108, 112–115
Claim Lattice. *See also* Extended Claim Lattice; Coverage
  algorithm for inserting cases in, 129–130
  changed by hypothetical modifications of the cfs, 84
  comparing cases on same branch of, 143
  definition/construction of, 40, 42, 55–57, 129–130
  example of, 56, 130–131, 136
  use of, in comparing arguments, 154–155
  use of, to find most-on-point cases, 57, 60
  use of, to recognize counterexamples, 146–147
  use of, by 3-Ply Arguer, 42, 62, 77
Clancey, W. J., 207, 218–221
Cohen, R., 208
Coherence view of legal reasoning, 231
Common employee scenario, 94, 98, 101
Comparing arguments, 16–17, 75–76, 80–83, 146, 154–155. *See also* Argument Evaluation Criteria; Evaluating a precedential argument
  example of, 147
Comparing cases. *See also* Dimensions, use of, in comparing cases; On Pointness; Relevant differences; Relevant similarities
  Hypo's metrics for, 127–128
Comparison of Hypo's output and legal treatise notes, 191–193
Comparison of Hypo's output and the opinion of the court, 193
  in *Amoco* case, 189–190
  in *Crown* case, 187–188
  in *Structural Dynamics* case, 191
  in *USM* case, 185–186
Competitive-Advantage Dimension, 95–96, 105, 108, 111, 114, 116, 118–122
Computational complexity, problems of, 206, 216, 243
Concept/case organization, 226–227
Conflicting answers, 142
Context-sensitive computation of salience/significance, 157–174
Control, flow of, in Hypo, 39–40
Controlling inference, 6, 205–208, 210, 218–219, 252. *See also* Computational complexity, problems of
Counterexample(s), 15, 63–64, 70–71, 144–145, 197, 200. *See also* As-on-point or partial counterexample; Boundary counterexample, More-on-point counterexample; Potentially more-on-point counterexample
  configurations of, 144–147
  definition of, 31–32, 68
Coverage, 129–130
Credit assignment problem, 252
Crown case
  Argument Records for, 64–66, 72–74
  Case Analysis Record for, 54–55, 60–61

Index

comparing Hypo's and court's analyses of, 186–188
hypotheticals for, 79–80, 149–154
hypothetical variant of, 81–84, 86, 154–155
Interpretation Frame for, 53–54
Legal Case Frames for, 47–51
squib for, 45–46
3-Ply Arguments for, 70–71, 75–78
Cuban missile crisis, 201–202
Current fact situation, 35, 40
Cyrus, 215

Data General case
as counterexample, 68–72, 83, 122, 139, 147, 151–155, 178
described in context-sensitive manner, 167–174
Deductive reasoning, 2–4, 205
Depth of inference, 206–207
Derivational analogy, 212
Descriptions of precedent cases, 167–168
Diagnosis, 216, 218–220
Dimensional analysis process, 35–40, 98, 103
steps of, 52
Dimensional Index, 35, 103–104, 107, 207, 252–253
Dimensions, 28, 33, 36–38, 107–108, 206–207. *See also* Focal slot; Near-miss Dimension; Prerequisites of Dimensions; Pro-defendant Dimensions; Pro-plaintiff Dimensions; Range information associated with a Dimension
adding, 126
advantages of, 125, 126
associated text for use in 3-Ply Arguments, 72
comparison information contained in, 66–67, 118–119
determining whether a Dimension applies, 40, 52, 55, 116
examples of, 108
extreme values along, 85, 122, 123, 146, 151, 154
learning new, 246
list of, 273–278
long and short names for, 273–278
magnitudes of, 66–67, 114, 128
modification method, 85
pro-plaintiff direction for, 118–119
relation between claims and, 108, 112–115

sources for, 115
use of, in comparing cases, 95, 98, 107, 122
use of, for computing distinctions, 66–67, 120
use of, for computing counterexamples, 68–69
use of, in computing hypotheticals, 84–86, 149–154, 237
use of, in constructing Claim Lattices, 56–57
use of, in Dimensional Analysis, 52, 54–55, 98
use of, for drawing analogies between cfs and cited case, 70
Directed acyclic graph, 56
Distinctions. *See* Relevant differences
Distinguishing a counterexample, 71, 197
Distinguishing the cited case, 14–15, 26, 66–68, 71, 77
example of, 120–121
salient features when, 163, 172
use of, in adversarial reasoning, 196–197
Domain. *See* Adversarial case-based reasoning, application outside the law, suitable domains for; Trade secrets misappropriation
Domain model. *See also* Causal model
strong versus weak, 202–204, 214–215
Doyle, R. J., 221–222
Dworkin, R., 231
Dyer, M. G., 226

EBR. *See* Example-based reasoning
Evaluating a precedential argument, 157, 166–167, 198, 226. *See also* Comparing arguments
Evaluating Hypo's performance
criteria for, 183, 254
proposed experiments for, 193
Example-based reasoning, 217–218
Expert systems, 1, 4–6, 251
Explainer, 39, 43, 64, 75–86, 148
Explanation, 5, 35–36, 43, 154–155, 207, 218–222, 252
and argument, 219–220
Explanation-based learning, 221
Extended Claim Lattice, 57, 60, 136–139, 143
definition of, 56, 129
Extended Hypo, 238–247

Factors, 17–18, 26–34, 37–38, 66, 158–159
  case representation with, 26–34
  combination scheme for, 175–176
  conflicting, 28–29, 105, 176, 201, 252
  in an example of everyday reasoning, 199
  as expert knowledge, 26–27
  interaction among, 240, 241
  magnitude of, as distinguished from weight, 27, 175
  represented by Dimensions, 28
  in trade secrets law, 17–18
  weight of, 27–28, 175–178
Fact situation, editing of, 46
Factual Predicates, 36–37, 40, 46, 52–54, 98–102, 115–116, 124, 261
Flavors, Hypo's use of, 305–307
Flowers, M., 207–208
Flow of control in Hypo, 39–41
Focal slot, 38, 40, 114
  use of, to compare cases, 107, 118
  use of, to compute distinctions, 67, 120
  use of, to compute hypothetical modifications, 85–86, 150–151, 237
Focal slot prerequisite, use of, in Dimensional Analysis, 55, 123–124
Frames. *See* Legal Case Frames
Full-text retrieval systems, 18–19, 193

Gardner, A., 225–228
Gentner, D., 212
Gilburne, M. R., 17, 245
Global Catalog, 102–104, 306
Goldman, S. R., 226

Hafner, C. D., 19, 227
Hammond, K. J., 212–213
Heuristics for modifying cases hypothetically, 43, 85, 148–154
Holyoak, K. J., 212
Hybrid hypotheticals, 148–149, 152
Hypo Generator, 39, 43, 80, 84–86, 149–152
Hypo's architecture, overview of, 35, 38–39
Hypo's basic control loop, 39–40, 51, 80
Hypo's contribution to artificial intelligence, 251–253
Hypo's data structures. *See* Argument Record; Case Analysis Record; Claim Lattice; Dimensions; Interpretation Frame; Legal Case Frames

Hypo's key elements, 36
Hypo's knowledge sources, 36
Hypo's modules, 39
Hypo's reasoning process, 25–26, 33–34, 36
Hypotheticals, 26, 35–36, 43, 72, 78–80. *See also* Cfs spinoff; Heuristics for modifying cases hypothetically; Hybrid hypotheticals; Suggested Hypotheticals to Consider
  computing of hypothetical variations of the cfs, 84–86, 122–124
  example of, in *Amexxco* case, 21–22
  example of, in *Crown* case, 72, 147, 152–154
  line-drawing, 242
  purpose of posing, 84, 147, 197, 233–237, 241–243, 247
  Supreme Court examples of, 233–237
Hypo-XL, 238–247

Implementation of Hypo, 305–307
Improving an argument. *See* Suggested Hypotheticals to Consider
Indexing, 6, 206, 215, 252
Indexing a case in the CKB, 103, 107, 116–117. *See also* Dimensional Index
Inputs, Hypo's, 20, 25, 36, 40
Inputting a case already in the CKB for analysis, 50–51
Inputting cases into the Case Knowledge Base, 105, 126. *See also* Fact situation, editing of
Interpretation Frame, 40, 52–53, 99–102, 116, 120

Johnston, R. L., 17
Jurisprudence, 229–232
  Hypo's contribution to, 230–232, 253–254
Justification in legal argument, 11–12, 26, 29, 196–198, 229–232, 238. *See also* Rationale in legal argument

Kedar-Cabelli, S., 213
Keyword searches, 19, 245
Kolodner, J. L., 215
Koton, P., 216
Kuhn, T. S., 205

Lakatos, I., 205
Legal argument, 10, 12
  components of, 11

Index 327

evaluating, 16–18
precedents to cite in, 13–14
responding to, 14–16
strengths and weaknesses in, 12–13
Legal Case Frames, 36–37, 47–50, 87–88, 94–95, 103, 259. *See also* Top-level Legal Case Frame; Underlying Legal Case Frame
Legal cases, 25, 29, 158. *See also* Legal precedents
Legal database, 1, 18, 245
combining Hypo with, 245, 246
Legal domain as a challenge to artificial intelligence, 2–3
Legal memorandum, 11
Legal precedents, 105
finding (*see* Bibliographic tools)
as resolving competing factors, 28–33, 163
Legal predicates, 197, 204, 227–228, 238–240
open-textured, 204, 225–226
reasoning with abstract, 238–241
Legal principles, 231–232
Legal reasoning. *See* Analogical legal reasoning; Coherence view of legal reasoning; Logic-based models of legal reasoning; Rule-based models of legal reasoning
Legal rules, 225–226, 239, 241
Levi, E. H., 204, 229
Lexis, 18, 193, 245–246, 254
Logic, 6, 158
Logical ambiguity, 241
Logic-based models of legal reasoning, 228
Lynch v. Donnelly, 233–235, 237

McCarty, L. T., 217, 223–225
McGuire, R., 207–208
McKeown, K. R., 219
Manager. *See* Session Manager
Matching, 211–213
Matching based on a static hierarchy of features, 145, 175, 213, 252
May, E. R., 201, 205
MBRTalk, 216
Mediator, 215
Meldman, J. A., 227–228
Memory organization, 208, 210, 215, 226. *See also* Concept/case organization
Michaelsen, R. H., 228
Milgrim, R. M., 17, 239

Modifying cases hypothetically. *See* Hypotheticals
Modularity, supported by Dimensions, 126
Modus ponens, 210
MOP. *See* Most-on-point case(s), definition of
More on point, 31, 129, 160
More-on-point counterexample,
definition of, 68, 145, 162
example of, in *Crown* case, 68
example of, in *USM* case, 147
finding, 68, 146
salient features of, 164, 173
Most analogous cases, 142, 230
in Cyrus and Mediator, 215–216
relaxing the criteria of analogy, 244–245
selecting, 139, 142
Most-on-point case(s)
definition of, 31, 130, 160
examples of, in *Crown* case, 61
examples of, in *Structural Dynamics* case, 136
examples of, in *USM* case, 131
selecting, 42, 57, 60, 143–144
use of, in arguments, 13, 60
use of, to compute most-on-point counterexamples, 67
use of, to find best cases to cite, 142
use of, to generate hybrids (hypotheticals), 148
Most-on-point near-miss cases
definition of, 143
selecting, 42, 60
use of, to generate hypotheticals, 80, 85, 148, 153–154
Movie permission example, 195–201
Mycin, 193, 207, 218

Natural language understanding, 2
Near-miss Dimension
definition of, 40, 52, 123–125
marked with asterisk (*), 57
use of, in computing hypothetical modifications, 85–86, 122–124, 149–150, 153
use of, in computing potentially more-on-point counterexamples, 68–69
use of, in constructing Claim Lattices, 57, 136
use of, in dimensional analysis, 55
Near win, 152
Neustadt, R. E., 201
New Jersey v. T.L.O., 235

Nimmer, R. T., 17, 18, 239
Nontrumped point, 75–76, 81, 83, 146

On pointness, 31, 56, 127–128, 160. *See also* More on point; Most-on-point case(s)
Open-textured predicates. *See* Legal predicates
Opinion, 105
  in *Amoco* case, 188–189
  in *Crown* case, 186–187
  in *Structural Dynamics* case, 190–191
  in *USM* case, 184
Organization of the Case Knowledge Base. *See* Case Representation Language; Dimensions; Legal Case Frames
Outcome of a precedent, 127–128
Output, Hypo's, 20, 25, 36, 281–299. *See also* Citation Summary; Comparison of Hypo's output and legal treatise notes; Comparison of Hypo's output and the opinion of the court; Hypotheticals, example of; 3-Ply Argument, example of;
Outsider-Disclosures-Restricted Dimension, 68, 86, 124, 150–152

Partial counterexample. *See* As-on-point or partial counterexample
Pedigree of legal case, 13–15
Perelman, C., 211
Plato, 6
Point, 12–14, 62, 70–71
Policy decision making, 201–202
Positioning. *See* Case Positioning
Post processing flavor instances, 306
Potentially citable, 127
Potentially more-on-point counterexample
  definition of, 68, 145–146, 165–166
  example of, in *Crown* case, 69, 147
  procedure to compute, 68–69, 146
  salient features of, 166
  use of, to pose hypothetical variants of the cfs, 68, 70, 80, 85, 148
Potentially trumping counterexample. *See* Potentially more-on-point counterexample
Potential most-on-point cases. *See* Most-on-point near-miss cases
Prerequisites of Dimensions, 28, 38, 40, 55, 115, 124, 149
Problem-solving analogical reasoner, 214

Pro-defendant Dimensions, 113–114
Pro-plaintiff Dimensions, 113–114
Protos, 217
Prototypes and deformations, 217, 223–224
PTCX (partial counterexample). *See* As-on-point or partial counterexample

Range information associated with a Dimension, 38, 107, 114, 118–119, 150
Ranking of features, 215–216
Rationale in legal argument, 11, 71, 240, 242. *See also* Justification in legal argument
Rawls, J., 231
Real estate appraisal, 202, 205
Rebuttal, 63, 70–72, 197
Regular Claim Lattice. *See* Claim Lattice
Reichman-Adar, R., 209–210
Relevance, definition of, 136. *See also* On pointness
  assessing relevance dynamically, 161, 251–252
  looser criteria of relevance, 138–139
Relevant differences, 66–68, 70–71, 80, 196
  definition, 29–31, 107, 159
  importance of, 229–232
Relevant similarities, 12–13, 25–26, 29–34, 66, 107, 196
  definition of, 29–34, 107, 159
  importance of, 229–232
Response, 14–16, 31, 63, 70–71, 196–197
Restatement of Torts, provisions on trade secrets, 17–18, 27, 257
Retrieving relevant cases, 25, 36, 40, 115, 215
Rissland, E. L., 217–218
Roles of precedents in arguments, 28–33, 157, 161, 167
Rule-based models of legal reasoning, 227–228
Run times, Hypo's, 305

Salience, 32–33, 157, 161, 167–168, 251–252
  example of context-sensitive computation of, 167–174
Schlobohm, D. A., 228
Secrets-Disclosed-Outsiders Dimension, 67, 108–109, 114, 116, 119–120, 123–124, 150–151
Security measures, 93–94, 105

Index 329

Security-Measures Dimension, 95, 98, 108, 110, 114–116, 118–122
Seed case for a hypothetical, 84–85, 148–152
Selecting best precedents to cite, 13–14, 36, 122. *See also* Best case to cite in an example of everyday reasoning, 200
Selector. *See* Best Case Selector
Sergot, M. J., 228
Session Manager, 39–40, 51, 84
Session Master List, 51, 84
Set theory notation, 158
Shepardizing, 19
Significance, 157
Simpson, R. L., 215
Slippery slope arguments, 148–149
Solution of a precedent case. *See* Outcome of a precedent
Sony Corp. v. Universal City Studios, 235–237
Sprowl, J. A., 18–19
Squib, 87
  for *Amoco* case, 270
  for *Crown* case, 45–46
  for *Data General* case, 269
  for *Structural Dynamics* case, 134–136
  for *USM* case, 88–89
Stanfill, C. W., 216
STARE, 226
Stare decisis, 3, 9
Statutes, 18, 255
Strengthening an argument, 83–84
  using an extended Claim Lattice to find how to strengthen an argument, 139
  example of, 147
Strength of an argument. *See* Comparing arguments
Structural Dynamics case, 131, 134–138
  comparing Hypo's and court's analyses of, 190–191
  squib for, 134-136, 143
Suggested Hypotheticals to Consider, 75, 79
  example of, for *Amexxco* case, 21–22
Symbolic Case Comparison, 35, 176–178. *See also* Comparing cases
  in Casey, 216–217

Tailoring the description of a precedent, 167–168
Target case for a hypothetical, 84–85, 148–152, 166, 174

Taxman II, 223, 225
TCX (trumping counterexample). *See* More-on-point counterexample, definition of
Thagard, P., 212
Theory of case-based argument, Hypo's computational, 157–167, 249–250
3-Ply Arguer, 39, 62–70, 75–76, 80, 85, 120, 146, 152–153
3-Ply Argument, 20, 35–36, 42, 64
  components of, 62–63, 71
  definition of, 20
  example of, for *Amexxco* case, 20–21
  example of, for *Crown* case, 70, 71, 76–78
  generating, 36, 39, 43, 70, 72, 76
  for hypothetical variant of the cfs, 81, 83–84
Top-level Legal Case Frame, 37, 88–89, 103, 105, 116–118. *See also* Dimensions, list of; Legal Case Frames
Toulman, S., 211
Trade secrets misappropriation, 4, 9–10, 17–18, 255, 257
Transformational analogy, 212
Trumping, 32, 68
Trumping counterexample. *See* More-on-point counterexample
Tutoring, 243

Underlying Legal Case Frame, 37, 88–89, 98, 100, 102. *See also* Legal Case Frames
Untrumped point. *See* Nontrumped point
USM case, 88–95, 100-101, 105, 116–118, 130–134
  comparing Hypo's and court's analyses of, 184–186
  Interpretation Frame for, 100–101, 117

Venn diagrams, 29–33, 107

Waltz, D., 216
Waterman, D. A., 227, 228
Weighting scheme. *See* Factors, weight of
Wellman, V. A., 229–230
Westlaw, 18, 193, 245–246, 254
Winston, P. H., 211

```
         Ashley, Kevin D.
KF
242         Modeling legal
A1       argument
A7
1990
```

	DATE DUE		

+KF242 .A1 A7 1990